Martha Nussbaum and Politics

THINKING POLITICS

Series Editors: Geoff M. Boucher and Matthew Sharpe

MARTHA NUSSBAUM AND POLITICS

Brandon Robshaw

EDINBURGH
University Press

Edinburgh University Press is one of the leading university presses in the UK. We publish academic books and journals in our selected subject areas across the humanities and social sciences, combining cutting-edge scholarship with high editorial and production values to produce academic works of lasting importance. For more information visit our website: edinburghuniversitypress.com

Edinburgh University Press Ltd
13 Infirmary Street
Edinburgh EH1 1LT

First published in hardback by Edinburgh University Press 2023

Typeset in 11/13 Adobe Sabon by
IDSUK (DataConnection) Ltd

A CIP record for this book is available from the British Library

ISBN 978-1-3995-0547-5 (hardback)
ISBN 978-1-3995-0548-2 (paperback)
ISBN 978-1-3995-0549-9 (webready PDF)
ISBN 978-1-3995-0550-5 (epub)

Contents

A Public Intellectual

I first encountered Martha Nussbaum in 1987. She appeared as a guest on Bryan Magee's BBC television series *The Great Philosophers*. At that time I had not studied philosophy, but took a dilettante-ish interest in it. The format of each programme was that Magee would interview a leading contemporary philosopher about the ideas of some great philosopher of the past, just the two of them sitting on a sofa, debating; and Martha Nussbaum was brought in as the Aristotle specialist.

Nussbaum would have been still in her thirties when the programme was recorded and was in fact the youngest contributor to the series (beating Peter Singer, who talked to Magee about Karl Marx, by one year). Magee introduced her by saying that she had 'established a reputation very young in Aristotle scholarship' (1988: 34). She had recently been made professor at Brown University and her book *The Fragility of Goodness* had been published the previous year. There were, no doubt, other, more senior Aristotelian scholars whom Magee could have chosen. But he could not have made a better choice. Magee stated that he employed two criteria in selecting which modern philosophers should discuss the philosophers of the past: they had to be experts in their subject, of course, but they also had to be skilled communicators (Magee 2004: 520). The second of these criteria was no less important than the first. And in Martha Nussbaum he found an expert communicator; a philosopher with the gift of making highly complex ideas seem lucid and comprehensible, to rival Magee's own gift (which is saying a good deal).

Nussbaum was the only woman guest over the whole series (there were twelve episodes), which in itself made her something of a trail-blazer. There were far fewer women philosophers then than there are now, and Nussbaum was one of the first to achieve a prominent public profile. But her contribution was notable not only because she was a young woman in a field of middle-aged men. Her exposition was sharp, smart and witty; she made ideas that were over two thousand years old spring to life. Despite finding much to disagree with in Aristotle's

1

work – his dim view of women and his defence of slavery, for example – Nussbaum strongly endorses his approach to philosophy:

> the philosopher must be someone who's attentive to and almost humble before the variety of human life and its great richness. But at the same time one who is committed to giving explanations, one who is committed to mapping that richness in a perspicuous way. In every area he strikes a kind of balance: between oversimplifying theorising that takes philosophy too far from the richness and complexity and even messiness of ordinary discourse and, on the other hand, a kind of negative or deflationary philosophising that says theorising is all a house of cards and there's no point in asking for and giving explanations. I think Aristotle has found the right balance, and has probably the best conception of the philosophical task that one can give to a student. (Nussbaum in Magee 1988: 54)

This characterisation of how philosophy ought to be done is an accurate description of the way that Nussbaum herself does it.

After this, Martha Nussbaum was on my radar, but for some time as a rather distant presence. She is a prolific author and every now and again I would read a review of one of her books and remember her performance on *The Great Philosophers*. It was not until decades later that I began to study philosophy seriously myself; when I did, I found myself immersed in Nussbaum. My PhD thesis was in political philosophy – 'Should a Liberal State Ban the Burqa?' – and I soon discovered that Nussbaum had written extensively and perspicuously on every aspect of the topic. She had written about liberalism. She had written about feminism. She had written about personal autonomy. She had written about multiculturalism. She had written about religious freedom. She had even written, explicitly, about burqa-wearing.

In the year 2012 I finally got to meet her, a quarter of a century after first seeing her on television. She gave a paper at a conference at Durham University which I attended. After her talk we had a brief conversation – fifteen minutes or so – about our views on the burqa, which did not entirely align. She was courteous, interested in what I had to say, and rapier-sharp in defending her own position.

Nussbaum: An Overview

Martha Nussbaum is one of the most important living philosophers, who has made influential contributions in many areas of moral and political philosophy. Her work has been widely reviewed and debated, and has garnered many honours. The following list is far from exhaustive, a mere sprinkling of greatest hits: she has been awarded no fewer than sixty-four honorary degrees from universities around the world; several of her books have won awards, such as the 2000 Book Award of the Year bestowed by the North American Society for Social Philosophy, for *Sex and Social Justice*; she was listed among the world's top 100 intellectuals by *Prospect* magazine in 2005 and made the same list in the American publication *Foreign Policy* not only in 2005 but in 2008 and 2010 as well; in 2016 she received the Kyoto Prize, which comes with an award of $500,000 and is 'the most prestigious award offered in fields which are not eligible for a Nobel, joining a small group of philosophers that includes Karl Popper and Jurgen Habermas' (Aviv 2016); most recently, in 2021 she received the Holberg Prize, an international award conferred by the Norwegian government, for her 'groundbreaking contribution to research in philosophy, law and related fields'.

Yet, to date, no synoptic account of her work has been published. That is a surprising fact, for which I canvas some possible explanations below. But first, a list of distinctive features of her approach which demonstrates that it's high time her oeuvre received the book-length treatment it deserves:

- For Nussbaum, philosophy's purpose is to provide ideas and principles that can be applied in the real world. She is no ivory tower intellectual; ideas should inform public policy. (This might be traced to her intellectual debt to Aristotle, with his emphasis on practice, rather than Plato's valorisation of timeless, absolute ideas.)
- Nussbaum is a public intellectual. It is noteworthy that she publishes not only for academic presses and journals, but also for newspapers and magazines such as the *New York Times*, the *New York Review of Books* and the *New Republic* (and appears on TV shows like *The Great Philosophers*; she has also presented a programme on Plato on the Discovery Channel). She wants her ideas to have influence outside the academy.
- Nussbaum is a superb communicator. She writes in lucid, accessible prose and her works can be read for sheer pleasure, which is certainly not something that could be said of all academic philosophers. She has the gift of making the reader feel intelligent (unlike certain theorists who use jargon, abstruse terminology and appeals to authority to baffle and bully the reader into acceptance).

3

- Her work is exceptionally wide-ranging, covering ethics, political philosophy, animal rights, personal autonomy and global justice, among many other areas.
- Although Nussbaum's work tackles contemporary issues, she is a scholar of the history of philosophy. Her books provide excellent introductions to such philosophical giants as Plato, Aristotle, Kant, Mill and Rawls, relating their ideas to today's world.
- Nussbaum's work is broadly in the tradition of analytic philosophy, but she is also a synthesiser. She brings together ideas and arguments from different centuries, relating them to one another and developing new theories from a synthesis of the old.
- For Nussbaum, philosophy does not exist in isolation, but can and should be informed by other disciplines, including the study of literature, psychology, economics, law, history and behavioural science.
- Certain themes are consistent throughout Nussbaum's long career: the Aristotelian concept of flourishing, the importance of the emotions, the principle of equal human worth and dignity. However, her work has never stood still and she often revisits, revises and reinvents positions.
- Nussbaum is one of the most important exponents of the liberal tradition in political philosophy, which in recent years has (undeservedly, in my view) fallen from fashion.
- Nussbaum has the ability to find things of value even in philosophical views with which she disagrees. Thus, she has important reservations about both Stoicism and utilitarianism, but she also finds many valuable insights in those traditions. She is never guilty of throwing the baby out with the bathwater.
- Finally, her philosophy is rooted in an idea of what it means to be human (again, following Aristotle).

It would, of course, be stretching matters to suggest Nussbaum's work has been neglected, given her media presence, the recognition she has received and the awards she has won. Nevertheless, it does seem rather odd that no synoptic account of her work has been published. Why should this be?

Nussbaum is an extremely prolific writer and among academics there can be a distrust (and perhaps envy?) of those who write 'too much'. A bizarrely hostile review of her work by Geoffrey Galt Harpham, 'The Hunger of Martha Nussbaum', appeared in the journal *Representations* in 2002, suggesting that her productivity was the result of some kind of neurotic compulsion. Harpham's theory is that such 'unseemly productivity' could only be the work of a 'closed-minded narcissist' or a 'deeply troubled person', or both (2002: 52–3). The fact that Nussbaum is a *populariser* of philosophy might also be a reason for distrust within the academy. And there might even be a dash of misogyny in the mix; on more than one occasion Harpham dismisses Nussbaum's thought with such sexually stereotyped adjectives as 'misty' and 'moony'.

In addition to these reasons there is also the matter of *intellectual fashion*. Harpham accuses Nussbaum of 'out-of-phase attitudes' (2002: 59), by which he means her attachment to ancient Greek philosophy, early modern thinkers such as Adam Smith and the liberal humanist literary critic Lionel Trilling. My own view is that philosophers have no duty whatsoever to be 'in phase' and all that matters is whether they find ideas of value in the texts they study and produce ideas of value themselves. I do not believe that value depends on fashion. But it is certainly true that Nussbaum swims against the tide in a number of ways. Her robust defence of political liberalism, for example, never popular with conservatives, has come to seem anathema in progressive circles too. Her brand of second-wave feminism (see Chapter 3) may appear old-fashioned at a time when gender and even biological sex have been put in question. Her commitment to ethical universalism is out of step in an era of identity politics. And her idea of human nature and of human flourishing is widely dismissed in postmodernist thought.

Leaving fashion aside, however, my contention is that Nussbaum's ideas can stand on their own merit and are a welcome challenge to prevailing orthodoxies in philosophy, cultural studies and progressive politics today. My aim is to demonstrate the continuing relevance of her arguments and approach.

Life and Work

Nussbaum frequently includes autobiographical elements in her own writings, so it seems not out of place here to touch on certain ways in which events in her life have inspired her philosophy.

At the age of sixteen, Nussbaum went on an overseas stay on an educational programme called the Experiment in International Living. She came to Britain and stayed with a family of factory workers in Swansea, South Wales. It was here that she fully realised how the effects of 'poverty, bad nutrition, bad sanitation (no indoor plumbing), and bad health conditions ... robbed people not only of flourishing lives but of desire and effort' (Nussbaum 2018: xiii–xiv). Here we see two ideas that will become of major importance in Nussbaum's work: the importance of human flourishing, and the way that *adaptive preferences* can stop people striving to achieve it (see Chapters 3 and 4). Nussbaum also says that this experience was responsible for her (many years later) working for an international development institute and development groups working for women's rights in India (see Chapter 4).

In 1969 she married Alan Nussbaum (who, like her, was studying classics at New York University, and who would later go on to become a linguist and philologist at Cornell). Alan Nussbaum was Jewish, and Martha as well as taking his name converted to Judaism. Her father was dismayed that she had married a Jew and refused to come to the wedding. Nussbaum notes that two things about Jewish culture attracted her: its concern for social justice, and its argumentativeness. And these are most useful qualities for a political philosopher.

Martha and Alan divorced in 1987. But Martha kept both the surname and the religion. She retains her maiden name 'Craven' as a middle name and her books appear under the name of Martha C. Nussbaum. Her Judaism has continued to be important in her life and thought. She states in *The Monarchy of Fear* that she has 'become more involved in the life of my congregation than I was back then', and clearly her own experience informs her work on religious freedom (see Chapter 6).

After graduating, Martha Nussbaum gravitated towards philosophy. She obtained her Master's degree and PhD at Harvard, where she went on to teach classics and philosophy, and where she met John Rawls, who became a friend and mentor. Nussbaum also mentions Stanley Cavell, Hilary Putnam and Bernard Williams as mentors and influences on her work (2018: xviii). In 1982, Nussbaum applied for a tenured post at Harvard, but was turned down (and for a while considered bringing a sexual discrimination suit). She moved instead to Brown University, where she taught until 1994, when she moved to the Chicago School of Law.

From 1986 onwards, Nussbaum published articles and books in a swift and steady stream. The very titles of the books – *The Fragility of Goodness, Love's Knowledge, Cultivating Humanity, The Therapy of Desire, Women and Human Development, Frontiers of Justice, From Disgust to Humanity, Anger and Forgiveness, The Monarchy of Fear* and so on – by themselves indicate the tenor and the territory of her thought. She is interested in humanity, in the emotions, in justice and in the real world. She is committed to using philosophy to make the world better, hence the positive words we find in her titles – goodness, love, knowledge, cultivating, development, forgiveness – and believes improvement to be possible; on the other hand, she does not think the task is easy, hence the warning words like fragility, disgust, anger, fear.

Nussbaum also had long-term relationships with the Nobel Prize-winning economist Amartya Sen and with the legal scholar and author Cass R. Sunstein, both of which resulted in fruitful intellectual collaborations (see Chapters 4 and 5).

The Plan of this Book

Martha Nussbaum has written twenty-eight books. According to a feature in the *New Yorker* magazine by Rachel Aviv, she's also written 509 philosophical papers – but that feature was written in 2016, so no doubt the total is higher by now. Nussbaum is also a tireless reviewer of other philosophers' work; in 2012, Oxford University Press published a book-length collection of her reviews, *Philosophical Interventions.*

Indeed, between my submission of the proposal for this book and my commencing work on it, Nussbaum had already published another two books. It is therefore impossible, given the scope of this introduction to her work, to discuss everything she has written. Instead, I have opted to introduce eight major areas of her thought, each area represented by one or two of her books. Fortunately, this lends itself to a chronological approach, in that she has explored different areas at different points throughout her career. The areas are not discrete, however, but interconnected in multiple ways. All her thought stems from the fundamental Aristotelian principle that human beings have a nature and that certain essentials are required for it to flourish. But the question of what is required for flourishing leads naturally on to the philosophy of education; and also to the claim that women and men require the same essentials to flourish; which leads to the capabilities approach, systematically setting out what those essentials are; which later widens into consideration of what other species require in order to flourish; and so on.

The chosen areas and books are:

- Ancient Greek philosophy: *The Fragility of Goodness* (1986); *The Therapy of Desire* (1994)
- Education: *Cultivating Humanity* (1997); *Not For Profit* (2010)
- Feminism: *Sex and Social Justice* (1999)

- The capabilities approach: *Women and Human Development* (2000)
- Animal rights: *Animal Rights: Current Debates and New Directions* (edited with Cass Sunstein, 2004); *Frontiers of Justice* (2006)
- Religious freedom: *Liberty of Conscience* (2008); *The New Religious Intolerance* (2012)
- The emotions: *Upheavals of Thought* (2001); *Hiding from Humanity* (2004); *Anger and Forgiveness* (2016)
- Global justice: *The Cosmopolitan Tradition* (2019).

A Note on the Word 'Liberal'

Throughout the book I refer to Nussbaum and her ideas as 'liberal'. Nussbaum herself consistently styles herself a 'political liberal'. This might cause some confusion for North American readers, where the word 'liberal' generally signifies a commitment to 'left-wing' or progressive causes. And to add to the confusion, in many contexts Nussbaum *does* take a position which would be identified with the progressive or left-wing side of things. But that is not what I mean by the word 'liberal' in this book.

Liberal in the sense used here suggests no affiliation to any political party. It has a more neutral sense, meaning a commitment to the liberty of the individual (consistent with not infringing the liberty of others) and to the principle that all individuals are fundamentally equal. There are many disagreements among liberals as to both the implications and the applications of these principles. But the following characterisation of liberalism by Jonathan Quong (2011: 14–15) would be accepted by most:

(a) Persons are free and equal, at least from the political point of view. Persons are free in the sense of being rational agents, capable of practical reasoning, with plans and projects for their own life, and with the capacity to understand and respond to moral reasons. Persons are equal in the sense that each person has the same fundamental moral status: there are no natural superiors or inferiors among us.

(b) All sane adults have certain basic rights and liberties which include at least some form of freedom of thought and conscience, freedom of expression and association, rights to democratic participation and other political rights that are essential or important for a functioning democracy, a right to bodily integrity and freedom from assault, a right to private property (however property is justly distributed), as well as equal rights under the rule of law.

(c) The protection of these rights and liberties should be one of the main functions of any legitimate state.

(d) Even if these rights are viewed as defeasible, they have a certain priority in our political reasoning, and are not easily defeated by conflicting considerations.

Nussbaum is not only a liberal in this sense but a *political* liberal (as indeed is Quong). The term *political liberal* was coined or at least given currency by John Rawls, in his book *Political Liberalism*, first published in 1993. A political liberal is one who believes that all citizens must be treated justly and granted equal rights and liberties, but that the state should not tell them what kind of life they should lead. On that issue the state should be neutral. As Quong puts it, 'Because we disagree about what makes life worth living, it would be wrong for the government to take sides on this question' (2011: 2). Or as Rawls puts it, a politically liberal state should be concerned only with what is *right*, not with what is *good* (2005: 173).

Political liberalism is contrasted with *perfectionist* liberalism. Perfectionist liberals believe that liberty is valuable only when it is used to live a worthwhile life; and therefore the state should steer people towards worthwhile lives. Perfectionist liberalism therefore allows for a higher degree of *paternalism* – that is, obliging citizens to do (or not to do) certain things for their own good.

Nussbaum places herself firmly in the tradition of political liberalism. Some have disputed this, arguing that her capabilities approach implies perfectionism (see Chapter 4). My own view is that there is a continuum rather than a cleavage between political liberalism and perfectionist liberalism, and that Nussbaum has not moved very far along the continuum and is much closer to the political liberalism end of things.

Still, it is true that Nussbaum's thought takes its bearings, initially, from Aristotle, and Aristotle is generally counted as a perfectionist (though not a liberal one) because he has a definite idea of what makes for human flourishing. So, let us begin with Aristotle and the ancient Greeks.

Chapter 1

Nussbaum and the Ancient Greeks

Tragedy, the Luck-Proofing of Life,
and Practical Rationality

Martha Nussbaum's political philosophy is rooted in her moral philosophy, which is in turn rooted in the ethics of ancient Greek writers and thinkers. It is worth noting that Nussbaum's first orientation was towards classics, and in particular classical drama; she graduated with a BA in theatre and classics from New York University in 1969, before going on to specialise in philosophy at Harvard. Her first book, *The Fragility of Goodness* (first published in 1986) focuses on three major lines of ancient Greek ethical thought: the moral ideas embodied in Greek tragedy, particularly the work of Aeschylus and Sophocles; Plato's moral theory; and Aristotle's virtue ethics. These ideas are developed and related to moral and political theory in the modern world. Moreover, they form the roots of the future development of her work as it branches in different directions.

The Fragility of Goodness announces several themes that will continue to be important throughout Nussbaum's work. One of these is an acceptance that there is such a thing as human nature. But human nature is wide, various, rich and complex. Nussbaum is not a perfectionist – that is, she does not hold that there is one best kind of life which is suitable for everyone. Nevertheless, she does hold that, since we are the kind of creatures that we are, there are certain goods to which it's essential we have access. At an individual level, these goods should inform how we relate to one another personally; at a political level, governments should provide or facilitate access to them.

Another key theme is the centrality of personal relationships in any conception of a good life. For Nussbaum, relationships are one of the supreme goods of life, if not *the* supreme good, and this view informs all her later writings on morality and politics.

A third feature to note is not so much a theme as an approach or method: the use of literature to illuminate philosophical theory. In *The Fragility of Goodness* Nussbaum draws on Greek tragedy not

10

just for examples of moral dilemmas (although she does do that) but also because she finds philosophical ideas there, expressed in literary form. Throughout the rest of her career Nussbaum continues to use imaginative literature (as well as drawing on other intellectual disciplines such as economics and psychology) in her philosophical work and this book is a harbinger of the interdisciplinary approach she has employed throughout her career.

The Fragility of Goodness

Nussbaum begins with a quotation from the Greek lyric poet Pindar, which sets the theme and tone of the enquiry that is to follow: 'human excellence grows like a vine tree, fed by the green dew, raised up, among wise men and just, to the liquid sky' (Nussbaum 2013a: 1). The question Nussbaum addresses is explored as much in literature as in philosophy. That question is, how important is *luck* in pursing the goal of an excellent life? Pindar's vine tree will flourish if it is fed by the dew, but if through brute bad luck it is not so fed, it will wither and never achieve excellence. So, as Nussbaum frames the question, 'How much luck do these Greek thinkers believe we can humanly live with? How much *should* we live with, in order to live the life that is best and most valuable for a human being?' (2013a: 4)

Nussbaum points out that this question, so central to the Greeks, has been largely neglected through long periods of philosophical history, and in particular since the late-Enlightenment German philosopher Immanuel Kant. In his *Groundwork of the Metaphysics of Morals* (1785), Kant argues that the supreme principle of morality is the Categorical Imperative: an unconditional principle which it would be irrational to deny and which it is our duty to follow whether we like it or not. Kant's emphasis on reason, and his sharp distinction between moral and non-moral values, make the vagaries of fortune appear contingent and irrelevant to morality. Part of Nussbaum's mission here, then, is to return to centre stage a problem that for too long has been confined to the wings.

Nussbaum's move here should be seen in the context of a debate about moral luck which began to assume more prominence from the 1970s onwards. Egalitarian liberalism, represented in its most developed form by John Rawls, is attentive not just to bad things that happen to individuals, but to the fact that starting points can be bad in the first place.

So Nussbaum was not the first to bring luck back into moral philosophy. Her friend and mentor Bernard Williams had already reopened this area in his collection of essays *Moral Luck* (1981) and Nussbaum affords him due credit in *The Fragility of Goodness*. Williams had argued that we frequently make moral judgements of other people's actions based on how things turn out: he offers the example of Gauguin, who left his wife and children to go and paint in Tahiti. This was (perhaps) morally justified in that it brought great works of art into the world for others to enjoy; but Gauguin could not have known in advance that he would succeed. Indeed, as Williams says, he might have suffered an injury on the way to Tahiti that prevented him ever painting again. It was luck – events outside his control – that decided whether his action was morally justifiable.

Nussbaum is concerned with another side of the problem: not so much whether outcomes will luckily turn out to provide moral justification for our actions, but with the fact that the desired outcomes that our moral actions might seem to deserve can be derailed by brute bad luck. (Nussbaum also argues that Williams, though attentive to the importance of luck in Greek tragedy, underestimates the extent to which it figures in Greek philosophy too.) Nussbaum's enquiry has a three-part structure:

- an exploration of the way tragedy shows luck as a powerful force in shaping human lives;
- an examination and critique of Plato's attempts to 'luck-proof' life through the use of reason; and
- an analysis – and endorsement – of Aristotle's aim of striking a balance between the claims of practical rationality and the insights of tragedy.

Tragedy

Nussbaum points out that before the Greeks there was no clear demarcation between literature and philosophy:

> epic and tragic poets were widely assumed to be the central ethical thinkers and teachers of Greece; nobody thought of their work as less serious, less aimed at truth, than the speculative prose treatises of historians and philosophers. Plato regards the poets not as colleagues in another department, pursuing different aims, but as dangerous rivals. (2013a: 12)

The Greek tragedians (and epic poets too, but Nussbaum concentrates on tragedy) are rivals to Plato because they take *moral conflict* seriously. They depict moral conflicts as ineliminable and insoluble. For Plato, as for later moral philosophers in the Kantian and utilitarian traditions, in any apparent conflict there is always a right thing to do. Reason will tell you what it is. But tragedy forcefully, *dramatically* denies this.

Nussbaum focuses mainly on two Greek tragedies to explore this idea: Aeschylus's *Agamemnon* and Sophocles' *Antigone*. In *Agamemnon*, the eponymous king has had a tragic dilemma thrust upon him. He must lead the expedition to conquer Troy and bring back Helen. Zeus commanded him to do so; it would be both impious and cowardly to refuse. But, as the Chorus report near the beginning of the play, the goddess Artemis then intervened: Agamemnon's avenging fleet was becalmed in the port of Aulis and could not embark (so the seer Calchas divined) unless Agamemnon sacrificed his own daughter, Iphigenia.

The dilemma was not of Agamemnon's making. He in no way earned or caused it. Yet he must respond. If he refuses to fulfil Artemis's condition he defies Zeus; moreover, then the fleet will remain stranded and those aboard will starve. If he does fulfil Artemis's condition then he murders his own daughter. But he must either fulfil the condition or not fulfil it; no third way or compromise is available.

Agamemnon is seized by anger and grief. Both choices are horrible but they cannot both be avoided. Yet the instant he has judged that the *less* horrible choice is to make the sacrifice, 'something strange takes place', as Nussbaum puts it (2013a: 35). Agamemnon's attitude towards the decision changes as soon as he has made it. He is now confident that he is doing the right thing and expresses no further regrets. It is this change of heart that is condemned by the Chorus, rather than the sacrifice itself.

Nussbaum draws two lessons from Aeschylus's presentation of the dilemma. One is that sometimes there is no unambiguously right thing to do: the playwright 'shows us not so much a "solution" to the "problem of practical conflict" as the richness and depth of the problem itself' (2013a: 50). The second thing Aeschylus shows us is that pain, grief and remorse are inevitably bound up with the things we most value. We could avoid tragedy only by forswearing a range of deep ethical commitments. A life containing no possibility of tragedy would be a severely impoverished one.

In *Antigone*, the tragic conflict is played out between two characters rather than within one. Creon, King of Thebes, represents law, order, civic values and the security of the *polis*. Antigone, his niece and the fiancée of his son, represents familial obligation and piety. These values collide when Antigone's two brothers, Eteocles and Polynices, slay each other in battle at one of the gates of Thebes. Eteocles, who was fighting to defend the city, is buried with full military honours by Creon. But Polynices, who fought with the attacking force, is refused burial and left outside the city to be eaten by kites and vultures. This for Creon is a matter of principle: Polynices was a traitor to the city, and traitors should never be honoured. That is his duty, as he perceives it, and he will not be swayed from it.

But Antigone is Polynices' sister. For her it is a sacred duty that her brother *must* be buried. This indeed is the only duty she recognises. She defies Creon's order and slips out of the city to bury Polynices – with tragic results that include her own death, and the death of Creon's son and wife. Creon survives but is left a broken man.

Nussbaum's analysis of this tragedy is that both Creon and Antigone attempted to *simplify* their moral commitments so that they could be fully expressed in a single sentence: either 'Never bury dead traitors' or 'Always bury dead family members'. She relates this point to Hegel's discussion of the play in *The Philosophy of Fine Art* (1853). For Hegel, both Creon and Antigone hold positions that are narrow in themselves and contradictory with each other and the task is to effect a *synthesis* between them, so that future moral conflicts can be eliminated. Nussbaum partly endorses this view but with two important reservations. One, that although it's true that both positions are too narrow, Antigone's position in the context of the drama *is* superior to Creon's (one is reminded here of E. M. Forster's famous dictum, 'if I had to choose between betraying my country and betraying my friend, I hope I should have the guts to betray my country'; 1970: 76); and two, that eliminating all potential conflict is neither a feasible nor a desirable aim (Nussbaum 2013a: 67).

For Nussbaum, the characters who best articulate the nature of the dilemma and who propose not a solution but a response to it, are Creon's son Haemon and the blind seer Tiresias. Both urge flexibility, sensitivity, a willingness to be open to others. Haemon, for example, says to his father:

The world is full of different words, different voices.
Listen to the words, the voices.

Do not be a prisoner in yourself
Although you are a King of others.
For if any man thinks that he alone is wise
Then, my father, he's in danger of being mad. (Sophocles 1996: 30)

Haemon and Tiresias suggest, says Nussbaum, that:

Responsiveness (to other people, to the world of nature) may bring not immobility, but a finer and more supple sort of motion. And it is not simply that this way of proceeding is safer and more prudent. Haemon and Tiresias do say this. But they also indicate . . . that this way is also richer and more beautiful. To be flexibly responsive to the world, rather than rigid, is a way of living in the world that allows an acceptable amount of safety while still permitting recognition of the richness of value that is in the world. (2013a: 80)

Two points need to be made explicit here. First, Nussbaum is not arguing that such a flexible, sensitive approach on the part of either or both Creon and Antigone would definitely have averted the tragedy. It might not have done. But had it failed, still Creon and Antigone would have had a better, richer understanding of themselves, their values and the place of those values in life. And second, if the flexible approach were to work in *this* case, that is no guarantee that it must always do so. The vagaries of luck in human affairs mean that we can never expect more than 'an acceptable amount of safety' – unless, of course, there is a way to luck-proof life, and it is Plato's attempt to do just this that Nussbaum goes on to consider.

Plato

To make sense of the argument that follows, we need first to note an important opposition between two words of ancient Greek: *tuchē* and *technē*.

Tuchē could simply be translated as 'luck'. It does not necessarily imply randomness. It denotes whatever events of life human beings have no control over (Nussbaum 2013a: 89, n.1). It does not denote events of life over which humans *can* have no control, however. By extending our possibilities of control we reduce those areas of life where *tuchē* holds sway. And we can extend our possibilities of control through the use of *technē*.

Technē is variously translatable as art, science, skill, craft or know-how. It is the root, of course, of the modern English word 'technology', but does not imply mechanisation or automation. *Technē* means 'knowing how to do it' and is applicable in such diverse realms as carpentry, flute-playing and political organisation. Citing a range of ancient sources, including Hippocrates and Aristotle, Nussbaum identifies four essential features of *technē*: (1) universality, (2) teachability, (3) precision and (4) concern with explanation (2013a: 95). In any given field of endeavour, *technē* can reduce or perhaps (but this is the question at issue) even eliminate *tuchē*.

Nussbaum is wary of ascribing a single view to Plato. For one thing, his position alters over time. For another, even within a single dialogue alternative views are proposed and the dialogues seldom end conclusively. However, Nussbaum does offer a broad schema of Plato's response to the question of *tuchē* versus *technē*. In his early dialogues, she argues, the view that *technē* can do away with *tuchē* altogether is adumbrated. In the middle-period dialogues, this view is developed and strongly argued for. In the later dialogues, some doubt is cast on this confident view.

Protagoras is an example of an early dialogue in which the question is explored. Both Socrates and his interlocutor Protagoras agree that *technē* can be used to counter *tuchē*. However, Protagoras takes a conservative view, maintaining that existing *technē*, such as knowledge of how to manufacture goods, build houses and construct workable political systems, is enough to keep *tuchē* at bay most of the time. He upholds a plurality of values – as opposed to the 'unity of the virtues' for which Socrates will argue throughout his career – which, as Nussbaum says, 'keeps alive the possibility of tragedy'. A legislator following Protagoras's interpretation of *technē* will be skilled at avoiding, minimising or navigating conflicts, but will neither eliminate them completely nor expect to.

Socrates' view is more radical. He argues in this dialogue that there is only one goal to aim at: 'a life free from pain, a pleasurable life' (358b). And that goal can be achieved through an accurate weighing up of pleasures and pains. If there are two conflicting options, we can simply measure the amount of pleasure each would yield and choose the one that would yield the most. (As Nussbaum notes, this anticipates the single-value utilitarianism of Jeremy Bentham; 2013a: 123.)

The duel between Protagoras and Socrates is more evenly matched than the duels between Socrates and his interlocutors in most of the later dialogues. Protagoras is no pushover and as a result of the argument Socrates does change his initial position, that virtue cannot be taught. Nevertheless, on balance Socrates seems to win the argument. He succeeds in getting Protagoras to concede that virtue is a unity, rather than the five separate elements of goodness (knowledge, good sense, courage, respect for what's right, and piety) which Protagoras had earlier argued for. At the end of the dialogue Protagoras tells Socrates, with proleptic irony, 'I wouldn't be surprised if you ended up as a pretty famous name in philosophy' (361e). Nussbaum, however, is in sympathy with the initial position of Protagoras, that there is a *plurality* of values which need to be kept in balance – a position essential to the Aristotelian virtue ethics which she espouses and indeed (to look forward) to the capabilities approach she promulgates later in her career.

The view that *technē* can be deployed to eliminate *tuchē* is argued for at greater length and with more conviction in the middle-period dialogue, the *Republic*. Early in the dialogue (Book 1) Socrates converses with the old man Cephalus, who says that many elderly people bemoan the fact that they can longer enjoy the pleasures of their youth – sex and drinking and feasting – but that he is content to be released from these appetites. He quotes with approval Sophocles' saying that being released from the sexual urge is like 'being a slave who has got away from a rabid and savage master' (329c). This sets the general direction of the argument that is to follow, but Socrates will go much further than Cephalus in disvaluing the unreliable pleasures of appetite. He will argue that the best human life is 'the life of the philosopher, whose soul the *Phaedo* describes as akin to the forms it contemplates: pure, hard, single, unchanging, unchangeable. A life, then, of *goodness without fragility*' (Nussbaum 2013a: 138, my italics).

Nussbaum points out that the *Republic* makes two distinct claims about the role of reason in living a good life. One is about the *procedure* for living a good life and the other is about the *content* of a good life. The procedural claim is that 'the best life is a life "ruled" by reason, in which reason evaluates, ranks and orders alternative pursuits' (2013a: 138). This claim is argued for in Book 4, where reason is conceived as the controlling part of the soul which selects, orders and arranges which objects should be pursued. But as Nussbaum says, that argument offers no reason why 'the *content* of a life plan should not include appetitive activities as intrinsically valuable activities that get selected and arranged alongside the others' (2013a: 139). It should be noted that if reason played this role only, it could minimise but never eliminate the incursions of *tuchē* into a person's life.

17

The claim about content, however, is designed to eliminate *tuchē* – to luck-proof life. For *this* claim states that the best kind of human life is the life of the philosopher – where reason isn't used to determine what is valuable but is itself the valued thing. The best life is spent in intellectual contemplation – contemplation of the *truth*, which does not change, perish or decline and is invulnerable to the depredations of *tuchē*. This claim is cashed out fully in Book 9 of the *Republic*.

Socrates identifies three valuable and defining features of intellectual contemplation. First, its *purity*. It does not gain value as a relief from some other activity but stands alone; moreover the *objects* of philosophical contemplation (e.g. mathematical truths) are clear and pure. Second, its *stability*. Intellectual contemplation does not ebb and flow as the appetites do, and its objects are constant. Third, *truth*: philosophy leads to a grasp of how things really are in themselves, not as they appear to be (see Nussbaum 2013a: 147–8).

The consequence of such a view is *asceticism*. If intellectual activity is the most worthwhile of all activities, then appetitive pursuits are a distraction from the most valuable goal in life. Of course, one needs to eat and drink to stay alive and carry on contemplating, but satisfaction of these needs would be only instrumentally, not intrinsically valuable.

As Nussbaum points out, 'this standpoint is nothing like that of the ordinary human being' (2013a: 153). Ordinary human beings do ascribe intrinsic value to pleasures such as food and sex. Their lives go better when those needs are fulfilled. Plato of course would not deny this but would hold that ordinary people are simply deluded about what is valuable. Nussbaum does not agree with Plato about that, but she is sensitive to the attraction of his position (it is indeed typical of Nussbaum that she can see the strength of positions with which she disagrees).

Plato himself in the later dialogues does to some extent move away from the hard-line, ascetic, luck-proof theory of value in the *Republic*. In the *Symposium* – a dialogue on the nature of love – Socrates once again puts forward that theory but this time it is challenged with perhaps greater success. Socrates claims that what one loves in the beloved is *kalon* (beauty/value/goodness); and since all *kalon* is qualitatively the same (an exemplar of the ideal form of beauty) it does not matter who or what manifestation of *kalon* one loves. Therefore any object of love is *replaceable* – not by a good-enough substitute, but by something identical in essence. Ultimately, the philosopher will pass from beautiful things to an awareness of 'the Beautiful' in itself. If one is able to make this ascent – from perceiving individual instances of beauty to apprehending its universal, ideal form – then 'the lover escapes, gradually, from his bondage to luck' (Nussbaum 2013a: 181). If we follow Socrates and see beauty *in and for itself* then we have 'an object of love that is always available' (2013a: 182). We can never be disappointed, jealous or bereft. We are luck-proofed.

But at this point in the dialogue, enter Alcibiades. He is drunk, charming, charismatic, beautiful and crowned with violets – an irruption from the real (as distinct from the ideal) world. His speech about love focuses on the particular: on Socrates himself. Socrates is lovable because he is *him*. This is the opposite of Socrates' rarefied, form-loving view. And it is not luck-proofed. For if you love the particular you can fail to win the person you desire; or having won them, you can lose them. As Nussbaum points out, these visions of love are *alternatives*; you can't have both (2013a: 198). But the dialogue itself does not come down conclusively on one side or the other.

In the late dialogue *Phaedrus*, Plato seems to go further in distancing himself from the luck-proof position. It begins with the young man Phaedrus reading to Socrates a speech by the orator Lycias, in which Lycias argues that is wiser to accept the addresses of a suitor who does not love than one who does. Socrates is unimpressed by the speech. When challenged by Phaedrus to extemporise a better one, Socrates covers his head out of embarrassment, or so he claims, and delivers a high-flown speech about the demerits of lovers – they are suffering from a malady, ruled by desire, they are jealous, possessive and so on. He refrains from continuing with the merits of the non-lover, claiming he has said enough. But then Socrates commits a volte-face. He uncovers his head and, quoting a recantation of the poet Stesichorus, says 'This story isn't true'.

He now proceeds to argue that madness is not simply an evil. The distinction between madness and self-possession is too simplistic. 'Certain states of madness or possession are said to be both helpful and honourable, even necessary sources of the "greatest goods"' (Nussbaum 2013a: 213). Socrates' speech of recantation makes three points. As summarised by Nussbaum they are:

1. The non-intellectual elements are necessary sources of motivation energy.
2. The non-intellectual elements have an important guiding role to play in our aspiration towards understanding (2013a: 214).
3. The passions, and the actions inspired by them, are intrinsically valuable components of the best human life (2013a: 218–19).

On this view, then, the intellect is not pure and isolated from human desires but inextricably bound up with them. Therefore, 'Unlike the life of the ascending person in the *Symposium*, this best human life is unstable, always prey to conflict' (Nussbaum 2013a: 221). The *Phaedrus* gives us a 'rehabilitation of *mania*' and a 'new acceptance of the goodness of the risky and mutable' (2013a: 230).

This suggests a more complex view where *technē* cannot make life invulnerable to *tuchē* – a view endorsed and articulated in more detail by Aristotle.

Aristotle

For Nussbaum, of all the ancient Greek thinkers it is Aristotle who best captures the relationship between luck and the good life. As she puts it: 'Aristotle returns to and develops a conception of a human being's proper relationship to *tuchē* that returns to and articulates many of the insights of tragedy' (2013a: 237).

Unlike Plato, Aristotle regards appearances (*phainomena*) as evidence of how things are; they are not to be *opposed* to truth or reality, but instead provide evidence of it. 'Plato, then, is Aristotle's central target when he tells us that the *phainomena* are our best and only *paradeigmata* [examples]' (Nussbaum 2013a: 242). Aristotle's view is thus anthropocentric: that is, it's based on what and how phenomena appear to *human*s. The term 'anthropocentric' is often used in contemporary discourse to imply a failing – a limited, parochial or relativistic view. But that is not the sense intended here. Nussbaum means that Aristotle's ethics are rooted in human nature and faculties; and since it is the theory of a good life for humans that we seek, there is no better place to root them. As Nussbaum argues, one might have a notion of, for example, *time* that applied to all creatures; but not a notion of good. For the idea of good is species-relative (Nussbaum 2013a: 292).

Moreover, not only is the good species-relative; it is also *plural* and goods are *incommensurable* (2013a: 294). There is no single measurable standard, such as pleasure, underlying all goods. (This is, of course, a direct contradiction of the argument put forward by Socrates in the *Protagoras*, referred to above.)

The answer to what is good in a human life, then, must be sought in the practical sphere. But our knowledge of the practical sphere is incomplete and imperfect. Each new event may include features never before encountered. On this view, what is good may depend on

20

context. Aristotle, then, is concerned with the *particularity* of goods. And particularity means vulnerability to loss. Goods are not replaceable on a like-for-like basis, as Plato argued. Love of an individual person means love of *that* individual person.

It might seem from this discussion that Aristotle recommends a kind of pick-and-mix approach where the particularities of what makes for a good life depend simply on the preferences of the individual. Nussbaum anticipates this criticism: 'it is now time to say that the particular case would be absurd and unintelligible without the guiding and sorting power of the universal' (2013a: 306). One needs a sense of what is good, in the universal sense (universal for human beings, that is) in order to perceive value in individuals. To love what is good in an individual presupposes a general understanding of what counts as good. At the same time, coming to know examples (*paradeigmata*) of goodness as instantiated in individual men and women adds to and refines our conception of goodness: there is thus a 'two-way illumination' between the universal and the particular.

One might note here that this conception of our understanding of the good as a work in progress – an understanding that is imperfect but constantly developing – is in line with Nussbaum's liberal political philosophy, which aims at improvement rather than utopia.

Aristotle's account thus makes way for the passions as both motivators and guides in our efforts to live the good life. Moreover, satisfaction of appetites is itself (in moderation) intrinsically valuable and an essential part of the good life. By downgrading the role of *technē*, Aristotle makes more space for *tuchē*: he defends 'an attitude to contingent particulars that renounces the Platonic aspiration to control and unblemished activity' (2013a: 310). And thus vulnerability is admitted into the picture, since passions and appetites can always be thwarted or unsatisfied.

Is Aristotle's view circular, however? The standard for ethical deliberation is the view of a competent, wise, ethical judge. But who says they are competent and wise? They are judged wise only because they already endorse Aristotle's theory. Nussbaum concedes that there may be some circularity but argues that all complex ethical theories have an element of the circular; and Aristotle's circle is, after all, large and interesting (2013a: 311–12). And, as Nussbaum emphasises, it is not a fixed circle. Our notion of what is wise is subject to modification through experience.

Aristotle thus steers a course between two extremes – that luck has nothing to do with living a good life, and that luck has everything to do with it. For Aristotle, living well means acting well and our actions are always liable to impediment or disruption. Like Nussbaum, Aristotle looks to tragedy for his example and finds it in the fate of Priam, King of Troy. King Priam lived well – but then was deprived by war of children, family, friends, power and freedom and was finally killed ignominiously.

But this is an extreme case. In general, excellence of character (which means excellence in action) helps to preserve *eudaimonia* (a happy or flourishing life). As Nussbaum sums it up: 'In short, an Aristotelian conception of *eudaimonia*, which bases excellent activity on stable goodness of character, makes the good life tolerably stable in the face of the world. But this stability is not limitless' (2013a: 334). It cannot be limitless because activities essential to *eudaimonia* – activities of citizenship, friendship, love and so on – involve relations with others. Aristotle states that *philoi* (friends and loved ones) are the 'greatest of the external goods' (*Nicomachean Ethics*, 1169b10, quoted in Nussbaum 2013a: 354). This, inevitably, makes us vulnerable to loss. It is also a very different conception of love from the rather chilly ideal proposed by Domitia in Plato's *Symposium*.

One other difference between Plato and Aristotle is that Aristotle, unlike Plato, says very little about erotic love. Nussbaum surmises that this is because Aristotle, a heterosexual, had sex only with partners whom he regarded as inferior. This view might seem rather awkward for a modern Aristotelian (as might his views on slavery), but as Nussbaum points out, the difficulty stems rather from his own character, situation and culture than from his philosophical method. On this view, a neo-Aristotelian can be a better Aristotelian than Aristotle himself was.

Overall, then, Nussbaum endorses Aristotle's position that vulnerability to *tuchē* is an essential part of *eudaimonia*, but that the risk of loss or disaster can be managed and minimised by *tuchē*, as well as by practical wisdom (Aristotle's term for practical wisdom or judgement is *phronesis*). But it is worth remarking that Nussbaum acknowledges the attraction of Plato's position and notes that Aristotle himself took it seriously, even though he did not subscribe to it. It is typical of Nussbaum to admit the complexity of the questions she explores. This quality is one of the things which make her such a clear writer. Writers who proceed from over-simple premises are soon led to elaboration, obfuscation and evasion, in order to defend the simplicity with which they began.

With *The Fragility of Goodness*, Nussbaum made an important contribution to breaking up the duopoly of Kantianism and utilitarianism which had held sway over Anglo-American moral philosophy for decades if not over a century. Thanks in large part to Nussbaum (as well as other philosophers of the time such as Elizabeth Anscombe, Philippa Foot and Bernard Williams) virtue ethics came to be seen as a serious alternative to deontology and utilitarianism, to be further developed by, among others, Rosalind Hursthouse (1999). Nussbaum helped pave the way for the duopoly to become a triopoly.

The Therapy of Desire

Nussbaum returned to the philosophy of the ancient world eight years after the publication of *The Fragility of Goodness*, in her book *The Therapy of Desire*, first published in 1994. Here, her focus is on the Hellenistic rather than the classical period (the classical period is conventionally dated as from 480 to 323 BCE; the Hellenistic period from 323 to 31 BCE). Nussbaum's conception of the purpose of philosophy is that it must be 'for the sake of human beings, in order to address their deepest needs, confront their most urgent perplexities, and bring them from misery to some greater measure of flourishing' (2013b: 3).

The goal of flourishing is, of course, an Aristotelian one, but like the Stoics and unlike Aristotle Nussbaum does not restrict access to it. Everybody, not just free-born male citizens, has the same need and the same right to flourish. Philosophy should help not just the philosopher (as she points out, it is a rare privilege to be a philosopher) but others too to flourish. For Nussbaum, philosophy must be engaged with the real world. It can, she contends, 'perform social and political functions, making a difference in the world by using its own distinctive methods and skills' (2013b: 3). One aspect of Hellenistic thought which Nussbaum enthusiastically endorses is its 'combination of logic with compassion' (2013b: 9) – and indeed this is a neat description of her own approach to philosophy. It is worth noting that to take on the Hellenistic philosophers implies a challenge to Nussbaum's own position, as set forth in *Fragility*, that the most valuable kind of human life comprehends emotional attachments, which necessarily involve risk.

The Hellenistic schools – to be precise, the Epicureans, the Sceptics and the Stoics – all conceive of philosophy as a way of addressing life's most painful problems. Hellenistic ethics had been largely neglected by modern Western philosophy at the time Nussbaum was writing. That there has subsequently been a resurgence of interest in it is at least partly due to her efforts.

Nussbaum allows one exception to her claim that contemporary thinkers had ignored the Hellenistic thinkers: Michel Foucault, in volume 3 of his *The History of Sexuality* (1984), discusses them in some detail, but Nussbaum is not in agreement with his approach. She does endorse his claim that the Hellenistic philosophers 'are not just teaching lessons, but also engaging in complex practices of self-shaping' (Nussbaum 2013b: 5). But, Nussbaum points out, magic, ritual and religion also do this. Nussbaum claims that Foucault misses what is distinctive about philosophy – that it is 'an art that deals in valid and sound arguments, an art that is committed to the *truth*' (2013b: 5, my italics). It can thus free us from the tyranny of custom, creating a community of free beings who can think for themselves. But this is just what Foucault cannot acknowledge, because he thinks all knowledge is a form of power – which is just what Nussbaum denies. (This is one of Nussbaum's earlier clashes with what has come to be loosely termed 'postmodern' thought. Here, though her disagreement with Foucault is radical, she treats his position with respect; in some of her later disagreements with postmodernists, that respect is absent or far more qualified.)

Nussbaum's programme is 'to investigate [the] idea of a compassionate "medical" philosophy by studying its development in the three major Hellenistic schools, Epicurean, Stoic and Skeptic' (2013b: 40). The Epicureans were followers of the materialist philosopher Epicurus (341–270 BCE), who taught that the goal of human life was happiness, to be secured by absence of pain and mental anxiety. He emphasised the values of friendship, self-sufficiency and being satisfied with little. The Epicureans formed communities to live according to these values. The Stoics believed that happiness results from virtue alone, and that a wise person would not undergo passionate emotions. Notable Stoic philosophers include Seneca, Epictetus and the Roman emperor, Marcus Aurelius. Sceptics aimed at tranquillity through a lack of attachment to beliefs. A notable Sceptic of the Hellenistic period was Sextus Empiricus (160–210 CE).

The metaphor of philosophy as medical treatment, or therapy, runs throughout the whole book. Also running through the book is the character of Nikodion, a female student who studies at the feet, successively, of Epicurean, Sceptic and Stoic philosophers (principally Epicurus, Lucretius, Sextus Empiricus and Seneca), in search of philosophical therapy for her problems: her unsatisfied desires, her anger, her fear of death, her itch to know things. Nikodion was, it seems, an actual pupil of Epicurus, but little is known about the real-life woman so the Nikodion who appears here is a fictional creation, able to range across space and time (and, when she studies with Aristotle early in the book, to assume male form, since he had little truck with female philosophers).

Nussbaum explores the arguments put forward by these philosophers, and how they might cure Nikodion's ills, in some detail. For example, Nussbaum asks us to visualise Nikodion taking a walk on a spring morning, relishing the beauty of the green leaves, the smell of the air, and the sparkle of sunlight on water, and being struck by the realisation that this moment, like all moments, is fleeting; and one inevitable day, all moments will be stopped forever by Death. This seems to Nikodion to be unacceptable: 'It is an illness that must, she thinks, have a cure' (Nussbaum 2013b: 193).

There follows a fascinating exploration of the thought of Epicurus and Lucretius, who both offer arguments that death is nothing to fear. In his long poem *De Rerum Natura*, which draws on the thought of Epicurus, Lucretius presents several arguments to show that we should not fear death:

1. A state of affairs can only be bad for a person who exists as a possible subject of experience; but after a person's death, they no longer exist as an experiencing subject; so death cannot be bad; so death is nothing to fear.
2. The 'symmetry' argument: the time before our death will be no different (as far as we are concerned) from the time before our birth. If the latter does not trouble us, neither should the former.
3. The 'banquet' argument': life is like a banquet of many courses, with its own structure; the end of the banquet is what gives the whole its shape and meaning.
4. The 'population' argument: if nobody died, but babies continued to be born, the world would soon be over-populated to an unendurable degree. (See Nussbaum 2013b: 201–4)

Nussbaum forensically examines the arguments, and the responses of modern philosophers such as Thomas Nagel and Bernard Williams, at a level of detail which we cannot reproduce here. The upshot is as follows. Lucretius's arguments do offer rational reasons that should *abate* the dread of death; but they do not remove it altogether nor is it desirable that they should. Lucretius's poem offers two different voices or perspectives on death: the personified voice of Nature, and a godlike indifference in which all human concerns are trivial. Nussbaum endorses the first of these but not the second. The godlike perspective, she argues, would take away the possibility of human virtue (an invulnerable and immortal god would have no use for the virtue of courage, for example) and omit much or most of what is valuable in human lives: 'the component of friendship, love, and love of country that consists in a willingness to give up one's life must be absent as well' (Nussbaum 2013b: 227).

The voice of Nature, on the other hand, does offer reasons why we should accept the fact of death. The banquet argument does suggest that death need be no bad thing: a banquet that lasted forever would be meaningless – not a banquet, in fact. The population argument urges upon us a fact of nature: that new people must be born, loved, nurtured and enabled to grow to adulthood. To make this possible, older people must die to make room. By accepting death on an individual level we consent to the wider good.

However, considering death in this light does not prevent *premature* death from being a tragedy. Just as the banquet could go on too long, it could also end too soon, when one has barely consumed the starter. Nikodion therefore is not wrong to fear premature death; and, as Nussbaum points out, most deaths are in some sense premature. Therefore Nikodion should embrace her fear of death along with her delight in life. Death is, as Nussbaum puts it, 'a condition of our best possibilities' (2013b: 231) – we could not get rid of it without ceasing to value the things that we do and ought to value.

Nussbaum, therefore, does not fully endorse Lucretius's therapy for Nikodion, but offers a modified, more nuanced and humanised therapy of her own instead.

What, then, are Nussbaum's overall conclusions? First, she amply demonstrates that the Hellenistic schools did view the function of philosophy to be therapeutic – a view that Nussbaum herself agrees with. In terms of how *successful* the three main schools are in fulfilling that function, she argues that they all have much to teach us, in that all see dispelling false beliefs as a vital part of therapy and all have interesting arguments to offer in doing so. But she concludes that the Stoic approach is the best, since, unlike Scepticism and Epicureanism, Stoicism sees accurate and honest reasoning as one of the *goals* of a healthy mind, rather than merely a means to achieving it. The Stoic conception of therapy, then, is the most promising one as it acknowledges an essential element of human nature: the fact that we are rational creatures.

However, Nussbaum does not fully endorse Stoicism for she cannot endorse its goal of achieving *ataraxia*, or a state of mental serenity – which she reads as aiming to get rid of human passions. This is not only unachievable but profoundly undesirable. It ignores the most valuable goods of life. A balance needs to be struck between over-reaction to life's inevitable ills and continuing to value the precious but fragile goods of love, friendship and community. This steering a balance between undesirable extremes is something we see again and again in Nussbaum's philosophy (which probably reflects the pervasive influence of Aristotle on her thought).

A further criticism of the Hellenistic schools is that they are politically *quietist*. They do not challenge the status quo. The therapy they propose is aimed at the individual, not at the institutions under which the individual lives. They teach indifference in the face of calamity, rather than seeking structural ways of reducing the likelihood or impact of calamities. Nussbaum endorses this criticism to some extent. Certainly she does not accept that *ataraxia* or *apatheia* is all that is necessary for flourishing, nor that all painful problems can be solved or treated at an individual level. Again she argues that, of the Hellenistic schools, the Stoics do best. They show that our emotions and desires are shaped by society; and they do propose an ideal – the ideal of community (2013b: 11–12). Moreover, the ideal of universal human equality is at bottom a Stoic idea. One can say that to study the 'inner world' is a necessary if not a sufficient condition for a practical political philosophy (2013b: 12). The two key Stoic ideals of community and equality, then, could form the basis for a more worked-out *political* philosophy.

At the end of the book Nussbaum, echoing the charges she made against Plato in *Fragility*, concludes:

> Abandoning the zeal for absolute perfection as inappropriate to the life of a finite being, abandoning the thirst for punishment and self-punishment that so frequently accompanies that zeal, the education I recommend looks with mercy at the ambivalent excellence and passion of a human life. (2013b: 510)

Two points are worth drawing out from that conclusion. First, it is a statement of anti-perfectionism. It reflects Nussbaum's belief that there is no one kind of perfect life for human beings; and, of the plurality of good lives in conformity with human nature, none is likely to be realised fully. Second, it suggests a widening of the purpose of philosophy. Philosophy is not just therapy for the troubled individual but can be therapy for a troubled society – hence the looking forward to education, the subject of her next book.

The Therapy of Desire was successful in achieving a secondary and perhaps unintended outcome: the rekindling of both scholarly and popular interest in a neglected period of philosophy. In his review for the *London Review of Books*, Bernard Williams commented: 'she has certainly redeemed [the Hellenistic philosophers] from celebratory entombment in the history of philosophy' (1994). In 1999, the journal *Philosophy and Phenomenological Research* published a *Symposium* on the book, with contributions from Martin Fischer (questioning Lucretius's 'existence requirement' as necessary for having bad experiences), Robert C. Roberts (challenging the Stoics' and Nussbaum's claim that emotions are a kind of judgement), Richard Sorabji (agreeing with, but offering further qualifications to Nussbaum's endorsement of Stoic philosophy as therapy) and Brad Inwood (arguing that Stoic morality was more dogmatic and authoritarian than Nussbaum acknowledges). Despite the criticisms, all the contributors engage enthusiastically with the book, and Fischer and Sorabji in particular praise it highly.

The *Symposium* concludes with Nussbaum's response to the critical essays. Philosophers' replies to their critics can be revealing. Often the tone is lordly, tetchy, or an uneasy combination of both. Nussbaum's responses are courteous and reasonable, defending her positions, noting where agreement exists, trying to clear up misunderstandings and granting that, as always in philosophy, there is more to be said. It is true that she accuses Inwood of misreading her, which might sound like fighting talk, but she does regret any 'unclarity in expression' on her part that may have led to the misunderstanding (Nussbaum 1999: 818).

This scholarly interest was to be followed in the next few years by a growth in popular interest in Hellenistic philosophy and in Stoicism in particular. For example, popular philosophy books published subsequent to *The Therapy of Desire* include *A New Stoicism* (Becker 1998), *A Guide to the Good Life: The Ancient Art of Stoic Joy* (Irvine 2008), *Travels with Epicurus* (Klein 2012), *The Daily Stoic* (Holiday, 2016), *Stoicism and the Art of Happiness* (Robertson, 2019), *How to Be a Stoic* (Pigliucci 2017) and *The Little Book of Stoicism* (Salzgeber 2019). One cannot know for sure how much of this was a result of

Nussbaum's influence, and other sources such as Pierre Hadot's *Philosophy as a Way of Life* (1981) should be mentioned here, but it would be surprising if there were no causal connection at all.

Summary

The Fragility of Goodness and *The Therapy of Desire* are significant stages in Nussbaum's political thinking for a number of reasons. Both exhibit features of her approach to philosophy which will remain consistent throughout her career:

- the project of returning to classic texts and reappraising and readapting them for contemporary purposes;
- the conviction that philosophy is no idle pursuit but ought to be *helpful* to humanity;
- a commitment to a clear, elegant and readable style, making her work appealing to those outside the confines of the academy.

More specifically, in *Fragility* Nussbaum identifies some of the chief goods of human life – love, friendship, relationships, community – which help to determine what politics is *for*. In addition, *Fragility* moves towards a form of virtue ethics, turning away from the utilitarianism which had been a salient feature of political thought, at least in Anglo-American philosophy, since Bentham and Mill – thus paving the way for her development of the capability approach.

Therapy continues the movement from moral to political philosophy (not that Nussbaum sees the two as distinct; for Nussbaum, normative political theory is based on normative moral theory, and both are based on an idea of human nature). Although *Therapy* is concerned with treating the philosophical ailments of the individual, it ends with the claim that understanding one's inner self is not sufficient alone. Community and a principle of human equality are also necessary (it's because Stoicism comprehends these things that Nussbaum judges it to be superior to other Hellenistic schools). And so is education, which is the subject of Nussbaum's 1997 book, *Cultivating Humanity*.

Chapter 2

Nussbaum and Education

Socratic Scrutiny, World Citizenship
and the Narrative Imagination

Cultivating Humanity (1997) marks a distinct turn from the question of what makes for a good human life to the question of how to get it; or, one might say, from moral to political philosophy. The book continues Nussbaum's practice of drawing on other disciplines. Like the Greeks whose ideas have inspired her, she makes no sharp distinction between philosophy and other arts, and *Cultivating Humanity* is an interesting hybrid of philosophy, literary criticism, history, case studies and autobiography.

Cultivating Humanity also features another hallmark of Nussbaum's work: its engagement with the real world. She is no ivory tower philosopher, noting in her preface that 'philosophy should not be written in detachment from real life' (1997: ix). The book grew from her two decades of experience teaching at Harvard, Brown, the University of Chicago and dozens of other campuses where she was a Visiting Professor, and she first began to outline the ideas of the book in articles for the *New York Review of Books* and the *New Republic*, rather than in scholarly journals which would have reached only a small, specialist readership.

One of those articles was a lengthy (nearly 8,000 words) response to Allan Bloom's *The Closing of the American Mind* (1987). Bloom's book, subtitled *How Higher Education Has Failed Democracy and Impoverished the Souls of Today's Students*, is an attack on the values of American students, castigating them for, among other things, their ignorance of books and their love of rock music, but most importantly of all, their *relativism*. Bloom begins the book with the claim that 'almost every student entering the university believes, or says he believes, that truth is relative' (1987: 25). This relativism results in an unlimited open-mindedness which, Bloom argues, is paradoxically a *closing* of the mind, since it requires a total suspension of the critical faculty. Praised by conservatives, damned by progressives, the book became an unexpected best-seller and is often credited with having kick-started the so-called 'culture wars'.

Nussbaum's article, which appeared in the *New York Review of Books* and was later included as a chapter in her collection of reviews, *Philosophical Interventions* (2012a), is not only a trenchant critique of Bloom's position (as well as his scholarship and the vagueness of his arguments), but also an early manifesto for her own philosophy of education. It should be said that Nussbaum does agree with Bloom's diagnosis that relativism is rife and that this is not a good thing. However, Nussbaum disagrees very strongly indeed with his prescription. The prescription rests 'upon his understanding of the texts of ancient Greek philosophy and of the nature of the philosophical life' (2012a: 40). In the early portions of the book, Nussbaum says, Bloom's defence of the ancient conceptions of philosophy might lead us to expect a plea for an education enabling 'each and every person . . . to have both the opportunity and the incentive to engage in studies that awaken the rational search for a good life' (2012a: 46). But when he comes to the business of making recommendations, he offers a philosophy of education that is 'not practical, alive, and broadly distributed, but contemplative and quasi-religious, removed from ethical and social concerns, and the preserve of a narrow elite' (2012a: 46).

Cultivating Humanity

Cultivating Humanity, appearing ten years after that review, sets out in full Nussbaum's own philosophy of education, and could be seen as both a rebuttal of and an alternative to Bloom's position. Indeed, in the first chapter she restates her disagreement with Bloom:

> There is a widespread fear – reflected, for example, in Allan Bloom's book *The Closing of the American Mind* – that critical scrutiny of one's own traditions will automatically entail a form of cultural relativism that holds all ways of life to be equally good and thereby weakens allegiance to one's own . . . But this of course is not what Socratic scrutiny implies. Rather, it implies that we should cling to that which we can rationally defend, and be willing to discover that this may or may not be identical with the view we held when we began the enquiry . . . If Bloom and others do think that American traditions are so fragile that mere knowledge of other ways will cause young people to depart from them, why are they so keen on endorsing and shoring up these fragile traditions? (Nussbaum 1997: 33)

Cultivating Humanity focuses on the curriculum and teaching practices of American universities, so there is no treatment of primary and secondary education, nor of education systems in other countries. But the liberal principles grounding Nussbaum's recommendations could, of course, be transferred and applied to earlier stages of education or to other systems. The book is subtitled 'A Classical Defense of Reform in Liberal Education'. What does Nussbaum mean by 'reform'? In the context of the 1990s, she is referring to changes in the humanities curriculum to include what were then new subjects such as women's studies and African American studies – which Nussbaum is strongly in favour of. But the idea of reform also has a wider and more timeless application: it is a call for a rethink of the *purpose* of higher education which, Nussbaum argues, is already under way and needs to be supported. Note that she wants these changes to occur within the framework of a 'liberal education' – a phrase which has gone out of fashion somewhat, but Nussbaum makes a cogent case for it and it is, in my view, an ideal urgently deserving of rehabilitation. What, then, does, Nussbaum mean by a liberal education?

A Liberal Education

In general terms, she is talking about the kind of broad, multidimensional education that produces a well-rounded individual: an education that cultivates the person to fulfil the demands of citizenship and to live a rewarding life. Note that the purpose of this kind of education is not purely vocational. Enriching the inner life is as important as, and not isolated from, equipping the student to function well in the world. This kind of education should be for everyone, does not treat books as authorities, aims to cultivate independence of thought, is pluralist, and accepts norms of reason and objectivity.

Nussbaum's ideas on education fit well into a liberal tradition of seeing education as a means of encouraging rationality and a critical spirit, rather than simply delivering knowledge. The tradition can be traced at least as far back as John Locke's *Some Thoughts Concerning Education* ([1693] 1996). Locke concentrates on the early education of children by their parents, whereas Nussbaum focuses on the education of young adults at university level. Nevertheless, much of Locke's advice would be endorsed by Nussbaum: for example, his insistence that children should not be subjected to physical punishment, that they should be treated as rational creatures, and that learning should be made pleasurable rather than imposed as a compulsory task (1996: 33, 58, 113–14).

Rather more contemporaneously, philosopher of education Israel Scheffler offers an account of the purpose of education congruent with Nussbaum's approach. Scheffler argues that the goal of education is to teach self-sufficiency, which requires 'self-awareness, imaginative weighing of alternative courses of action, understanding of other people's choices and ways of life, decisiveness without rigidity, emancipation from stereotyped ways of thinking and perceiving . . . empathy . . . intuition, criticism and independent judgment' (Scheffler 1973: 124). And, he says, educators should 'surrender the idea of shaping or molding the mind of the pupil. The function of education . . . is rather to liberate the mind, strengthen its critical powers, [and] inform it with knowledge and the capacity for independent inquiry' (Scheffler 1973: 139). Nussbaum endorses this liberatory function. What is distinctive about her approach is (a) the application of liberal principles to a modern, multicultural world and (b) the specificity of her proposals.

Three unstated but fundamental principles underlie Nussbaum's model of education. First, that there is such a thing as objective truth. Second, that the goal of education is to discover or at least approach closer to the truth. And third, because we don't yet know what the truth is, the goal of achieving it must be pursued by allowing a plurality of views and voices to be heard.

All three of these principles were under challenge at the time Nussbaum was writing (paradoxically, of course, her own principles commit one to the view that they *should* be challenged) from what may broadly be termed postmodernism: an umbrella term for a range of theories which are intellectually indebted to French thinkers of the late twentieth century such as Michel Foucault and Jacques Derrida. What they have in common is (a) a scepticism about grand explanatory narratives; (b) a mistrust of the claims of reason; and (c) a tendency to a relativist view of truth, holding it to be inseparable from ideology and power.

If anything, this radical scepticism appears to be even more prevalent in academia today. Nussbaum was fully aware of this challenge and explicitly positioned herself against it in *Cultivating Humanity.*

She identifies three capacities necessary for cultivating our humanity as she sees it:

- a Socratic examination of life;
- 'world citizenship', requiring knowledge and understanding of other cultures besides one's local culture; and
- 'narrative imagination', i.e. the ability to put oneself in another's shoes, which is best served by the study of literature. The importance of literature and the humanities is, of course, a recurring theme in Nussbaum.

Socratic Self-Examination

Nussbaum makes a distinction between what she terms the 'Old Academy' and the 'Think-Academy'. The Old Academy is the traditional model of education: the transmission by authorities of accepted wisdom and pieties. The 'Think-Academy' follows the Socratic model of questioning – not swallowing traditional norms without thought but subjecting them to rational scrutiny and criticism. This latter approach is at the heart of a liberal education.

Historically, the Old Academy was associated with conservatism. Socrates was of course tried and found guilty of corrupting the young, and some conservative commentators accuse modern colleges and universities of doing the same thing (Nussbaum 1997: 15). But as Nussbaum points out, Socratic reason today is often rejected by the left as well as the right: 'It is fashionable today in progressive intellectual circles to say that rational argument is a male western device, in its very nature subversive of the equality of women and minorities and non-western people' (1997: 18–19). Nussbaum argues that these modern, or rather postmodern, opponents are as mistaken as their right-wing predecessors: 'Socratic argument is not undemocratic. Nor is it subversive of the just claims of excluded people. In fact, as Socrates knew, it is essential to a strong democracy and to any lasting pursuit of justice' (1997: 19). This claim – that justice relies on and is allied to reason – is a central thesis of the book, and underpins her critique of postmodernism.

Nussbaum's statement of the importance of Socratic questioning runs as follows:

> Liberal education in our colleges and universities is, and should be, Socratic, committed to the activation of each student's independent mind and to the production of a community that can genuinely reason together about a problem, not just trade claims and counter-claims. (1997: 19)

Two points are worthy of note here. First, the statement bears the influence of John Rawls in its espousal of the idea of *public reason*. In his book *Political Liberalism*, Rawls argues that political questions are to be debated and decided by *public reason* – that is, by appeal to publicly available values and standards, which all reasonable citizens can accept. Personal or sectarian values and standards cannot be used to evaluate public policy (see Rawls 2005).

Second, Nussbaum's point applies even more pertinently to the academic culture of today. Mistrust of reason in the humanities seems to have become more firmly entrenched since 1997; the postmodern, broadly Foucauldian claim that reason, truth, logic and objectivity are tools of the oppressor tends to be presented, or assumed, with the same kind of dogmatic certainty that Nussbaum associates with the Old Academy. Nussbaum regards such claims as inaccurate, condescending and unsupported by empirical evidence, often showing ignorance of the cultures they claim to be defending (1997: 38).

For Nussbaum, the Socratic ideal of the 'examined life' is a 'central educational goal for democracy' (1997: 28), and equally valuable to all ethnic or cultural groups within a democratic society. She makes five claims for Socratic education:

1. It is for everyone (1997: 30).
2. It can and should be tailored to the student's circumstances and context (1997: 32).
3. It should be pluralistic (1997: 32).
4. Books should not be treated as authorities (1997: 33).
5. It requires the ability to reason logically – for example, to be able to tell the difference between a valid and an invalid argument (1997: 35–6).

It will be seen that these claims place Nussbaum firmly in opposition to the central tenets of what is loosely called postmodernism. Nussbaum does allow that some work of value has been done by postmodern thinkers. She concedes that the work of Michel Foucault contains 'important insights and remains the only truly important work to have entered philosophy under the banner of "postmodernism"' (Nussbaum 1997: 40). On the other hand, she also criticises Foucault's writing for its 'historical incompleteness' and 'lack of conceptual clarity' (1997: 40).

Nussbaum does agree with the postmodern claim that there are problems with a naive view of unmediated access to objectivity. But rather than junking the ideal of objectivity, one should instead be alert to bias, pursuing objective truth 'in a more nuanced way, taking account of the shaping role of our categories' (Nussbaum 1997: 40). Denying the very possibility of achieving or even approaching truth is, in Nussbaum's view, intellectually disastrous: 'What is deeply pernicious in today's academy, then, is the tendency to dismiss the whole idea of pursuing truth and objectivity as if those aims could no longer guide us' (1997: 40).

Nussbaum is not content simply to state the value of Socratic reasoning and leave it at that. She goes on to exemplify the point by discussing a variety of higher education institutes in America that already build an element of critical enquiry into their curriculums: Bentley College in Massachusetts, which, although a business college, has a compulsory philosophy module for all students; Harvard's Core Curriculum which contains a one-semester moral reasoning requirement and a one-semester social analysis requirement; St. Lawrence University, a liberal arts college that offers a cross-disciplinary Cultural Encounters programme, encouraging students to 'think Socratically about central moral and political issues' (Nussbaum 1997: 44). She records the experiences of individual students who have benefited from such programmes. As is usual with Nussbaum, she aims to show that her principles can be instantiated in the real world and calls on empirical evidence to prove it.

Citizens of the World

Nussbaum states that a central goal of education must be to 'to educate people who can operate as world citizens with sensitivity and understanding' (1997: 52).

She advocates a form of cosmopolitanism, the roots of which go back as far as the ancient Greek Cynic Diogenes, who claimed 'I am a citizen of the world'. The idea is that, although we belong to and have affiliations with the local community of our birth, we are also part of the global community of all human beings, who share common concerns and values such as justice, in virtue of our shared human nature. This was also the view of the Stoic philosophers such as Seneca, Cicero and Marcus Aurelius (Nussbaum had already discussed this in *The Therapy of Desire*: [1994] 2013b: 341–4). She points out that this view is *not* a specifically Western one: it was shared by the Indian poet and writer Rabindranath Tagore, whose cosmopolitan views stemmed from Bengali traditions, and she also cites in support the philosopher Kwame Anthony Appiah, who says, of African identity: 'We will only solve our problems if we see them as human problems arising out of a special situation, and we shall not solve then if we see them as African problems generated by our being somehow unlike others' (quoted in Nussbaum 2997: 53).

This kind of cosmopolitanism, though alert to cultural differences, regards all humans as fundamentally equal and in essentials alike. It will be seen, then, that Nussbaum is an ethical universalist, not an ethical particularist. Her cosmopolitanism, however, does not take a political form: that is to say, she does not advocate the formation of a world government. For Nussbaum, cosmopolitanism is fully compatible with the existence of the nation-state (her later, more developed views on cosmopolitanism are explored in Chapter 8).

It follows that a liberal education needs to be multicultural and multi-faith. It is to be expected that the curriculum will mainly focus on students' home culture, 'but in a way that reminds the student of the broader world of which the Western traditions are a part' (Nussbaum 1997: 68–9). All school pupils, from first grade onwards, should have been taught about the major world religions, Nussbaum argues. At university level, Nussbaum reviews a number of programmes already run by universities at the time of writing which encouraged multicultural, or intercultural understanding. At Reno, for instance, there was an elective programme where students studied one chosen culture other than their own; St. Lawrence at the time offered the Cultural Encounters programme already referred to, designed by Cornwell and Stoddart, which included a requirement to study the culture of either Kenya or India, to live abroad for a month, and to learn a foreign language. But the precise details of any particular programme are not the key point: the key point is that the *purpose* of a liberal education is to produce world citizens, and there are many ways in which that could be achieved. Nussbaum presents the goal of world citizenship, which emphasises commonalities at the same time as exploring difference, as an alternative and preferable approach to identity politics (see Nussbaum 1997: 71–2). Since Nussbaum wrote *Cultivating Humanity*, identity politics has arguably taken over large sections of the academy in the humanities, and the very phrase 'world citizenship' now sounds a little quaint. Which does not, of course make it any the less worthwhile a goal.

37

The Narrative Imagination

To become world citizens, we must enter into a sympathetic, imaginative understanding of other lives; and it is here that the arts have a vital role to play. Nussbaum urges that we should study art and literature from other ages and cultures. Literature stimulates 'the compassionate imagination' (Nussbaum 1997: 93) and as global citizens our compassionate imagination should be all-embracing; we should therefore make sure we include works that give voice to 'members of other cultures, ethnic and racial minorities, women, and lesbians and gay men' (1997: 100). As is her usual practice, Nussbaum offers a concrete example: a student at Reno, Eric Chalmers, was given the task of writing a letter to his parents in the persona of a gay man – an activity designed to extend the sympathetic imagination and one that is 'closely connected to the Socratic activity of questioning one's own values' (1997: 100).

For Nussbaum, literature can only perform its function of extending our imaginative functions when approached in a liberal humanist way: that is, responding to literary characters as if they were real people with real emotions, and problems, conflicts and dilemmas analogous to our own. For example, she cites Charles Dickens's *A Christmas Carol* (1997: 14) as a literary work where we can understand and respond to Scrooge's moral and spiritual transformation, putting ourselves in his shoes even though we have may have very little in common with him (we don't have to be white, male, middle-aged, miserly Victorian businessmen to get it).

Nussbaum therefore rejects two rival approaches which lie on either side of her own, not for the first or last time steering a course between undesirable extremes. On the one hand, she rejects a purely formalist approach, where the critic analyses texts in terms of structure, patterns, contrasts, oppositions and other formal features, without responding emotionally. At the same time, she rejects a politicised view based on group identities. This is not because there is any problem about taking political sides. On the contrary, it is good to have a spectrum of political views. The real problem is:

> the prevalence of an approach to literature that questions the very possibility of a sympathy that takes one outside one's group, and of common human needs and interests as a basis for that sympathy. The goal of producing world citizens is profoundly opposed to the spirit of identity politics. (Nussbaum 1997: 109)

Nussbaum's liberal humanism thus forms the basis for her world-citizen view, which is the exact opposite of the identity politics view. Her position is fundamentally antithetical to the notion that 'cultural appropriation' in literature is, in itself, a bad thing (of course, cultural appropriation *can* be done insensitively or exploitatively, and often is, but that is a different matter). Since Nussbaum wrote, the formalist approach associated with structuralism and some forms of post-structuralism has fallen from fashion somewhat, but her own liberal humanist approach is if anything even more out of favour. The group-identity-based approach is in the ascendant. But Nussbaum's conception of literature as appealing to universal human sympathies, and thus able to *widen* our sympathies, still seems to have much to recommend it.

The Study of Non-Western Cultures

If the aim of education is to produce world citizens, then it should produce citizens who know something about the world; and for Western students, that means learning about non-Western cultures. But Nussbaum notes two potential pitfalls in studying cultures other than one's own: *descriptive chauvinism* and *descriptive romanticism* (Nussbaum 1997: 118). Both of these errors may be seen as forms of what Edward Said termed 'Orientalism' (1978). Following Foucault, Said defines Orientalism as a discourse about Middle Eastern and Asian cultures, which represents the Orient in terms of a series of oppositions with Europe – rationality/irrationality; order/disorder – where the privileged term is associated with Europe. Nussbaum, however, does not follow Said's Foucauldian approach, nor agree that such characterisations of the Other are as entrenched or systematic as Said presents them. Instead, she takes them to be *mistakes* which we can watch out for and correct or avoid.

Descriptive chauvinism is 'recreating the other in the image of one-self' – making the strange into the familiar. What's different is then often ignored, downgraded or reinterpreted to make it less different.

Romantic chauvinism is 'the expression of a romantic longing for exotic experiences that our own familiar lives seem to deny us' (Nussbaum 1997: 123). This kind of chauvinism often involves valorising the exotic as a repository of essential qualities which the effete West has neglected or forgotten – much as avant-garde artists of the early twentieth century valorised 'primitive' art as being in closer touch with the emotions than the over-sophisticated Western tradition. The example of romantic chauvinism that Nussbaum offers is significant; she cites Derrida's reading of Chinese culture as '"a powerful movement of civilisation developing outside all logocentrism"' (1997: 126). This reading, Nussbaum says, is simplistic, citing the Chinese scholar Zhang Longxi's verdict that 'Derrida's discussion of Chinese culture gives no evidence of serious study' (1997: 126), and that in fact the Chinese tradition of language, thinking and writing is in many respects comparable to the Western tradition. (The accusation of lack of serious scholarship is one that Nussbaum repeatedly presses against postmodern theorists – see her critique of Judith Butler in Chapter 3.)

Romantic and descriptive chauvinism are not the only intellectual vices Nussbaum identifies: she also warns of 'normative chauvinism' (the assumption that one's own culture is always best); 'normative Arcadianism' (the assumption that non-Western cultures are spiritual, perfect and unspoilt); and 'normative skepticism' (the suspension of all normative judgement of other cultures) (see Nussbaum 1997: 130–8). In her later work Nussbaum is particularly critical of the last of these, as in her condemnation of FGM (female genital mutilation) (see Chapter 3). It is worth noting that these intellectual vices can come from both the political right and the political left, with the right more likely to incline to the vice of the chauvinism and the left more likely to incline to the vices of romanticism, Arcadianism or normative scepticism. Again, we see Nussbaum steering a middle course – or perhaps it is more accurate to say, a balanced course, sensitive to nuance and complexity.

To avoid these pitfalls, we need to see all cultures as *real*. Cultures must not be seen as monoliths, but as rich, diverse and containing 'argument, resistance and contestation of norms' (Nussbaum 1997: 127). Moreover, cultures have a present and future as well as a past; they are not preserved in aspic and it is necessary to appreciate this to see them as real. As well as the study of a non-Western culture, Nussbaum makes two more specific prescriptions: 'All students should gain some understanding of the major world religions' (1997: 145) and 'All students should also master a foreign language' (1997: 145).

The Role of African American Studies

Nussbaum's vigorous defence of African American studies is of specific relevance to education in the United States, but the principles underlying it have a more universal application. She presents a more nuanced, humanistic and perhaps idealistic (her critics would say naive) justification than that currently on offer. But she is alert to the fact that her position is contested. She poses the question of how to think about race:

> Should the goal be an inclusive, humanistic vision of culture such as that envisaged by W.E.B. Du Bois, in which black culture is embraced by all Americans, even as black Americans embrace all of culture? Or should it instead be the creation of an identity apart from others, and linked at times with the disparagement of other people and groups? (Nussbaum 1997: 150)

Nussbaum puts the question rhetorically; her preference is clearly for the Du Bois model. But from today's viewpoint it does appear that it is the latter goal which is currently in the ascendant.

Nussbaum argues strongly for the study of African culture and the African American experience as a discipline in its own right: 'a fuller pursuit of Veritas [truth], one that includes black Americans as inquirers and their history and traditions as part of the curriculum, is the only honourable solution to the social and intellectual legacy of racism' (1997: 165). But like other humanities disciplines the aim should be to learn and appreciate universal human values. Here, she quotes W. E. B. Du Bois, who saw students embarking on an intellectual journey 'beginning with the particular, and going out to universal comprehension and unhampered expression' ([1933], quoted in Nussbaum 1997: 169)

Nussbaum is very clear that African American studies should not only be for African Americans. She makes a robust defence of all subjects being open to all. Whites should not feel unwelcome if they choose African American studies; as conversely, no subjects should be closed to Blacks. She also argues trenchantly against the idea that different (i.e. less demanding) intellectual norms should be required of African American studies: 'One of the most pernicious developments in debates about race and the curriculum, as in debates about women's studies, has been the suggestion that standard structures of argument, and logic itself, are racially tainted and not for African-American students' (1997: 177).

Nussbaum contrasts her inclusive approach with what she terms a retributivist approach – 'a curriculum that is unbalanced in a direction opposite to that of earlier imbalances, Afrocentric where the old curriculum was Eurocentric' (1997: 178). She approvingly quotes Henry Louis Gates, who sums up the alternatives thus: 'We Liberal

Reformists say: Do unto others as you would have them do unto you and – hope for the best. The Left says: Let's do unto you what you *did* unto others; and then see how you like that' (Gates quoted in Nussbaum, 1997: 178). Although Nussbaum concedes that there is a limited place for *some* retribution – 'when it prompts us to uncover prejudice that has been parading as objectivity' (1997: 178) – such an approach should never permit distortion of the truth to support a particular narrative. (Later in her career, Nussbaum will develop a cogent moral critique of retributivism in general; see Chapter 7, 'Nussbaum and the Emotions'.)

It is worth pausing here to note Nussbaum's foundational commitment to objective truth and universal values. This view was already under attack within the academy when Nussbaum wrote *Cultivating Humanity* and has become even more unfashionable since then in many disciplines. Nevertheless, I contend, with Nussbaum, that a belief in truth and objectivity is fundamental to philosophy and all academic disciplines (and indeed to daily life). Such a belief is not to be confused with the naive view that the truth is always easy to discover and everyone agrees on what it is. The truth may be as intricate and hard to find as a crown of feathers, to borrow Isaac Bashevis Singer's metaphor. But without a belief that there *is* such a thing as objective truth and that it matters, we can't reason with each other. Nussbaum's robust defence of it is urgently needed today.

Not For Profit

The Black former mayor of Atlanta, Andrew Young, criticised courses in African American culture as being of little practical use – indeed he tried to dissuade his own daughter from majoring in Black studies: '"If you are paying for an education, you ought to get people to teach you things [you] can't learn on [your] own. Spend your time in math, finance, accounting, and sciences"' (Young quoted in Nussbaum 1997: 149). This criticism could of course be levelled at any liberal arts course: it's better to study subjects that you can make a career and earn money from. Nussbaum's response is to agree that, yes, one must think about jobs and there is nothing wrong in that, but at the same time we must not neglect what makes education valuable:

> the narrow vision of education suggested by [Young's] statement, increasingly prominent in a world anxious about job security, threatens to do

away with some of education's most important benefits for all students, white as well as black. We have to think not only about how we will earn enough to live, but also about why we live and what makes life worth living. (Nussbaum 1997: 172)

Nussbaum returned to the idea that education should not be all about earning money in her short 2010 book *Not For Profit*, where she argues not only that a liberal education is necessary for the individual to flourish, but that it is a necessary condition for democratic societies to function. *Not For Profit* is less optimistic about the prospects for liberal education than was *Cultivating Humanity*. Thirteen years on, Nussbaum now believes:

We are in the midst of a crisis of massive proportions and grave global significance. No, I do not mean the global economic crisis that began in 2008 . . . I mean a crisis that goes largely unnoticed, like a cancer; a crisis that is likely to be, in the long run, far more damaging to the future of democratic self-government: a world-wide crisis in education. (2010: 1)

The solution is the same as that proposed in *Cultivating Humanity* – a liberal education that encourages students to think for themselves rather than training them to become money-making machines – only now Nussbaum calls for it with much greater urgency.

Women's Studies

In *Cultivating Humanity* Nussbaum offers a vigorous defence of women's studies as an academic discipline, with a particular focus on philosophy – that is to say, ethical and political philosophy which focuses on the role of women in society. Nussbaum's own stance is clearly that of a liberal feminist, in the tradition of John Stuart Mill/ Harriet Taylor Mill and her own contemporary, Susan Moller Okin. She starts from a commitment to the foundational liberal principle of equality for all citizens (women and men) and to the goal of maximal freedom for each citizen, compatible with not infringing the freedom of other citizens. She would subscribe to Okin's straightforward characterisation of feminism as:

the belief that women should not be disadvantaged by their sex, that they should be recognized as having human dignity equal to that of men, and that they should have the opportunity to live as fulfilling and as freely chosen lives as men can. (Okin 1999: 10)

A further point to add is that Nussbaum, like other liberal feminists, holds that equality for women can be achieved within the framework of liberal institutions; no revolutionary overthrowing of the liberal state is called for. This is a position which she will develop and expand in her next two books *Sex and Social Justice* (1999) and *Women and Human Development* (2000), the subjects of Chapters 3 and 4.

In *Cultivating Humanity*, however, although her position as a liberal feminist is clear, she does not spend time attacking other forms of feminism, such as radical, Marxist or postmodern feminism. On the contrary for Nussbaum a key positive feature of women's studies is that different feminist positions can be examined, compared and argued over in the Socratic tradition she espouses, leading to new understandings. Nussbaum stresses the range of topics covered on different courses at different universities – examples include feminist positions on pornography, on abortion, and on clashes between cultural norms and universal norms – and notes approvingly that these are all treated as matters to *debate* rather than to arrive at a conclusion preordained by the teacher. She notes too the range of philosophical positions taken by feminist philosophy teachers, which include 'Rawlsian liberals, Utilitarians, followers of the "discourse ethics" of Jurgen Habermas, postmodernists, analytic philosophers of science, theorists of "care ethics", Wittgensteinian communitarians, and many others, including religious ethicists both conservative and liberal' (1997: 207). This is a significant instance of Nussbaum's commitment to pluralism – a commitment to which she remains constant throughout her career.

As usual, Nussbaum's emphasis is on the practical application of ideas. For her, women's studies is valuable for its real-world effects, a way of helping us 'strive to build a society that is both rational and just' (1997: 221). As we see in the next chapter, she has little time for feminism which is not about effecting change in the world we inhabit.

Most of the feminist philosophy Nussbaum discusses in this section is *by* women – such as Susan Moller Okin, Cynthia Freeland, Marilyn Friedman, Mary Ann Glendon and others – but there is no suggestion that it should be exclusively *for* women. Just as African American studies should not be confined to Black students, so men should not be made to feel uncomfortable about taking women's studies courses (Nussbaum 1997: 204).

The 'New' Liberal Education

Nussbaum places the word *new* in scare quotes in her conclusion, to signify that the kind of education she is arguing for is not really new at all; indeed it is as old as Socrates. But in the context of American higher education, it *is* new (or was new in 1997), representing a move away from traditional teaching of the humanities to include the new perspectives of women's studies, African-American studies, the study of human sexuality and so on. It is (or was) to quite a large extent already in place in American universities, as evidenced by the copious examples of good practice Nussbaum cites. Nevertheless, Nussbaum sees liberal education as under threat, from, on the one hand, right-leaning ideologues who say education should be career-oriented and, on the other, left-leaning postmodern critics who want to dismantle the Western canon and liberalism itself. *Cultivating Humanity* is thus a *re-statement* of the value of liberal education. Nussbaum says that, like Seneca, we live in a time divided between two ideas of liberal education. The first is an education suited for well-born, free people; and the second – the *new* one – is an education suited to *producing* free citizens. Free citizens are world citizens, reasoning citizens, who have 'ownership of their thought and speech' (Nussbaum 1997: 293). Such students will not reject all tradition out of hand, but will evaluate it for themselves.

Here is Nussbaum's final statement of the programme:

> We must therefore construct a liberal education that is not only Socratic, emphasizing critical thought and respectful argument, but also pluralistic, imparting an understanding of the histories and contributions of the groups with whom we interact, both within our nation and in the increasingly international sphere of business and politics. (1997: 295)

Three Objections

1. Neglect of science

One criticism that might be levelled at Nussbaum's programme for a liberal education which produces world citizens is that it has very little to say about science. Indeed, the word 'science' does not appear even once in the index of *Cultivating Humanity*. Science is accorded a few brief mentions in *Not for Profit*, but mostly to note that it is not endangered in the way that humanities subjects are, and to decry the narrowly vocational conception of the science that is studied in Institutes of Technology (see Nussbaum 2010: 131).

Nussbaum focuses pretty much entirely on humanities courses and has nothing to say about either how STEM (science, technology, engineering and mathematics) subjects might be enriched by modules in humanities subjects, or about how humanities subjects could be enriched by including elements of science, technology or mathematics. It may be countered that, traditionally, the idea of liberal education has emphasised the liberal *arts* – classics, literature, history, philosophy and the humanities generally. However, Nussbaum's whole programme is based on the idea of questioning tradition, so it offers no good reason to stick to the traditional liberal arts and exclude mathematics and the sciences. Since the purpose of a liberal education is to fit the student for citizenship in the modern world – a world which is rapidly being changed by science and technology – one would have thought some knowledge of science would be of practical use, as well as personally enriching. The omission seems all the odder since Nussbaum in many respects takes her bearings from Aristotle, who *was* what we would call a scientist. Nussbaum's own central belief in human nature ultimately rests on science (that our species has its own unique nature is, ultimately, a scientific claim). Moreover, scientific knowledge is a paradigm for the kind of culturally independent (non-relative) truths about a shared world that Nussbaum so prizes. Scientists form a global community, sharing knowledge and procedures, building on each other's results. Science offers a compelling example of how well questioning and improving on traditional beliefs can be made to work.

This, however, is not a fatal objection to Nussbaum's goal of liberal education. It is merely an objection to the *curriculum* she proposes. But the success of her project does not depend on any *specific* curriculum – indeed it is in line with her philosophy of education that the curriculum should always be up for debate. Nussbaum could easily accept that the study of science in some form could be part of the curriculum for a world-citizen-building education, and her proposal would be the stronger for it. And indeed she would no doubt agree, as she says 'Science, rightly pursued, is a friend of the humanities rather than their enemy' (Nussbaum 2010: 8).

2. Critique from the right

Nussbaum's educational theory has attracted criticism from the political right. David Frum, in a 1998 review of *Cultivating Humanity* for the journal *The Public Interest*, seems perturbed by the rise of 'political correctness' on American campuses and cites the example of the student whose task was to write a letter to parents in the persona of a gay man - which Nussbaum gave as an instance of good practice – as evidence of 'the crisis in American higher education' (Frum 1998: 105). He argues that it doesn't occur to Nussbaum that 'a genuine questioning of "all beliefs" might overturn liberal idols as much as the traditional ones she opposes' (1998: 106). But in any case, Frum does not believe that Nussbaum wants to question all beliefs. She has her own liberal political agenda and wants to stick to it: 'Nussbaum is not for disinterested pursuit of truth but political "reform"' (Frum 1998: 108). Frum also accuses Nussbaum of applauding 'the narrow political agendas of race and gender that dominate American universities' (1998: 109).

Stephen Eide, a social policy researcher and Senior Fellow at the Manhattan Institute, wrote a scathing critique of Nussbaum's educational philosophy, as expressed in both *Cultivating Humanity* and *Not For Profit*, in a 2014 paper, 'Martha Nussbaum: The Voice of Convention' for the journal *Academic Questions*. Eide claims that Nussbaum 'speaks for the status quo' (2014: 185), defending a view of education that was already dominant when she was writing – a liberal view that resisted, on the one hand, education for profit-making and, on the other, postmodernist assaults on the Western canon. Eide tends to support her resistance to the latter trend. But he does not agree that universities have a duty to 'shape a liberal political culture' (2014: 194). He states that Nussbaum's 'respect for the moral imagination does not extend to conservatives' (2014: 197).

Eide also points to a tension between reading literary texts in order to develop compassion and empathy, and reading literary texts to pursue whatever truths they lead us towards. Nussbaum favours both but does not acknowledge that these aims may be in conflict (David Frum also made this point.) In order to guarantee that classic texts only deliver the correct, compassionate messages, Eide says, one would have to select from an extremely narrow range, since 'not every great book is written for the purpose of teaching tolerance, strengthening democracy, and promoting world citizenship' (2014: 196).

Eide disagrees, too, with Nussbaum's rejection of education-for-profit. Studying – or indeed practising – business is, he claims, no less likely to produce tolerant, decent, world-minded citizens than is studying the humanities, quoting Montesquieu's idea of 'gentle commerce' as a means of producing friendly relations between individuals and nations.

Eide does agree with Nussbaum that the future of the humanities is under threat. In his view she might have got something right about the diagnosis but is wrong about the treatment: 'the humanities need to develop a more energetic spirit of doubt and self-criticism. Nussbaum can't take the lead there. She's too blinded by convention' ((2014: 198).

Both Frum and Eide make some cogent points. There is indeed a tension between the pursuit of the truth wherever it leads and any pre-existing political philosophy. This tension has peculiar force for liberalism which, more than other political philosophies, actively champions free enquiry. Some might say 'So much the worse for liberalism', then. But I would argue, and I imagine Nussbaum would agree, that it is liberalism's recognition and embrace of this tension that makes it so rich a philosophical tradition – and also a much more realistic and flexible intellectual response to a changing and complex world than a reliance on tradition or dogma. Frum accuses Nussbaum of not really wanting to question all beliefs – of not being sincerely committed to her project of Socratic enquiry wherever it leads. But all questioning has to start somewhere. One needs a place to stand. Nussbaum does take certain liberal propositions as axiomatic – that all human beings share a nature, that all are of equal worth, that there is no moral difference between men and women, that there are no natural superiors or inferiors among us – but from that position, Socratic enquiry can proceed. Apart from these basic axioms, everything else is up for grabs, and Nussbaum explicitly and repeatedly champions political pluralism. Eide says that conservatives do not in fact feel welcome within humanities departments of American universities. That may be so, but it isn't Nussbaum's fault and it is not a consequence of her educational theory. Nussbaum noted approvingly the involvement of conservative religious ethicists in debates about feminism; and indeed Eide himself admitted that Nussbaum 'is careful to insist that illiberal points of view should be welcomed' (2014: 194).

Frum and Eide disagree with Nussbaum's liberal political affiliations, as they are of course entitled to do, but it does not follow that they must disagree with her ideal of a liberal education. They fail to differentiate between a liberal stance in the classroom (involving Socratic dialogue, free enquiry, openness to different viewpoints etc.) and liberalism as a political philosophy. Nussbaum subscribes to both, but there is no necessary connection between the two. In any case, even if Frum and Eide's arguments against Nussbuam's proposals were decisive – and I do not believe they are – it is quite unclear what model of education *they* would advocate instead.

3. Critique from the left

Nussbaum's optimistic programme of equipping students to be world citizens via a liberal education looks much more doubtful in 2023 than it did in 1997. Within humanities departments in the academy, both in the United States and Europe, liberalism is in decline if it has not already expired. I should reiterate here that I do not mean *liberal* in the loose sense of 'progressive' or 'Democrat-supporting' that is often employed in America, but rather liberalism in the Millian or Rawlsian form which Nussbaum endorses: that is, a commitment to the principles that citizens are free and equal and all entitled to the same rights – which should be as extensive as is consistent with not infringing on the rights of others. Many who would now style themselves as progressive reject these principles, arguing that by ignoring the facts of systemic racism and entrenched privilege, they serve to perpetuate the status quo (the same criticism as that levelled by Eide but from a left-wing perspective). For example, Nussbaum's liberal, non-retributive model of African American studies is distinctly out of favour, having been superseded by critical race theory (CRT) or variants thereof. (CRT is an interdisciplinary field which sees racial inequalities as systemic and immune to liberal reforms, since they are rooted 'in practices and values which have been shorn of any explicit, formal manifestations of racism' [Delgado 1995: xxix]. CRT holds that all whites are the beneficiaries of 'white privilege' – systematic advantages which cannot be repudiated. White people who dispute this analysis are said to display 'white fragility' [DiAngelo 2018].)

Nussbaum's ideal of global citizens all sharing the same universal rights is also hotly contested; many left-wing critics today view the concept of universal rights as a colonialist imposition of Western norms. The postmodernist scepticism of truth and objectivity is widely in evidence both in American and European universities, and identity politics is largely dominant. The question thus arises: if Nussbaum's theory of education is sound, why has it not prevailed?

Nussbaum's vision of education is less fashionable than it once was. But a theory's unfashionability is no reason, by itself, to reject that theory. Thus it is not, per se, a strike against Nussbaum's theory that it is no longer in the ascendant.

49

I am generalising here, but it seems that the postmodernist and/ or identity-based theories that currently dominate the study of the humanities are not open to debate and brook no dissent. It is not so much that they have disproved all other theories but that they do not allow them to be heard. They are as reliant on authority as the more traditional views they displaced. I maintain that Nussbaum's commitment to Socratic questioning, to the goal of producing world citizens and to the narrative imagination still has much to contribute to the debate. Indeed, these things are necessary for there to *be* a debate.

Summary

Cultivating Humanity and, later, *Not For Profit* offer a compelling, reasoned, evidenced educational theory which deserves to have a continuing influence on the philosophy of education and on curriculum design. It embodies the important Nussbaumian principle of seeking truth through reasoned enquiry rather than accepting traditional authority. Both books are also excellent examples of Nussbaum's gifts as a communicator, able to reach a wide audience outside the academy.

Cultivating Humanity introduces themes which will continue to be salient in Nussbaum's work. The idea of world citizenship and the political liberalism it is based on will find further expression in her later work on capabilities (see Chapter 4); and the liberal feminism it introduces is further developed in Nussbaum's 1999 book, *Sex and Social Justice*.

Chapter 3

Nussbaum and Feminism

Liberal Feminism, Adaptive Preferences and FGM

In 1999, Martha Nussbaum published *Sex and Social Justice*. Rather than being one sustained argument as her earlier books were, it is a collection of essays that Nussbaum wrote at various times during the 1990s. Some reflect Nussbaum's interest in literature – for example, one essay is a memoir about meeting the classical scholar Sir Kenneth Dover, while the final chapter is a literary appreciation of Virginia Woolf's novel *To the Lighthouse*, focusing on how it treats the philosophical problem of knowledge of other minds. These are only tangentially relevant to the main themes of the book. Nevertheless, the book does have clear themes overall, reflecting a decade of Nussbaum's thought on feminism, liberalism, and how to approach practical problems of injustice. It is significant in her oeuvre in that it is the first fully worked-out version of her liberal feminist position, which was adumbrated in *Cultivating Humanity* (1997); it also contains a trenchant defence of gay and lesbian rights. And it features the first appearance of her capabilities approach, which will be developed in her next book, *Women and Human Development* (2000) (see Chapter 4).

Sex and Social Justice includes, too, further criticism of postmodern theory, directed against its relativism, indeterminacy and what Nussbaum sees as its lack of engagement with the real world. In the same year, Nussbaum also published a short but famous (in some quarters infamous) attack on the postmodern gender theorist Judith Butler.

It is an over-simplification, but nevertheless a useful one, to divide the history of modern feminism into three waves:

- The first wave arguably began in the late eighteenth century, with Olympe de Gouges's *Declaration of the Rights of Woman and of the Female Citizen* (1791) and Mary Wollstonecraft's *A Vindication of the Rights of Women* (1792). However, first-wave feminism gets properly underway in the mid-nineteenth century, according to Marlene Legates' history of feminism, *In Their Time* (2001). Prior to that period, Legates says, feminist networks were either 'loosely organized or short-lived' (2001: 197). From the 1850s onwards, feminists in Europe and North America formed 'more permanent and sophisticated organizations' (2001: 197) and campaigned for a range of causes: the right to education, the right to follow professional careers, to escape economic and legal dependence on husbands, and for political inclusion. Legates states that this first wave lasted for three generations and culminated in the winning of the vote for women, in several countries, during or after the First World War (2001: 197). As Legates states, the first wave was really a variety of allied movements (2001: 197). But the single unifying idea was the need to achieve equal *rights* for women in a range of areas (although in practice the opportunities were mainly made available to white and relatively wealthy women).

- The second wave, associated with the post-war period and especially the 1960s, 1970s and 1980s, did not repudiate the goal of equal rights but began to concentrate more on the widening of *opportunities* for women, and changing attitudes – combating *sexism*, a term which first became current in the 1960s. Legates names the year 1968 as the one which 'marked a coming to feminist consciousness for many women in Europe and North America' (2001: 327). It was marked by student demonstrations, campaigns against beauty pageants, and the coining of the term 'Women's Liberation'. Second-wave feminists were also active in campaigning against sexual harassment and discrimination in the workplace, as well as securing legislative changes such the famous *Roe* v. *Wade* judgment of 1973, in which the US Supreme Court ruled that it was unconstitutional for states to make abortion illegal. The 2022 overturning of that judgment by the US Supreme Court is a reminder that the victories of second wave feminism should not be taken for granted.

- Writing at the start of the twenty-first century, Legates notes that there was 'an apparent contraction of feminism in the 1980s and 1990s' (2001: 375) and expresses the determined hope that the feminist struggle will continue. In fact, third-wave feminism was already on the move and would gather momentum in the decades ahead. It represents a departure from second-wave feminism in a number of ways. It is more concerned with diversity, highlighting the experiences of women of colour, working-class women and disabled women (the theorist Kimberlé Crenshaw coined the term 'intersectionality' to refer to the way that different forms of oppression intersect). It sometimes tends to stress the strength and energy of women rather than cast them as victims (the Spice Girls' slogan 'Girl Power' was a popular expression of this aspect of the third wave). There is also continuity with the second wave, in the #MeToo protests against male sexual harassment and predation. A marked discontinuity, however, is that, influenced by postmodernism, some third-wave feminists have a tendency to deconstruct some of the very categories, such as sex and gender, on which second-wave feminism was built. Judith Butler is exemplary of this tendency.

Of course, there are a number of continuities and parallels between these waves, and some feminist theorists cannot easily be identified with any one of them. Nussbaum's principles and priorities on the whole align with the second-wave feminism to which, generationally, she belongs. But her concern with the rights and opportunities of women of developing countries, as well as with those of gay men, accords with the value placed on diversity by third-wave feminists. In this chapter I explain and evaluate her brand of liberal feminism, arguing that it is far from outdated and deserves to remain part of current thinking. I also consider defensive responses to her accusations against Butler. I argue that Nussbaum's accusations are not without grounds, and that her liberal feminism is of more practical use in improving the lives of women than is Butlerian gender theory.

Statement of the Problem

As is her customary practice, Nussbaum starts her enquiry in the real world, with three real-life case studies which embody the issues she aims to address.

Case Study 1

She first describes the case of Saleha Begum, a Bangladeshi woman who became a farmer after her husband was disabled, in defiance of local tradition which was strongly against women working outside the home. She went on to organise a team of female labourers who applied for employment at a government-sponsored 'food for work' scheme – but their request was refused. Saleha did not give up, but appealed for help from the United Nations World Food Programme and the Bangladeshi government's Ministry of Relief and Rehabilitation; with their support, Saleha and her fellow women won the right to be hired. With the help of a local non-governmental organisation (NGO), the women went on to receive training in specialised areas – rearing poultry, cultivating silkworms, even doing paralegal and paramedical training. Saleha Begum then went on to stand for office in local government and although she lost, the margin of defeat was encouragingly narrow. This case study, then, is an example both of injustice towards women and of successful resistance to it.

Case Study 2

Nussbaum's second case is of a Bollywood film star, Sareetha. She married at sixteen, before she was a star, but she and her husband did not get on and he left her after a few months. Five years later – during which time they had had no contact – Sareetha had become a famous and successful movie star. Her husband decided he wanted her back and brought a legal case against her for 'restitution of conjugal rights', an outcome provided for by the Hindu Marriage Act of 1955. The first court found in the husband's favour. Sareetha appealed the verdict and the Andhra Pradesh High Court ruled in *her* favour, with the judge having some harsh words to say about restitution of conjugal rights: 'a savage and barbarous remedy, violating the right to privacy and human dignity' (Judge Choudary quoted in Nussbaum 1999: 4). The story did not end there, however. The husband took the case to the Supreme Court of India which reversed Judge Choudary's decision, on the grounds that under the present law Sareetha could not be forcibly returned to her husband's home anyway, as long as she paid a fine for not doing so, and that the Hindu Marriage Act served a useful social purpose in preventing marital break-up. Sareetha, being wealthy, was able to pay the fine, not return to her husband and continue making films. But a woman unable to pay the fine would have been compelled to return to her husband's home.

This case study illustrates a number of things. First, it calls attention to an institutionalised injustice against women: although in theory the law would also allow a woman to demand restitution of conjugal rights, as Judge Choudary pointed out, it works 'in practice only as an oppression to be operated by the husband for the benefit of the husband against the wife' (cited in Nussbaum 1999: 4). This institutionalised injustice remains: the Hindu Marriage Act was amended in 2010 to make divorce easier, but this would not have helped Sareetha, who was not divorced from her husband but only separated. But the case study does also suggest some grounds for optimism: fair-minded judges like Choudary are able to publicly challenge unjust laws, leading perhaps in the long run to change; while strong, independent women like Sareetha can, at least sometimes, pursue their life plans despite unjust laws.

Case Study 3

Nussbaum's third case concerns Joe Steffan, a student at the United States Naval Academy in Maryland. He was an outstanding student, selected as a battalion commander; but before graduation he confided that he was gay to a supposed friend, who promptly informed the authorities. Steffan was then denied the right to graduate. He brought a suit against the US Department of Defense, but lost. He took the case to the Court of Appeal, where a three-member panel of judges found in his favour. The case was then re-heard, but – in a pattern replicating Sareetha's experience – the final hearing once again found against him.

Nussbaum's Method

These brief case studies sum up the problem that Nussbaum wants to address: that all over the world, 'human dignity is frequently violated on grounds of sex or sexuality' (1999: 5). Three points can be drawn out from her method of proceeding. First, by starting with real-life case studies, she makes plain that the *purpose* of feminism, in her view, is to overcome real injustices that happen to real women; recall her definition of feminists in *Cultivating Humanity*: 'meaning, broadly, that they have a practical political interest in social justice for women' (Nussbaum 1997: 207). The practicality of this approach may derive from Nussbaum's immersion in Aristotle, an empiricist, or proto-empiricist, who held that philosophy should begin with investigation of *phainomena*.

The second thing to note is that Nussbaum's concern extends to gay men as well as women. Although the book as a whole focuses on the situation of women, she also wants to address the political and legal situation of lesbians and gay men. What is the connection? Both feminism and gay rights challenge the traditional hierarchical nuclear family. Throughout history gay relationships have often been less hierarchical than heterosexual ones. Finally, Nussbaum just hates injustice, so is naturally on the side of gay people who face oppression and persecution. Her feminism is motivated by the requirement of removing injustice – that is, individuals or groups being accorded lesser rights than others on arbitrary grounds, or treated with less than human dignity. It is thus an aspect of a wider liberalism that demands equal rights, freedoms and opportunities for all and extends to all victims of injustice, not just women (it just so happens, as an empirical fact, that women in many parts of the world are more likely to be victims of injustice than men). As Nussbaum puts it, 'In an important sense, the views expressed in this volume are not really about women at all but about human beings and about women seen as fully human' (1999: 9). It is worth noting that Nussbaum's idea of equal human worth, as inalienable and not to be diminished by 'any characteristic that is distributed by the whims of fortune' (1999: 5), seems to be grounded in a Rawlsian principle of fundamental human equality. It was to escape distortions occasioned by the 'whims of fortune' that Rawls set up his famous Original Position, where individuals make choices behind a Veil of Ignorance about the principles governing the state they will live in (Rawls 1971).

Third, it is significant that two of Nussbaum's case studies are Asian women from developing countries. A charge frequently levelled at second-wave liberal feminism is that it is practised in a white, well-educated, middle-class first world bubble. Nussbaum's approach is an ongoing, practical refutation of this charge.

Nussbaum's Liberal Feminism

Nussbaum sets out her conception of feminism clearly, identifying five salient features. They are:

- internationalism;
- humanism;
- liberalism;
- a concern with the social shaping of preferences;
- sympathetic understanding.

Let us take these one by one. On the first feature, *internationalism*, Nussbaum notes that feminism should not be insular; its concerns must extend beyond problems that beset women in the USA and the

West. This is a pre-emptive response to those who claim that liberal feminism is essentially 'white' or colonialist in its aims. Nussbaum is motivated by a desire for global justice and recognises that this is only part of the wider problem: distributive injustices also need to be addressed, although she does not do so in this book (that implied promise is kept in *Women and Human Development* [2000], to be considered in the next chapter, and *Frontiers of Justice* [2006], discussed in Chapter 5).

The second feature, *humanism*, involves two ideas. One, already noted, is that of universal equal human worth and dignity. This does not depend on sex, sexuality, class, wealth, nationality, abilities, or any other accident of fate. The second idea is that of universal equal human *need*. That is to say, all human beings need access to pretty much the same goods of life in order to flourish – a thought rooted in Aristotle's conception of *eudaimonia*. Of course, in addressing problems and injustices one needs to be sensitive to local conditions. *Solutions* to problems will vary according to culture; but Nussbaum believes that our fundamental human needs are trans-cultural. She is therefore strongly against cultural relativism:

> The approach defended here refuses to take that step [of relativism], arguing that an account of the central human capacities and functions, and of the basic human needs and rights, can be given in a fully universal manner, at least at a high level of generality, and that this universal account is what should guide feminist thought and planning. (Nussbaum 1999: 8)

Incidentally, it is worth pointing out that Nussbaum's humanism by no means commits her to ignoring the well-being of non-human animals. She explores our responsibilities towards other animals later in her career, in her 2004 book *Animal Rights: Current Debates and New Directions* (see Chapter 5). But the well-being of other animals is a matter of fulfilling *their* needs, which vary according to species and are not the same as human needs.

The third salient feature, *liberalism*, has been thought by some theorists to be an inadequate basis for feminism. Nussbaum strongly contests this view. She argues for a form of liberalism which she says derives from Aristotle, Kant and Mill (she might also have added Rawls), grounded in the specifically human capacities of choice and reasoning. It is true that, historically, liberals have not tended to be sufficiently alert to the particular injustices suffered by women, and many early liberal political theorists simply ignored or even defended women's subordinate position. But this, Nussbaum, argues, was a case of liberals being inconsistent – of not being liberal *enough*, in other words. As Nussbaum points out, John Stuart Mill identified and argued powerfully against this inconsistency as long ago as 1869, in *On the Subjection of Women*. Nussbaum characterises her version of liberalism as insisting on

> the separateness of one life from another, and the equal importance of each life, seen on its own terms, rather than as part of a larger organic or corporate whole. Each human being should be regarded as an end rather than as a means to the ends of others. (Nussbaum 1999: 10)

The last sentence is of course a conscious echo of Kant – but by emphasising that 'each human being' necessarily includes all women, Nussbaum gives the idea a feminist turn.

A possible objection here is that in stressing the separateness of each human life, Nussbaum neglects the extent to which we are social creatures who cannot live *without* being 'part of some larger organic or corporate whole'. But Nussbaum could answer that she has never ignored this fact: her first book, *The Fragility of Goodness*, argues specifically that our flourishing depends on relationships with others (see Chapter 1) and her capabilities approach gives social and personal relationships as among the fundamental capabilities required by humans (see Chapter 4). If Nussbaum stresses the separateness of human lives here, it is as a firewall against unjust interference or oppression from others – not to deny that others are essential to us. She makes this explicit when she says: 'liberal individualism does not entail egoism or a preference for the type of person who has no deep need of others' (Nussbaum 1999: 10).

Nussbaum's fourth feature, *concern with the social shaping of preferences*, takes account of the fact that one's preferences may be limited by lack of options available, or distorted by social pressure which valorises some choices while stigmatising others: the problem of *adaptive preferences*, in short (Nussbaum considers adaptive preferences in greater detail in her next book, *Sex and Social Justice*, and the capabilities approach developed by Amartya Sen and her is a response to it – see Chapter 4). Therefore, many of the choices and behaviours traditionally associated with men and women are socially constructed: 'even something as apparently deepseated as the character of a person's erotic desire may contain a socially learned component' (1999: 12). Nussbaum points out that liberals such as Rawls and Mill have long drawn attention to the fact that there is a social dimension to desire. I have noted previously that Nussbaum believes in human nature, but she does not reduce human nature to observable behaviour. It is indeed human to seek affirmation by responding to social norms; but that does not mean that any particular set of norms is necessarily the best for human flourishing. Therefore, 'a moral critique of deformed desire and preference is not antithetical to liberal democracy; it is actually essential to its success' (1999: 13). To this end, Nussbaum recommends a rigorous investigation into 'the social origins of desire, preference, and emotion, both through refined conceptual analysis and through empirical study, drawing on the excellent work that has recently been done in these areas in cognitive psychology and in anthropology' (1999: 13).

The fifth and final feature, *concern with sympathetic understanding*, demonstrates how important to Nussbaum are the emotions in moral and political thinking. But there is a dilemma here. Women have often been credited with a capacity for care and sympathy. Perhaps this is a capacity that men would do well to emulate, as feminists such as Carol Gilligan and Virginia Held have suggested (Nussbaum 1999: 13). But other feminists, such as Catharine MacKinnon and Claudia Card, have argued that women's apparently sympathetic nature is a consequence of subordination; they are sympathetic because they had better be (Nussbaum 1999: 13). Nussbaum accepts that 'emotions are in part made up out of socially learned beliefs' (1999: 13) – and so to that extent is wary of praising women for their sympathetic capacities. On the other hand, she is also certain that 'emotions of care and sympathy lie at the heart of ethical life' (1999: 14). Nussbaum is uncomfortably aware of the dilemma and does not want to reject either possibility:

> I try here, however uneasily, to combine a radical feminist critique of sex relations with an interest in the possibilities of trust and understanding. Each reader must judge in the light of his or her own sense of life the odd combination that results – of Kant with DH Lawrence, of MacKinnon with Virginia Woolf. (1999: 14)

The Capabilities Approach

Sex and Social Justice is the first of Nussbaum's books to feature the capabilities approach, although she had introduced and discussed the idea in several previous papers, the first, 'Nature, Function and Capability: Aristotle on Political Distribution', in 1988. The capabilities approach is the idea that in social policy the goal should be to equip citizens with the *capability* to exercise certain specified, essential functions, without attempting to ensure that they all perform the same functions, or perform them to the same extent. This approach is central to Nussbaum's feminism because she holds that the same capabilities are necessary for both women and men – they are capabilities required for *all* human beings to flourish.

Some have, of course, contested the notion that the same norms should apply to both men and women. Nussbaum distinguishes two forms of this objection. One, which she calls Position A, holds that men and women have the 'same general list of normative functions' (1999: 51) but that they should be exercised in different spheres; the other, Position B, that the list of functions is fundamentally different – for example, 'for men, citizenship and rational autonomy; for women, love and care' (1999: 51). Nussbaum rejects both of these positions. She allows that Position A could be consistent with a real concern for some form of gender justice (at least it doesn't neglect women's flourishing altogether), and also that this cautious approach could be of strategic help in winning gradual enlargements of freedom for women, being less likely to startle conservative men. Nevertheless, she notes that in practice such a view often does endorse traditional hierarchies, and is likely to continue to do so as long as the sphere ordained for women remains the under-valued domain of home and family.

Position B, famously defended by Rousseau, holds that men and women have entirely different innate capacities. But as was pointed out by Mill (and by Mary Wollstonecraft before him), we do not know that apparent differences in capacities between men and women are innate. We have never observed men and women in a pre-cultural state. In any case, as Mill pointed out in *On the Subjection of Women*:

> Even if [a presumption of fitness for an occupation] be well grounded in a majority of cases, which it is very likely not to be, there will be a minority of exceptional cases in which it does not hold; and in those it is both an injustice to the individual, and a detriment to society, to place barriers in the way of their using their faculties for their own benefit and for that of others. ([1869] 2008: 22–3)

Nussbaum's position, then, is that there is a shared norm of functioning for men and women and they should therefore have the same capabilities.

Nussbaum lists ten essential capabilities (1999: 41–2), including such things as being able to live a full-length life, being able to have good health, being able to move about freely, safe from violent assault, and being able to use one's senses, imagination and thought. There is no need to list them all here; they receive much fuller treatment in the next chapter. The capabilities approach is a central part of Nussbaum's political philosophy, of importance not only in her feminist theory but in her approach to global justice and to animal rights as well (see Chapters 4, 5 and 8).

Feminism and Religion

Women's rights and religious freedom are two fundamental liberal values. They are areas of major concern to Nussbaum, who has written extensively about both of them (see Chapter 6 for her ideas on liberty of religious conscience). However, Nussbaum acknowledges a tension between these two essential liberal values:

> the world's major religions, in their actual human form, have not always been outstanding respectors of basic human rights or the equal dignity and inviolability of persons. Some indeed, have gone as far as to create systems of law that deny the equal rights of persons and justify violations of their dignity and their person. (1999: 82)

As is her usual procedure, Nussbaum supports her claim with a series of real-life examples: six case studies of unjust treatment of women backed by religious authority. They feature *inter alia* a young, blind Pakistani girl who was raped and subsequently, under the Islamic Hudood Ordinance, sentenced to jail for fornication (the sentence was rescinded after international protest, but the rapist was never charged); support for violent reprisals against Iranian women who do not observe the dress code, by Prosecutor-General Abolfazl Musavi-Tabrizi; and the denial of the right of Jewish women to hold their own prayer services at the Western Wall in Jerusalem, by the Israeli Ministry of Religious Affairs.

What, then, from a liberal feminist perspective, ought to be done about such clashes between religious precepts and women's rights? Nussbaum's position is straightforward: 'the protection of basic human rights should have a very strong degree of priority, even when this interferes with some elements of traditional religious discourse and practice' (1999: 102).

Nussbaum identifies eleven specific rights that must be protected. These are the rights to:

- life and health;
- bodily integrity;
- free choice of employment;
- free mobility and assembly;
- political participation and speech;
- free religious exercise;
- own property and have full civil capacity;
- nationality (i.e. the right to move abroad and for women to pass their nationality on to their children);
- equal rights under family law;
- education (there should be no disparity in the education of boys and girls); and
- reproductive choice

It will be noted that this list of rights shows some overlap with the ten capabilities discussed below in Chapter 4, and which Nussbaum goes on to develop further in her next book.

It is all very well to list the eleven things needful, but how are they to be achieved? Nussbaum proposes the encouragement of 'pluralistic and religious discourse' on contested topics, so that all voices can be publicly heard. Very often, religious laws that deny human and, especially, women's rights are based on the narrowest, most conservative interpretation of a faith which is by no means accepted by the majority of its adherents; and Nussbaum points out that sometimes the interpretation is just plain wrong, as in the mis-identification of female genital mutilation (FGM) as an Islamic custom. As Nussbaum puts it: 'This is one area in which the old adage that it is best to drive out bad speech with more speech seems to be just right' (1999: 115): a classically liberal, Millian view.

Nussbaum argues that in countries where conservative religious traditions are strong, 'major state actors' – that is, politicians and public intellectuals – should insist on the need for diverse and plural interpretations of faith (1999: 116). The difficulty here, of course, is that this remedy presupposes that the liberals are in charge; but in theocratic states a liberal politician or intellectual might have considerable difficulty in getting elected, appointed or heard.

Western governments can play a part by putting pressure on regimes that violate women's human rights, and in acute individual cases by granting asylum to women fleeing such violations – Nussbaum cites the case of Fauziya Kassindja, who fled to the United States to escape genital mutilation. But, of course, granting asylum to refugees can only be a temporary and partial response to the problem.

More importantly, liberal feminists should do what they can to support and promote local grass-roots organisations that work for change. She gives the example of the Bangladesh Rural Advancement Committee, an NGO which works to improve women's literacy. Consistently with her earlier work, Nussbaum sees education as a crucial part of the solution; the best way to prevent conservative interpretations of faith from riding rough-shod over women's rights is 'to produce active, unintimidated, educated democratic citizens' (Nussbaum 1999: 116).

Nussbaum's Position on FGM

The practice of female genital mutilation raises the spectre of what Nussbaum calls 'judging other cultures'. Western liberals tend to feel, instinctively, that there is something dubious about making negative judgements of the practices of non-Western cultures. On the other hand, forced genital mutilation, performed on children without anaesthetic or their consent, with the deliberate aim of permanently impairing sexual function, and the unintended but frequent outcomes of infection, haemorrhaging, menstrual problems, infertility and even death, is a practice about which it is hard *not* to make a negative judgement. For Nussbaum, there is no dilemma here at all. FGM is a violation of human rights and dignity, rightly outlawed by the United Nations and indeed by the governments of most of the countries where it is practised. There is no good reason, in Nussbaum's view, for a liberal feminist to defend the practice.

Yet it has been defended, and often by people who would think of themselves as liberals. Nussbaum takes their arguments seriously enough to list and rebut them one by one. She identifies four separate theses:

1. It is morally wrong to criticize the practices of another culture unless one is prepared to be similarly critical of comparable practices when they occur in one's own culture . . .
2. It is morally wrong to criticize the practices of another culture unless one's own culture has eradicated all evils of a comparable kind . . .

3. Female genital mutilation is morally on a par with practices of dieting and body-shaping in American culture . . .
4. Female genital mutilation involves the loss of a capacity that may not be especially central to the lives in question, and one to which Westerners attach disproportionate significance. (Nussbaum 1999: 121)

Nussbaum deals with the first three fairly briskly. For (1), she freely agrees that it is salutary to be reminded that cultures should reflect on and be critical of their own shortcomings. This, though, would not be a reason for refusing help to non-Western women in need. And in any case, Nussbaum argues, American feminists *are* critical of their own culture, as evidenced by books like Naomi Wolf's *The Beauty Myth*.

For (2), Nussbaum claims that it is simply false. No culture in the world is morally perfect, yet it does not follow from this that we should ignore calls for help from other cultures. Nussbaum gives the example of the plight of Jews in Germany in the 1930s and 1940s: should the USA have refused to help or rescue any Jews from Nazi persecution on the grounds that anti-Semitism existed in America? It simply doesn't follow. And here Nussbaum calls in her principle of universalism: 'the fact that a needy human being happens to live in Togo rather than Idaho does not make her less my fellow, less deserving of my moral commitment' (1999: 122).

For (3), Nussbaum concedes that, if it were the case that dieting in America was as harmful as FGM in Africa, then American feminists might well be better off combating the evils of dieting than FGM, simply because they would be better placed to do something about it. But Nussbaum argues trenchantly that dieting is not morally on a par with FGM, for there are several crucial differences (she lists eight) between the practices, including the facts that FGM is carried out by force, that it is irreversible and that it is done to children.

Thesis (4) is discussed at greater length. Nussbaum examines the defence of FGM made by the Israeli philosopher Yael Tamir, who argues that 'hedonistic American feminists have ascribed too much value to pleasure' (1999: 126). Tamir denies that sexual pleasure is a universal human good; those who criticise FGM for impairing or destroying sexual enjoyment are exporting their own cultural values to cultures where those values do not hold. She adduces examples to show that a worthwhile life can be lived without sexual pleasure: 'Nuns take an oath of celibacy, but we do not usually condemn the church for preventing its clergy from enjoying an active sex life' (Tamir quoted in Nussbaum 1999: 127).

Nussbaum's response to this line of argument seems to me decisive. She points out that Tamir fails to make a crucial distinction: 'that between a function and the capacity to choose that function' (Nussbaum 1999: 126). (Here, again, is a deployment of the capabilities approach, to be further developed in *Women and Human Development*, 2000.) The nun has the capacity to experience sexual pleasure but chooses not to exercise it. The victim of FGM has had that capacity permanently removed.

That objection alone seems enough to discredit Tamir's analogy. But Nussbaum adds a further damaging criticism. The case against FGM does not in any case depend on the claim that life without sexual pleasure cannot be worthwhile, as Tamir seems to imply. As Nussbaum points out, people who are unable to see, or walk, can and do lead meaningful lives. But we would rightly deplore the deliberate blinding or maiming of people (and, one might perhaps add, especially children) without their consent.

American Feminism

Nussbaum includes a chapter, 'American Women', in which she considers both the condition of women in the USA and controversies among American feminists. Her starting point is a book by the philosopher Christina Hoff Sommers, *Who Stole Feminism? How Women Have Betrayed Women* (1994). Sommers divides feminists into two kinds: 'equity feminists' and 'gender feminists' (corresponding roughly to first-wave and second-wave feminists). Equity feminists – and Sommers classes herself as a member of this group – are those who seek formal equality between men and women, to be embodied in law. Sommers holds that this goal has very largely been achieved in America. Gender feminists, from whom she distances herself, are more extreme, undemocratic, unsatisfied with the progress already made, and committed to the overthrow of institutions such as marriage and the family (see Nussbaum 1999: 130).

Nussbaum disputes this analysis. She does agree with Sommers that in some respects American women have less to complain of than many women in other parts of the world. They may vote, hold political office, travel without a male escort, pursue their career of choice and so on. But she adds: 'It is quite wrong, however, to think (as Sommers seems to) that American women have no urgent complaints to press'

(Nussbaum 1999: 131). Nussbaum focuses on two areas: sexual violence and preference deformation. Sommers does of course acknowledge that there is violence against women in the USA but argues that it is not disproportionate and is mainly experienced in poor urban communities; gender feminists have exaggerated its extent to serve their agenda. Nussbaum responds with the findings of a large-scale empirical study of 1994 by Edward Laumann, *The Social Organisation of Sexuality* (published shortly after Sommers's book), which found that 22 per cent of women over the age of 13 stated they had been forced into sexual intercourse. Tellingly, only 3 per cent of men reported having forced a woman into intercourse – a disparity that suggests many men are unaware of how coercive their behaviour really is. The Laumann study also did not support Sommers's contention that rape is only a problem in 'poor urban communities' (Nussbaum 1999: 137). It is worth noting here Nussbaum's recourse to empirical data to settle the question; as always, her lodestone is what is demonstrably going on in the real world.

The most important part of Nussbaum's argument at this point, however, is her discussion of preference deformation. Nussbaum argues that the preferences and, hence, behaviour of individuals are often distorted by 'societal myths' about what is expected, acceptable, natural or unavoidable. One example that Nussbaum discusses is marital rape. Although rape within marriage was vehemently objected to by Mill as long ago as 1869 in *On the Subjection of Women*, societal attitudes towards it took a long time to change. Throughout the nineteenth century and much of the twentieth,

> the idea that men had a right to such conduct exercised a powerful hold over the imaginations of men, helping them to rationalize conduct that might trouble them, and over the imaginations of women, making many, at least, suppose they were fulfilling a duty and had no right to demand change. (Nussbaum 1999: 143)

Another example Nussbaum discusses is sexual harassment in the workplace. She notes that when she was a graduate student in the 1970s, 'every woman graduate student I knew at some time suffered some unwanted sexual attention from men in positions of power and authority' (Nussbaum 1999: 144). It seems clear that such frequent, institutionalised behaviour could hardly have been simply the aggregate of thousands of unrelated, independent preferences. Rather, men's preferences were distorted by the societal myth that such behaviour was natural or even beneficent; women's preferences were distorted by the myth that such behaviour was best tolerated and that complaining about it would be 'tasteless and unnecessarily punitive' (Nussbaum 1999: 144).

In both of these examples, change was eventually effected by the protests of radical or 'gender' feminists such as Catharine MacKinnnon, who in 1979 published *Sexual Harassment of Working Women*, which drew attention to the issue. As an 'equity' feminist, Sommers thinks that once we have laws enshrining equality the job is done; but as Nussbaum argues, formal laws granting women the right to vote, for instance, do not cover every area of life. New laws or new interpretations of laws to protect women may be necessary. Moreover, and more importantly, the preference formations that underlie which laws are enacted and how they are observed and interpreted also need to be addressed – and it is gender feminists who are doing that work.

Adaptive Preferences

Nussbaum discusses at length one specific type of preference deformation: the problem of *adaptive preferences*. This idea had already received the attention of philosophers. Jon Elster, in *Sour Grapes: Studies in the Subversion of Rationality* (1983), quotes the well-known La Fontaine fable about the fox and the grapes as a chapter epigraph: Renard, on the point of starvation, sees some grapes hanging out of reach; his reaction is to say that they were too green anyway, and fit only for '*goujats*' (boors). The sour grapes phenomenon, Elster says, is an example of *adaptive preference formation* (1983: 110). The fox had only two choices: lamenting the fact that he can't have the grapes, or convincing himself he did not want them anyway. He takes the latter course and indeed was perhaps wise to spare himself the misery of pining for the unattainable. Nevertheless, his preference has been distorted by his circumstances. Elster's conclusion is that social justice should not be grounded purely on 'given wants' (1983: 140); 'there is also the alternative possibility of changing the wants through rational and public discussion' (1983: 140).

Nussbaum agrees with this analysis, although she points out that not all adaptive preferences are of the sour grapes variety: often, unlike Renard, the agent is not even aware that other options exist. She cites the economist Amartya Sen's contention that 'women in many parts of the world exhibit preferences that are deformed [by having limited options], even when very basic matters such as physical health, nutrition and security are concerned' (1999: 151). It was in response to this problem that Sen pioneered the capability approach, which was taken up and developed by Nussbaum. The capability approach (or capabilities approach, as Nussbaum's version of it is commonly called) is not concerned only with the adaptive preferences of women but has a much wider, indeed universal application, and that will be considered in Chapter 4. For now, it is enough to note that Nussbaum's liberal feminism is not concerned with preference satisfaction alone, but with the question of whether women's preferences are such as will enable them to flourish. Changing laws to make marital rape or sexual harassment a crime is certainly an important step towards greater justice and democracy, but so too is changing attitudes. Nussbaum cites Aristotle in support of the view that 'moral education should play a central role in changing diseased preferences' (1999: 153).

Nussbaum concludes the chapter by noting that:

> American women have much to complain of. They are far too often victims of rape, of sexual coercion of many kinds, of sexual harassment and discrimination in the workplace. Moreover, the underlying attitudes that made these problems so difficult persist, producing pain of many kinds. On the other hand, the feminist movement that began in the 1970s has made considerable progress in articulating the underlying problems and in proposing solutions. This happened in large part through a criticism of the myths that underlay many men's (and women's) beliefs about sexual violence and its causes. (1999: 153)

It is characteristic of Nussbaum that she emphasises progress – actual gains that have been made. Unlike Sommers, however, she does not hold that since some gains have been made then no more are necessary. Nussbaum's approach is always to identify pre-existent or emerging injustices and work towards rectifying them. Pointing to past successes demonstrates that rectification is possible (though not, of course, easy).

Nussbaum's Attack on Butler

In the same year that *Sex and Social Justice* was published, Nussbaum's scathing attack on Judith Butler's brand of third-wave feminism appeared in the American magazine *The New Republic*. Butler's first and arguably most influential book, *Gender Trouble*, was published in 1990. In it, Butler questions the very idea of femaleness: 'Does being female constitute a "natural fact" or a cultural performance, or is "naturalness" constituted through the discursively constrained performative acts that produce the body through and within the categories of sex?' (1990: xxix).

Butler does not answer those questions directly (posing but not answering questions is a distinctive feature of her style), but the implied answers are (a) No, it is not a natural fact and (b) Yes, its apparent naturalness is constituted through discursively constrained performative acts. However, Butler claims that one does not need a fixed and agreed female identity to proceed with feminist politics; on the contrary, a radical questioning of the traditional categories of identity can open up new political possibilities. (She does not specify what those possibilities are.)

Butler challenges the distinction between sex and gender, claiming that biological sex is every bit as much an 'ontological construct' as gender. She also associates the male–female distinction with 'compulsory heterosexuality'. Butler's programme is to disrupt the traditional categories of sex and gender on which liberal feminists such as Nussbaum rely. To this end she proposes 'a set of parodic practices based in a performative theory of gender acts that disrupt the categories of the body, sex, gender, and sexuality and occasion their subversive resignification and proliferation beyond the binary frame' (Butler 1990: xxxi). The book is divided into three sections: 'Subjects of Sex/Gender/Desire', 'Prohibition, Psychoanalysis, and the Production of the Heterosexual Matrix' and 'Subversive Bodily Acts'. Butler considers the work of psychoanalysts and post-structuralists, such as Julia Kristeva, Foucault and Monique Wittig, using their work to deconstruct existing cultural/gender/medical norms, as well as finding evidence of those norms within their work. It is fair to say that the thrust of the book is critical rather than constructive: that is to say, Butler's project is to attack foundationalist assumptions on which traditional power hierarchies are based, but she does not propose anything to put in their place. Indeed, she appears to claim that it would be impossible to put anything in their place. In her conclusion she states:

> There is no ontology of gender on which we might construct a politics, for gender ontologies always operate within established political contexts as normative injunctions, determining what qualifies as intelligible sex, invoking and consolidating the reproductive constraints on sexuality, setting the prescriptive requirements whereby sexed or gendered

bodies come into cultural intelligibility. Ontology, thus, is not a foundation, but a normative injunction that operates insidiously by installing itself into political discourse as its necessary ground. (1990: 189)

This seems to mean that *any* categories of sex or gender would be normative – that is, would tell us what members of those categories should or should not do. The solution, according to Butler, is to deconstruct gender identity, and one way to do this is by parodying traditional gender norms, as is done by drag artists. Butler claims:

> The loss of gender norms would have the effect of proliferating gender configurations, destabilizing substantive identity, and depriving the naturalizing narratives of compulsory heterosexuality of their central protagonists: 'man' and 'woman'. The parodic repetition of gender exposes as well the illusion of gender identity as an intractable depth and inner substance. As the effects of a subtle and politically enforced performativity, gender is an 'act', as it were, that is open to splittings, self-parody, self-criticism, and those hyperbolic exhibitions of 'the natural' that, in their very exaggeration, reveal its fundamentally phantasmatic status. (Butler 1990: 187)

What she seems to be proposing is a feminism in which the identity of 'woman' would be superfluous, indeed an impediment to positive change. As she puts it:

> If identities were no longer fixed as the premises of a political syllogism, and politics no longer understood as a set of practices deriving from the alleged interests that belong to a set of ready-made subjects, a new configuration of politics would surely emerge from the ruins of the old. (Butler 1990: 189–90)

What that new configuration of politics would be, and how it would improve the lives of women or anyone else, is left blank. This style of feminism is fundamentally inimical to Nussbaum's positive, practical, goal-oriented liberal feminism. In her *New Republic* article, 'The Professor of Parody: The Hip Defeatism of Judith Butler' (1999), Nussbaum takes Butler to task on several counts:

- *Lack of engagement with problems faced by women in the real world*. Feminism, Nussbaum argues, should not just be 'fancy words on paper' but should be connected to concrete social proposals to reduce injustice and improve women's lives. She notes practical gains that have been propelled by feminist scholars, such as the reform of rape laws, legal redress for sexual harassment and domestic violence, benefits for pregnant women, and so on. Butler – in common with other American academic feminists of the time, Nussbaum says – takes no interest in such practical campaigns and also ignores the struggles of women outside the United States.

- *Obscurity*. Nussbaum criticises Butler's 'ponderous and obscure style', which is dense with allusions to other writers, without clear explanations of those writers' work; lacks argument or definition of terms, but depends on rhetoric and assertion; is unnecessarily abstract; and often fails to make Butler's own position clear, relying as it does on the heavy use of unanswered questions. (To this list of charges I personally would add Butler's manic over-use of the adverb 'precisely'.) Nussbaum suggests this obscurity is tactical; it is used to create a sense of profundity that will impress readers, especially those not well versed in philosophy. Although Butler identifies as a philosopher (or, to put it in her own words, 'Philosophy is the predominant disciplinary mechanism that currently mobilizes this author-subject'), Nussbaum argues that she is more in the tradition of the Greek sophists and rhetoricians, who sought to persuade rather than seek the truth.

- *Lack of originality*. Butler's main idea, Nussbaum says, is that 'gender' is a social artifice; but this idea is nothing new. It is to be found in John Stuart Mill, as well as contemporary feminist philosophers like MacKinnon and Andrea Dworkin and the psychologist Nancy Chodorow. In Nussbaum's view, Butler adds little of significance to this already well-established insight.

- *Lack of empirical underpinning*. Nussbaum's own approach to philosophy, deriving from Aristotle, is always to start from observable facts (not, of course, that what is observable should always be taken at face value). Butler, Nussbaum says, offers no empirical evidence to support her claims. For example, Butler asserts that there is no such thing as an agent prior to cultural forces that create and shape that agent, which would imply that babies are born completely inert, with no innate faculties or predispositions – but she offers no empirical support for this view (in fact, the empirical evidence goes the other way). Her assertion that biological sex is entirely a social construct also lacks empirical underpinning, and ignores facts such as the specific nutritional needs of adult human females, especially when pregnant or lactating.

- *Unwillingness to adopt a normative position.* Nussbaum accuses Butler of not offering any clue as to what rules, expectations or structures should be resisted or *why* they should be resisted. Butler, Nussbaum says, is unwilling to associate herself with any norms of what society ought to be like. She expressly rejects any such possibility when she says that universal norms 'colonize under the sign of the same' (there seems to be a suggestion there that we should have a norm against colonisation, but no reasons are offered for it). Thus Butler is reduced simply to hoping that new (presumably better in some unspecified way) political possibilities will turn up, but there is no indication of what they will be, or how and why we should work towards them.

- *Parody and subversion cut both ways.* Butler tacitly assumes that her readers will all want to resist the same things – unfair discrimination against gays and lesbians, unequal treatment of women and so on – but since that assumption is not founded on a normative theory, there is no reason why Butler's recommended tactics of parody and subversion should not be directed at other targets. Nussbaum cites the case of a law student she taught who was of a libertarian bent and asked why parody and subversion should not be used to resist the tax structure, or antidiscrimination laws. Another example (not mentioned by Nussbaum) is that, in *Gender Trouble*, Butler asserts that the medical model of femaleness is 'fiction', as a way of dismissing that model. But here she relies on the two-term hierarchy of fact/fiction, in which *fact* is privileged. What is to prevent a critic employing Butler's favoured technique of deconstruction and subverting that hierarchy, so that *fiction* becomes the privileged term? If Butler wants her tactics of parody, subversion and deconstruction to be directed at the appropriate targets, then a normative theory of justice and human dignity is what she needs, and that is what she lacks. Her politics are thus what Nussbaum calls 'naively empty'.

- *Quietism.* This is Nussbaum's most serious charge against Butler: that the resistance she recommends of parodic, subversive speech and acts is unlikely to change anything and indeed is not designed to do so. It is not clear how parody and subversion could have helped the people in Nussbaum's case studies, Sahela, Sareetha and Joe Steffan. Nussbaum claims that Butler's brand of feminism entails 'the loss of a sense of public commitment'.

Judith Butler did not respond directly to Nussbaum's accusations. But in the following issue of the *New Republic* a number of academics responded on Butler's behalf. Gayatri Spivak argues that Nussbaum was wrong to equate social construction theories with the specific claim that gender is performative; she states that Nussbaum's discussion of problems faced by women in India is 'matronizing' and says that many Indian feminists do indeed draw on the work of Butler. A joint letter from Seyla Benhabib, Nancy Fraser and Linda Nicholson objects to Nussbaum's dismissal of Butler as a proper philosopher – particularly since, as they point out, Nussbaum herself wants to bring literature and philosophy closer together. They concede that Nussbaum's article raised some worthwhile questions but object that its tone is unnecessarily vituperative. Joan W. Scott objects that Nussbaum presents a Manichean scheme in which there are 'good' feminists such as Nussbaum (and MacKinnon and Dworkin) and 'bad' ones who do not share Nussbaum's own ideas about normative justice and human dignity. She states that theory and practical political commitment operate on different levels and that the job of theory is not to specify how to reach political goals; to conflate theory and politics is to run the risk of creating reigns of terror where uncontested notions of the good are forcibly imposed, as by Robespierre or the Ayatollahs. Finally, Drusilla Cornell and Sara Murphy, while acknowledging that Nussbaum raises serious issues, argue that the dichotomy between feminists who get things done in the real world and those who merely deploy subversive-sounding words in academic journals is overly simplistic.

In the same issue Nussbaum replied to her critics, offering a succinct defence of her position in each case. My own view is that none of the critics dealt with her substantive charges against Butler, though in some cases they indicated areas which required fuller and more nuanced examination. But leaving aside the question of who won the debate, Nussbaum at the very least should be credited with starting that debate and raising questions that need addressing. Much postmodernist feminism makes *indeterminacy* central: one ought to be in the business of deconstructing differences, not defining or endorsing them. The rationale behind this seems to be that differences must be *normative*: that to define a woman (or any category of person) is to make claims about what they should and shouldn't do. This unevidenced claim exasperates Nussbaum. She sees no reason to accept the assertion that difference constitutes a normative category that can operate independently of universality, and every reason to dispute it.

Although Butler did not reply to Nussbaum's critique, in her preface to the 1999 edition of *Gender Trouble* she does answer the charge of opacity made by Nussbaum (and others). Her defence of her opaque style is twofold. First, she states that: 'It would be a mistake to think that received grammar is the best vehicle for expressing radical views, given the constraints that grammar imposes upon thought, indeed, upon the thinkable itself' (Butler 1999: xviii–xix). This does not seem a very convincing reply. Butler's prose is not criticised for being ungrammatical. It is criticised for prolixity, abstraction, imprecision, name-dropping and over-use of rhetorical questions. In any case, there is no problem about using received grammar to express radical views (Karl Marx managed it, after all.)

Butler's second line of defence is to point out that clear language can be used to tell lies. She writes: 'The demand for lucidity forgets the ruses that motor the ostensibly "clear" view. Avitel Ronell recalls the moment in which Nixon looked into the eyes of the nation and said "let me make one thing perfectly clear" and then proceeded to lie' (Butler 1999: xix). This, again, seems to be a response to an accusation quite apart from the one actually being made. Butler is correct that clear language is no guarantee of honesty. But nobody is maintaining that it is. The reason that clarity is valued is because it makes arguments easier to understand, appreciate and assess (as well as more enjoyable to read, which is not a negligible benefit). Perhaps those arguments contain dubious or untrue premises, but if so, clear expression allows the dubieties and untruths to be identified and contested. Obscure language is no more a guarantee of honesty than is clarity, but dishonesty shrouded in obscurity is harder to perceive.

Summary

Nussbaum offers a sophisticated defence of a liberal feminism which 'is *internationalist, humanist, liberal, concerned with the social shaping of preferences and desire,* and finally, concerned *with sympathetic understanding*' (Nussbaum 1999: 6). This type of feminism has a practical purchase on issues in the real world. It challenges masculine domination, systematic disadvantage, the violation of women's rights and the denigration of women. It provides a clear link between philosophical argument, legal redress and practical mobilisation, and seeks to empower individuals and collectives in their struggle for self-emancipation. In this it provides a valuable alternative to relativism and to the politics of indeterminacy.

Debates about and within feminism are both extensive and impassioned and certainly new ideas have enriched the field since Nussbaum wrote *Sex and Social Justice,* but I would contend that Nussbaum's liberal feminism remains relevant and deserves to continue to contribute to the debate. For a book-length defence of her work in this field (and that of other liberal feminists such as Susan Moller Okin and Jean Hampton), see Ruth Abbey's *The Return of Feminist Liberalism* (2011).

Sex and Social Justice is also significant in Nussbaum's body of work in that it contains the first clear statement of her capabilities approach – to be explored in the next chapter.

Chapter 4

Nussbaum and Capabilities

Human Nature, Human Flourishing
and the Ten Capabilities

In 1986, Martha Nussbaum took up a position as a research adviser at the World Institute for Development Economics Research (WIDER) in Helsinki – a post which she occupied for eight years, working one month every summer (she was concurrently a full-time professor at Brown University). It was during these years that her work began to focus on feminism (see previous chapter) and on international development. Nussbaum's most influential contribution was to bring philosophy to questions which had previously been primarily regarded as economic. As she puts it in her acknowledgements to her 2000 book, *Women and Human Development*:

> Aristotle's insistence on the ethical importance of a vivid perception of concrete circumstances had its own contribution to make, I felt, to a field that is frequently so preoccupied with formal modelling and abstract theorizing that it fails to come to grips with the daily reality of people's lives. (Nussbaum 2000: xv)

The Influence of Amartya Sen

It was while she was working at WIDER, too, that she met Amartya Sen, the economist and philosopher, with whom she had a relationship for several years (she and her husband, Alan Nussbaum, divorced in 1987). Sen was an important intellectual influence on Nussbaum and she credits his work for being 'a source of insight and inspiration, especially the way it combines a passion for justice with a love of reason' (Nussbaum 2000: xvi). Together she and Sen worked on and popularised the capabilities approach, a highly influential approach in both development economics and political philosophy. Put simply, the capabilities approach is the outcome of three propositions:

- All human beings have the right to flourish.
- Human flourishing can be broadly defined in universal terms.
- It is the task of governments to provide citizens with capabilities to flourish.

Nussbaum made many important and distinctive contributions to the theory, but it was Sen who pioneered it. In 1979 he published a paper, 'Equality of What?', in which he argues that merely allocating resources equally does not guarantee that all individuals will possess the same capabilities. For example, allocating equal resources to a disabled person and to an able-bodied person results in *in*equality. Moreover, switching from equality of resources to equality of well-being, measured in terms of happiness or preference-satisfaction (the utilitarian approach), is also unsatisfactory, for some individuals are easier to satisfy than others – in particular, those whom experience has taught to lower their expectations may too easily accept sub-optimal conditions, while those whom fortune has favoured will tend to be more demanding (this is the 'adaptive preference' problem discussed in Chapter 3).

Sen enlarged on these ideas in a short book, *Commodities and Capabilities* (1985), based on the Hennipman Lecture he gave at the University of Amsterdam in 1982. Here, he argues against both *opulence* and *utility* as ways of measuring outcomes. Instead, Sen proposes *functioning* as a criterion of a person's well-being – that is, 'what kind of life he or she is living, and what the person is succeeding in "doing" or "being"' (1985: 28). To succeed in doing or being one must, of course, have the *capability* to exercise the required functions. The goal, therefore, is to provide citizens with the right capabilities – that is, 'the various alternative functioning bundles he or she can achieve through choice' (Sen 1985: 27).

Other Influences

Nussbaum embraced and developed Sen's capability model, but it is fair to say that her own work had already started to lead her in that direction. The antecedents of the capabilities approach are to be found in Aristotle's view of human flourishing, as well as developments of the flourishing claim by Marx and Mill, all of whom influenced Nussbaum. In *Sex and Social Justice*, Nussbaum wrote:

> we do not want politics to take mere survival as its goal; we want to describe a life in which the dignity of the human being is not violated

by hunger or fear or the absence of opportunity. (The idea is very much Marx's idea, when he used an Aristotelean notion of functioning to describe the difference between a merely animal use of one's faculties and a 'truly human use'.) (Nussbaum 1999a: 40)

In *Women and Human Development*, she quotes Marx on this point in a chapter epigraph:

It is obvious that the *human* eye gratifies itself in a different way from the crude, non-human eye; the *human* ear different from the crude ear, etc. . . . The *sense* caught up in crude practical need has only a *restricted* sense. For the starving man, it is not the human form of food that exists, but only its abstract being as food; it could just as well be there in its crudest form, and it would be impossible to say wherein this feeding activity differs from that of *animals*. (Marx [1844] quoted in Nussbaum 2000: 34)

Nussbaum's alignment with her Harvard friend, colleague and mentor John Rawls, also predisposed her towards a capabilities approach. Rawls's *A Theory of Justice* (1971) is anti-utilitarian; his Original Position thought experiment, in which we are to imagine pre-social humans deciding on principles of justice to govern a state in which their own personal position is as yet unknown, is explicitly an alternative to utilitarianism in the sphere of public policy. The decisions made by the pre-citizens behind the Veil of Ignorance are not based on a calculated aggregate of happiness and misery, but on an apprehension of how any individual citizen could be affected by them; the rules of the Original Position make sure of that. The resulting principle of equal liberty – that basic liberties should be as extensive as is consistent with everyone having them, and that they should be equally available to all – carries over into the capabilities approach, in the sense that the proposed capabilities should also be equally available to everyone. Nussbaum's form of the capabilities approach also owes something to Rawls's political liberalism (see below). It is worth noticing that in his paper 'Equality of What?' (1980) Sen also credits Rawls. He does not in fact believe that the Rawlsian conception of equality is sufficient to cater to the diversity of human needs, but he does make the following claim: 'The focus on basic capabilities can be seen as a natural extension of Rawls' concern with primary goods, shifting attention from goods to what goods do to human beings' (Sen 1980: 278).

Nussbaum's Version of the Capabilities Approach

Sen ended *Commodities and Capabilities* (1985) with an appendix detailing the disadvantages that women in India suffer compared with men, across such areas as nutrition, health and mortality. Nussbaum begins *Women and Human Development* (2000) with a reflection on the same biases, stating that 'Women in much of the world lack support for fundamental functions of a human life' (2000: 1). She notes that, globally, women are likely be less well nourished than men and less well educated, that they face intimidation, sex discrimination and sexual harassment, and that in many countries they lack equality under the law. 'In all these ways, unequal social and political circumstances give women unequal human capabilities' (Nussbaum 2000: 1). This is not exclusively a problem of the developing world, but that is where it is at its most pressing:

> According to the *Human Development Report 1997* of the United Nations Development Programme, there is no country that treats its women as well as its men, according to a complex measure that includes life expectancy, wealth, and education. Developing countries, however, present especially urgent problems. Gender inequality is strongly correlated with poverty. (2000: 2–3)

Therefore, international political and economic theorising and action should be feminist (because that is where the need lies). Nussbaum aims to set out her own specific feminist approach – one that is grounded on 'a universalist account of central human functions, closely allied to a form of political liberalism' (2000: 5).

Rawls and Political Liberalism

The invocation of 'political liberalism' deserves some comment here. *Political Liberalism* is the title of an influential book by John Rawls, published in 1993. It is an update on *A Theory of Justice* – not inconsistent with the earlier book, but locating it in a wider theoretical framework. *A Theory of Justice* argued for a form of egalitarian liberalism based on social contract theory. *Political Liberalism* does not recant that position, but accepts that it is only one among many reasonable positions. The book is thus an attempt to answer the question: 'how is it possible for there to exist over time a just and stable society of free and equal citizens, who remain profoundly divided by reasonable religious, philosophical, and moral doctrines?' (Rawls [1993] 2005: 4).

Rawls's answer commits the state to *neutrality* regarding competing doctrines: it is not to favour one ideology, religion or worldview over others. But the competing doctrines must be held by *reasonable persons*: which is to say, those persons who 'desire for its own sake a social world in which they, as free and equal, can co-operate with others on terms all can accept' (Rawls [1993] 2005: 50). The stability of the state is to be underpinned by an *overlapping consensus*. In other words, citizens may disagree as much as they like about competing doctrines, but all must sign up to a consensus (even if for different doctrinal reasons) that all are politically equal and that differences are to be solved through public reason, not force. This entails a commitment to *reciprocity*: reasonable persons 'insist that reciprocity should hold within that world so that each benefits along with others' (Rawls [1993] 2005: 50). The reciprocity requirement rules out doctrines held by those who consider certain others to be natural inferiors, whose interests can be given less or no weight. It would rule out a doctrine which held that women's interests counted for less or are more easily set aside than those of men.

When Nussbaum identifies as a political liberal, then, this is what she means: that she holds a fundamental commitment to the principle that all citizens are free and equal, but would not regard it as justified to impose any doctrine or ideology upon citizens. Her aim, as she puts it, is to provide the philosophical underpinning for a set of 'basic constitutional principles' that all states should respect (Nussbaum 2000: 5).

Some philosophers have questioned whether Nussbaum really is a political liberal. Serene Khader (2011), while sympathetic to Nussbaum's view, describes it as perfectionist. This issue is explored later in this chapter. First, let us look at Nussbaum's version of the capabilities approach. There are some significant differences from Sen's formulation.

The Ten Capabilities

Sen does not offer a detailed, comprehensive list of the capabilities that we should aim for. In 'Equality of What?' (1980) he does offer some examples of basic capabilities: 'The ability to move about . . . the ability to meet one's nutritional requirements, the wherewithal to be clothed and sheltered, the power to participate in the social life of the community' (Sen 1980: 278). However, he does not get any more specific than that, and indeed explicitly refuses to do so. In his 2005 paper, 'Human Rights and Capabilities', Sen says he is reluctant to endorse 'one pre-determined canonical list of capabilities' because to have 'such a fixed list, emanating entirely from pure theory, is to deny the possibility of fruitful public participation on what should be included and why' (2005: 158).

Nussbaum, by contrast, fleshes out this aspect of the approach by listing ten specific and fully explained capabilities which all human beings should have (and which ideally all states should include in their constitutions). For this reason, while Sen's version of the theory is often described as the *capability* [singular] approach, Nussbaum's version is more commonly referred to as the *capabilities* [plural] approach. Nussbaum's list first appeared in *Sex and Social Justice* (1999) and is given again in *Women and Human Development* (2000). It is almost unchanged, but one difference is that Capability 5 (Emotions), now includes the capability to feel 'justified anger', which Nussbaum included after discussion with the American feminist Marilyn Friedman. (Nussbaum will later re-revise her opinion on the desirability of anger; see Chapter 7, 'Nussbaum and the Emotions'):

1. *Life* (being able to live a normal human lifespan).
2. *Bodily Health* (being able to have good health, including reproductive health, and adequate nourishment and shelter).
3. *Bodily Integrity* (being able to move freely without risk of assault; making one's own sexual and reproductive choices).
4. *Senses, Imagination and Thought* (being able to use the senses, imagination and thought in a 'truly human' way, cultivated by education, and having opportunities to use these powers).
5. *Emotions* (being able to have healthy attachments to things and people, to love, to grieve and to feel justified anger).
6. *Practical Reason* (forming one's own conception of the good, including liberty of conscience).
7. *Affiliation* (A: capability for social interaction, friendship and freedom of assembly; and B: protection against discrimination on grounds of sex, race, caste etc.).
8. *Other Species* (being able to live in relation to the world of nature).
9. *Play* (being able to enjoy recreational activities).
10. *Control Over One's Environment* (A: political – being able to make political choices, including freedom of association and of speech; B: material – being able to hold property). (Nussbaum 2000: 78–80; my parenthetical explanations are summaries of Nussbaum's)

Three points need to be made about this list. First, it is *universal*. Nussbaum holds that all adult human beings – both men and women – should be endowed with these capabilities, because we all have the same shared human nature. The same capabilities would not, of course, be suitable for other species (see Chapter 5). Objections to Nussbaum's universalism are considered below.

Second, these are *capabilities*, not required functions. They should be made *available*, so that all citizens are capable of benefiting from them, but there is no obligation for any citizen to do so. A person might prefer not to realise one or more of the capabilities, or to do so only to a small extent. The point is that they *could* if they wanted to. For example, although the capability to play is one of Nussbaum's ten essentials, an individual 'may prefer to work with an intense dedication that precludes recreation and play' (2000: 87). For this reason, 'Where adult citizens are concerned, *capability, not function, is the appropriate political goal*' (Nussbaum 2000: 87, italics in original). Therefore:

> for political purposes it is appropriate that we shoot for capabilities and those alone. Citizens must be left free to determine their own course after that. The person with plenty of food may always choose to fast, but there is a great difference between fasting and starving, and it is this difference I wish to capture. (2000: 87)

Third, the list is *provisional*. Nussbaum refers to it as 'the current version of the list' (2000: 77). It is true that some of the capabilities are so fundamental that it is hard to imagine any reason for their being dropped. As Nussbaum says, 'it would be astonishing if the right to bodily integrity were to be removed from the list; that seems to be a fixed point in our considered judgements of goodness' (2000: 77). Nevertheless, in principle the list could always be amended and updated, perhaps as technology changes our lives, or as we discover more about human needs and psychology. And in fact, in their 2007 book *Disadavantage*, Jonathan Wolff and Avner De-Shalit, while accepting the ten capabilities on Nussbaum's list, added four more to it:

11. Complete independence (ability to do as you wish without dependence on others).
12. Doing good to others.
13. Living in a law-abiding fashion.
14. Understanding the law. (Wolff and De-Shalit 2007: 190–1)

Other Differences from Sen

Sen's and Nussbaum's versions of the theory do have many essential points in common. For instance, they both urge the Rawlsian priority of liberty for the individual (the individual is the 'moral unit' for both of them); they both take the political liberal view that governments should not urge or encourage any single comprehensive vision of a good life but should limit themselves to providing citizens with the capabilities to realise their own vision. They also both agree with the Kantian conception of each person being an end in themselves, and both reject cultural relativism. But there are important differences too.

For Sen the primary use of the capabilities approach is to provide a standard of comparison of quality of life between nations. Nussbaum agrees: but she also wants to go further and use capabilities as a basis for constitutional principles that citizens should be able to demand by right. Another difference is that for Nussbaum the notion of reaching a *threshold* is more important than full capability. That is, the pressing goal is to get each person to a threshold where they can avail themselves of the capabilities to at least some extent; progress towards that goal is at different stages in different parts of the world. The ultimate goal may be to consider just distributions once everyone in the world is above the threshold, but that day is still a long way off. Sen does not use the notion of a threshold. However, as Nussbaum points out, he also has not explicitly committed to the goal of complete capability equality, so, Nussbaum says, 'to the extent that his proposal is open-ended on this point, he and I may be in substantial agreement' (2000: 12).

One final difference lies in Sen's and Nussbaum's presentation of the capabilities approach. Nussbaum's is more accessible, more easily graspable. Sen certainly writes with clarity and elegance, but much of his discussion is at quite a high level of abstraction, and he has a tendency to use algebraic notation to express economic models. For example, in *Commodities and Capabilities* (1985: 13), he explains the freedom that an individual has in terms of choice of functionings thus:

$$Qi(Xi) = [bi = fi)(c(xi)), \text{ for some } fi(.)EF, \text{ and for some } xiEXi]$$

– which no doubt makes very good sense to an economist or mathematician if those values are defined (and Sen does of course define them) but is somewhat intimidating to the layperson.

Nussbaum, on the other hand, has a warmer, more human style and as is her wont she includes case studies describing the lives of actual individuals, whom she met while working with development projects in India. This makes the ideas much more accessible and Nussbaum may be fairly said to have popularised the capabilities approach as well as developing it.

Two Case Studies: Vasanti and Jayamma

Nussbaum focuses throughout on India, as supplying examples of the obstacles to full capability that women face. She makes this choice consciously, because of her own observations, study and familiarity with India; it supplies an example of a nation where women do theoretically have equal constitutional rights but the reality is one of great inequality. (We might note here a continuity with Nussbaum's earlier educational prescription that world citizens should acquire in-depth knowledge and understanding of one other culture (1997, see chapter 34).

She starts by describing the contrasting lives of two Indian women, both of whom, in their different ways, are struggling to thrive amid conditions that scarcely supply the capabilities with which to do so. She begins each story with a vivid physical description so that the women spring off the page as real, living, breathing humans with whom one is ready to empathise. Vasanti is a

> tiny dark women in her early thirties, [who] wears an attractive electric blue sari, and her long hair is wound neatly into a bun on top of her head. Soft and round, she seems more comfortable sitting than walking. Her teeth are uneven and discoloured, but otherwise she looks to be in reasonable health. (Nussbaum 2000: 16)

Jayamma is described thus:

> The first thing you notice about her is the straightness of her back, and the muscular strength of her movements. Her teeth are falling out, her eyesight seems clouded, and her hair is thin – but she could be a captain of the regiment, ordering her troops into battle. (2000: 17)

Each woman faces different impediments to what they would freely choose to do and be. Vasanti, a high-caste Hindu Gujarati woman, was married to a man who was both a gambler and an alcoholic; he took advantage of the money offered by local government for men who elect to have vasectomies and proceeded to spend the money on drink. He became violent towards her and eventually she left him and lived with her brothers, working in their shop making saris. With the help of her brothers she took her husband to court to make him pay maintenance. But the course dragged on for years, like the Jarndyce and Jarndyce lawsuit in *Bleak House*, without a judgment being reached. Her brothers lent her money to buy a machine to assist in her sari-making. With the help of the Self-Employed Women's Association (SEWA), she got a bank loan to repay her brothers (who had families of their own to support) and now works with SEWA, earning 500 rupees a month – a reasonably decent living from which she is able to save.

Jayamma, a Keralan, is of a lower caste than Vasanti. For years she worked in a brick-kiln, carrying planks loaded with bricks on her head (hence her upright posture) and earning no more than five rupees a day. Women in the brick industry were not permitted to do the less arduous, more skilled and higher-paid jobs, so Jayamma carried bricks on her head until she was in her sixties, when she was no longer physically up to the job. Her husband died and she is unable to claim a widow's pension since she has able-bodied sons, though in fact her sons do nothing to support her.

Nussbaum points out that there are important differences between these cases. Vasanti is of the lower middle class, while Jayamma is at the bottom of the economic ladder; Vasanti is of a higher caste than Jayamma. Moreover, to understand either woman one needs to know something of the facts that have shaped their lives: the reality of how the caste system limits opportunities, the prevalence of domestic violence, the government vasectomy programme, lack of education for women, differences between country life and city life in India and between Gujarat and Kerala, the gender divide within the brick-making industry and so on and so on. What Nussbaum is at pains to stress is the particularity of each woman's life. As she says, 'The problems faced by Jayamma and Vasanti are particular to the social situation of women in particular caste and regional circumstances in India' (Nussabuam 2000: 21). At the same time, Nussbaum points out that though circumstances, problems, expectations and practical possibilities differ widely, both within India and throughout the world, the *needs* of women are fundamentally the same:

The body that labours is in a sense the same body all over the world, and its needs for food and nutrition and health care are the same – so it is not too surprising that the female manual labourer in Trivandrum is in many ways comparable to a female manual labourer in Alabama or Chicago, that she doesn't seem to have an utterly alien consciousness or an identity unrecognizably strange, strange though the circumstances are in which her efforts and her consciousness take root. (Nussbaum 2000: 22)

We can now more clearly see the nature of Nussbaum's objection to cultural relativism. Nussbaum does not deny, indeed she emphasises, how local cultural factors shape both preferences and opportunities. But at a deeper level, we do all share the same needs because we share the same human nature. *Solutions* to problems can and must vary according to local conditions. But being denied the opportunity to flourish is, universally, a problem.

Nussbaum's Universalism

Some have criticised Nussbaum's espousal of universal values. In the hostile, *ad hominem* review of Nussbaum's oeuvre previously referred to in the Introduction, Geoffrey Galt Harpham wrote:

> Nussbaum, it has been asserted, has mistaken the ethos of the academic first world for a set of universal norms; by presuming that everyone wants the same things, she has blinded herself to cultural diversity; she has reduced the world's needs to a refrigerator list of to-dos . . . All these charges are to some degree justified. (2002: 74)

Mary Beard (whom Harpham quotes gleefully), in a review of *Women and Human Development* for the *Times Literary Supplement*, 'The Danger of Making Lists', described Nussbaum's capabilities list as 'a frightful muddle, verging on the ludicrous' (2000). Beard does show some sympathy for Sen and Nussbaum's general project of concentrating on what functionings people are capable of – 'how far they are capable of fulfilling a good life as a human being'. She also agrees with Nussbaum that cultural relativism can often be 'a convenient alibi for turning a blind eye to outrageous forms of injustice and oppression the world over' (2000: 6). But although she agrees, up to a point, with Nussbaum's diagnosis, she is dismissive of her prescription. She argues that the capabilities are ill defined and raise questions which are never answered. For example, under 'Bodily Integrity', Nussbaum gives the sub-capability of avoiding 'non-necessary pain', but what is to count as 'non-necessary'? Surely that will vary according to culture. Beard's summary is that the list 'is a set of criteria impossible to frame in anything other than a Western language – and probably in anything other than American English' (2000: 6).

Laurence Goldstein, in his 2007 foreword to a publication of Nussbaum's 2005 *Hochelaga Lectures*, writes in a friendlier but still critical spirit: 'It is difficult to reconcile [Nussbaum's internationalist stance with her] sensitivity to cultural difference and respect for cultural diversity, because some cultures embrace practises to which she herself is strongly morally opposed' (Goldstein 2007: 8). Nussbaum herself, however, anticipated such criticisms and answered them in her chapter 'In Defence of Universal Values' (2000). Indeed she states the problem rather more clearly than her critics:

> Where do these [cross-cultural] categories come from it will be asked. And how can they be justified as appropriate for lives in which those categories are not explicitly recognized? The suspicion uneasily grows that the theorist is imposing something on people who surely have their own ideas of what is right and proper. And this suspicion grates all the more unpleasantly when we remind ourselves that theorists often come from nations that have been oppressors, or from classes in poorer nations that are themselves relatively privileged. Isn't all this philosophizing, then, simply one more exercise in colonial or class domination? (2000: 35)

Nussbaum identifies three 'respectable arguments that deserve to be seriously answered' (2000: 41) against universal norms: the *argument from culture*, the *argument from diversity* and an *argument from paternalism*. I shall take them one by one and show how Nussbaum answers them, before looking at possible replies to Beard's specific criticisms of the capabilities list.

The Argument from Culture

Indian culture – in both its Hindu and Muslim traditions – contains

> powerful norms of female modesty, deference, obedience, and self-sacrifice. We should not assume without argument that these are bad norms, incapable of constructing good and flourishing lives for women. Western women are not so happy, the objector adds, with their high divorce rate and their exhausting careerism. Feminists condescend to third-world women when they assume that only lives like their own can be fruitful. (Nussbaum 2000: 412)

The same argument could be applied in defence of traditional norms in any non-Western culture, of course, not just India.

Nussbaum's answer to this line of argument is threefold. In the first place, she points out that the capabilities approach does not rule out adherence to traditional female norms of modesty, obedience to men and so forth. Any woman who chooses to follow those norms is entirely free to do so. The only caveat is that 'certain economic and political opportunities [should be] firmly in place' (2000: 41), so that she has the capability to adopt a different kind of life if she chooses. (Nussbaum did not add – but could have done – that a 'traditional' life chosen in this way is considerably more meaningful than following a traditional life because it is imposed.)

In the second place, Nussbaum adverts to the problem of adaptive preferences. It may well be that women appear to be satisfied with traditional norms, but only because they fear reprisals if they challenge them and see no alternative but to accept them. If new alternatives become available, attitudes can quickly change. Nussbaum illustrates this with an anecdote about a group of women she met in a desert area of Andhra Pradesh, who initially resisted participating in a government project of forming women's collectives as they thought it could only bring trouble, but over time came to see that taking part brought worthwhile advantages, such as being able to lobby for access to health care and other government services. The attitudes of their menfolk changed too, when they saw the benefits the project brought. Therefore, we should not be too quick to conclude that 'women without options really endorse the lives they lead' (Nussbaum 2000: 43).

In the third place, Nussbaum points out that cultures are neither unchanging nor monolithic. There is no such thing as a single culture of India (a country, as Nussbaum points out, with seventeen official languages, four major religions and vast regional differences). Within the many cultures of India there are many traditions of protest by women against unfair treatment; Nussbaum cites evidence from the Indian Constitution, from the *Mahabharata*, from the stories of Rabindranath Tagore, from the Muslim feminist Rokeya Sakhawat Hossain and others to make the point. It is simply a mistake to believe that feminist ideas are a Western import, incompatible with the culture(s) of India.

The Argument from Diversity

This argument starts from the premise that what makes the world such a rich and interesting place is its diversity of cultures. Just as we value the beauty and complexity of the world's many languages, and think it deeply regrettable when a language dies out, so too we should value the dazzling range of world cultures – and protect them in the same spirit as endangered languages are often protected by governments.

Nussbaum distinguishes two versions of this argument. One is that diversity is valuable per se. The other is that *American* culture has many flaws – it is overly materialist and militarily aggressive, for example – and we don't want all cultures to go down that road. But that second version of the claim is not an argument against universal values. It simply implies that if there are universal values they should not be American. So it is the first claim, that cultural diversity is a good in itself, that Nussbaum needs to counter.

Nussbaum's answer is to point to a disanalogy between languages and cultures. Languages do not harm people. But cultural practices (can) do. Therefore, when seeking to preserve cultural diversity, we need to ask whether the practices to be preserved are harmful to individuals and communities. As Nussbaum points out, one could not make much of a case for preserving the cultural practice of the unfair division of labour in the brick-kilns where Jayamma worked, or Vasanti's husband's traditional practice of wife-beating, merely on the grounds that they contribute to a rich and diverse tapestry of human life. One needs to ascertain whether a practice is harmful, or whether it generates more goods than harms, before deciding whether there is a case for preserving it. But to ascertain this, one needs a framework of universal norms. We should note that this reply does not dismiss the value of cultural diversity. At no point does Nussbaum suggest that there is only one worthwhile culture, or a small number of them. Winnowing out harmful practices still leaves room for a vast and rich variety of cultural traditions and customs.

The Argument from Paternalism

The argument from paternalism is perhaps misleadingly labelled; it is really an *anti*-paternalist argument (paternalism could be defined as restricting a person's liberty *for their own good*).

The argument runs like this:

1. Requiring societies to follow a set of universal moral norms is paternalist.
2. Paternalism is bad because it fails to respect people's autonomy.
3. Conclusion: therefore we should not require societies to follow a set of universal moral norms.

Nussbaum accepts that this argument does raise issues which deserve to be taken seriously. She makes three points in reply. First, her capabilities approach is designed to *avoid* paternalism, because it does not require that individuals avail themselves of the capabilities. It requires merely that the capabilities are available. Second, the anti-paternalist objection itself implicitly relies on a universal norm: the norm that autonomy should be respected. And finally, Nussbaum points out that 'many existing value systems are themselves highly paternalistic, particularly toward women' (2000: 52).

Reply to Beard

We are now in a position to assess Beard's accusation that Nussbaum's capabilities are based on Western values and could not even be framed in non-Western languages. She gives the specific example of being able to avoid non-necessary pain. Beard's point is that different cultures judge for themselves what is necessary. Let's take the case of FGM, which offends against Nussbaum's 'Bodily Integrity' capability. Beard dismissively describes Nussbaum's discussion of FGM as 'inevitable', seeming to suggest that there is something not only predictable but otiose about it. I contend, on the contrary, that it is a most illuminating example, which demonstrates the limitations of what Nussbaum called the argument from culture. Let us enquire how the pain of FGM could be justified as 'necessary'. It seems that any such justification would rely on a cultural context where three conditions obtained: (1) it was regarded as necessary for women to be unable to experience sexual pleasure; (2) undergoing FGM was necessary for a woman to get a husband; and (3) continuing the tradition was itself regarded as necessary.

Now, Beard might say that in certain cultures all those things hold true and therefore it would be wrong to say that the pain of FGM was always unnecessary. But let us look at those 'necessities' more closely. Conditions 2 and 3 we can set aside, for they are parasitic on the very existence of the tradition. They are not anterior to the tradition but dependent on it. If the tradition were removed, one could not say that those necessities were no longer being met, for they would no longer *be* necessities.

Condition 1 – 'It's necessary for women to be unable to experience sexual pleasure' – is more complex. It depends on an ambiguity about who the beneficiary is. If it is the woman herself, the claim is false. It's not just a Western convention that individuals value sexual pleasure (clitorises work the same in South Sudan as in Sacramento). To have the possibility of that pleasure irrevocably removed is neither necessary nor a benefit to the woman concerned. (As Nussbaum argues in her previous book, *choosing* not to indulge in that pleasure is a different matter: 'the person who has normal opportunities for sexual satisfaction can always choose a life of celibacy and my approach says nothing against this'; 2000: 87.) If, however, the beneficiary is not the woman herself but her husband or community, then Condition 1 depends on an implied claim that disbenefit to the woman is of no account compared to the benefits enjoyed by husband or community. But this claim is strongly contested, *not* just in the West but, as Nussbaum has pointed out with a wealth of examples, throughout the developing world. For Beard or anyone else to hold that the traditionalists should have the final word on what counts as necessary seems a far more egregious example of Western meddling than Nussbaum's capabilities.

In any case, even if it were otherwise – even if there were *no* opposition to unfair treatment of women within India and other developing countries – the problem of adaptive preferences would remain. Perhaps women accept unfairness only because they see no alternative. When they have the full range of capabilities that Nussbaum proposes, then we shall see. But it is not an imposition of American values to offer that opportunity. As Nussbaum puts it:

> When we speak simply of what people are actually able to do and be, we do not even give the appearance of privileging a Western idea. Ideas of activity and ability are everywhere, and there is no culture in which people do not ask themselves what they are able to do, what opportunities they have for functioning. (2000: 100)

Moreover, Nussbaum's objections to the cultural diversity argument and the anti-paternalist argument have bite here. It's not persuasive to argue that FGM should be permitted in order to preserve cultural diversity, for the reason given by Nussbaum: cultural diversity does not require that all harmful practices should be protected (otherwise nineteenth-century American plantation owners might have argued that slavery should continue in order to preserve cultural diversity). And it is not paternalist to offer women the capability of bodily integrity. Nor is bodily integrity something that only Westerners value, or that can only be described in American English.

Further Replies to Beard

In her review of *Women and Human Development*, Mary Beard made two other criticisms of Nussbaum's capabilities list. Nussbaum states that an individual who lacks any one of the capabilities will fail to have a good life. Beard claims, citing an unnamed earlier commentator, that this statement rules the disabled 'out of the picture at a stroke, from Stephen Hawking to Stevie Wonder' (2000: 6). Presumably what she has in mind is Nussbaum's Capability 2, Bodily Health. Those with disabilities or illnesses do not have the capability of good health that Nussbaum says is indispensable to a good life.

Clearly, however, Beard has not exercised the principle of charity here. She chooses to be witty rather than fair-minded. She cannot genuinely believe that Nussbaum thinks disabled people are incapable of flourishing. Nor do Nussbaum's own comments on the matter support that interpretation. Nussbaum's explanation of Capability 2 does call for 'good health', specifically mentioning reproductive health and adequate shelter and nutrition. She does not say anything specifically about disability. But we should recall that the capabilities are supposed to be a basis for *government policy*, so it would follow that governments ought to provide disabled people with the support, equipment and therapy, as well as the social basis, needed to give them the best health possible given their condition, and to have the other capabilities to the fullest extent possible. But governments cannot, of course, wave away all disability and sickness with a magic wand:

> Thus, governments cannot hope to make all citizens healthy, or emotionally balanced, since some of the determinants of those positive states are natural or luck-governed. In these areas, what the government can aim to deliver is the *social basis* of these capabilities. The capabilities approach insists that this requires doing a great deal to make up for differences that are caused by natural endowment or by power, but it is still the social basis of the good, not the good itself, that society can reliably provide. (Nussbaum 2000: 82)

In *Women and Human Development*, Nussbaum is concerned to establish on secure foundations the general principle of the capabilities approach and does not explore in much detail how it is to be applied to specific groups. It is worth remarking, however, that Nussbaum does focus on the problem of securing social justice for disabled people in her 2006 book, *Frontiers of Justice* (see Chapter 5).

Beard's other criticism of the capabilities list is that Nussbaum offers little guidance about *how* they are to be provided for everyone, and is naively optimistic to think that they can be put in place just by calling for them.

This is an interesting and important criticism. The task of translating philosophy into effective social policy is a real and difficult one. I do not think that Nussbaum would disagree with that general point. But three additional points should be made.

First, the capabilities approach was never intended as a magic spell that cures all ills simply by being expressed: it is a list of goals to work *towards*. Of course, the work still has to be done.

Second, Nussbaum does in fact provide some ideas about how to set about that work. She supports, for example, the establishment of women's cooperatives and collectives such as SEWA. She also sees legal change as one of the ways forward: she is in favour of constitutional guarantees, and cites legislation and court judgments in India that have benefited women (as well as some that have failed to do so). She offers tactical advice, arguing, for example, that secular feminists should make common cause with religious feminists in challenging abuses and injustices based on conservative interpretations of religion. And she argues that work towards securing the capabilities for all must go on at many levels: 'from local collectives, to regional NGOs, to government programs, to international agencies and human rights programs' (Nussbaum 2000: 299).

Third, Nussbaum *is* optimistic, if that means that she believes that progress towards justice for women (and others) is achievable and has, to some extent and unevenly, already been achieved. Without optimism of this kind there would be no motivation to work towards international development. But the catalogue of ongoing injustice towards women that Nussbaum records demonstrates that she is a realistic rather than a naive optimist. Perhaps she would be better described as a meliorist.

Is Nussbaum a Perfectionist?

Nussbaum defines herself as a political liberal. The main alternative within the liberal tradition to political liberalism is perfectionist liberalism. According to Thomas Hurka, perfectionism is a moral theory which starts from an account of the good human life, or the intrinsically desirable life. And it characterizes this life in a distinctive way. Certain properties, it says, constitute human nature or are definitive of humanity – they make humans humans. The good life, it then says, develops these properties to a high degree or realizes what is central to human nature. Different versions of the theory may disagree about what the relevant properties are and so disagree about the content of the good life. But they share the foundational idea that what is good, ultimately, is the development of human nature. (Hurka 1993: 3)

Perfectionism in this broad sense is not necessarily liberal. Indeed, it may be inimical to liberalism if the good life is narrowly interpreted and if it is the role of the state to promote the good life. Plato's *Republic* ([c. 380 BCE] 2008) is perfectionist but it is not liberal.

Our concern here, however, is with *liberal* perfectionism. As Jonathan Quong (a political liberal) puts it, liberal perfectionists hold that 'It is at least sometimes permissible for a liberal state to promote or discourage particular activities, ideals or ways of life on grounds relating to their inherent or intrinsic value, or on the basis of other metaphysical claims' (Quong 2011: 27). The perfectionist liberal Joseph Raz states the point in more extreme terms: 'It is the goal of all political action to enable individuals to pursue valid conceptions of the good and to discourage evil or empty ones' (Raz 2009: 133).

It might seem important for Nussbaum's project that she escape the label of perfectionist liberal, for perfectionism does tend to entail paternalism – if the state knows better than its citizens what a worthwhile life consists in, it will, as Quong says, promote certain activities and discourage others for people's own good. This would encroach on the personal choice that Nussbaum values so highly; as she is at pains to point out, it's important to 'respect the variety of ways citizens actually choose to live their lives in a pluralistic society' (2000: 51).

One might make the argument that in choosing those particular ten capabilities, Nussbaum *is* being perfectionist. She identifies what capabilities are needed for a flourishing human life and insists that governments should provide them. Serene Khader (2011), who is in agreement with Nussbaum that governments should provide the conditions necessary for people to flourish, refers to Nussbaum as a perfectionist, and she herself identifies as a 'deliberative perfectionist' – meaning that she is in favour of government intervention on perfectionist grounds but emphasises that it must be done sensitively.

94

My own view is that there is no dichotomy between political liberalism and perfectionist liberalism. Rather they occupy opposite ends of a continuum. Even if one's conception of political justice is restricted purely to very basic principles about what rights citizens should have, one has to make assumptions about what kind of rights are suitable – which depends on a theory, however skeletal, about what is good for people. Rawls himself, the very model of a political liberal, in *A Theory of Justice* acknowledges the need for a 'thin theory of the good' in order for rational choosers to have any basis for choice. He imagines that choosers in the Original Position would have such a thin theory:

> Other things equal, they prefer a wider to a narrower liberty and opportunity, and a greater rather than a smaller share of wealth and income. That these things are good seems clear enough . . . I have also said that self-respect and a sure confidence in the sense of one's own worth is perhaps the most important primary good. (Rawls 1999: 348)

But this inevitably opens the possibility of thickening one's theory of the good. If it is 'clear enough' that wider liberty and a greater share of wealth as well as self-respect and a sense of self-worth are good, then why not include other goods whose goodness is also clear enough? Martha Nussbaum's capabilities do just that. It is true that they are not required functions but *capabilities* – they should be made *available*, so that all citizens can benefit from them, but there is no obligation for any citizen to do so. But the fact that it is *these* capabilities and not others that are to be made available implies that they are good things for human beings to have. Nussbaum did not intend to move towards perfectionism. She intended simply to provide an improved framework for thinking about how economic policies can improve the lives of those in developing countries, and especially women, because 'the normative approaches characteristic of utilitarian economics are inadequate guides to public policy' (Nussbaum 2000: 299). Nevertheless, the capabilities approach does move liberalism in a perfectionist direction because it fills in more of the ingredients requisite for a good life. Simply making the capabilities available makes it more likely that they will be taken up and used – that is the point of them, after all. Providing a certain set of capabilities *encourages* certain functions. Nussbaum herself says:

There are some ways of life that people find deeply satisfying, and that probably do not involve unacceptable levels of indignity or capability inequality, which are likely to cease to exist in a regime of choice, simply because of social pressure, and the availability of alternative choices. (2000: 236)

The capabilities approach does embody a view, not of one particular model good life, but a fairly well-defined set of good lives. And indeed Nussbaum herself says that any theory of universal norms, if it is to have content at all, 'will say that some objects of desire are more central than others for political purposes, more necessary to a human's quality of life' (2000: 112). So by providing the capabilities for those objects of desire and ruling out others, the capabilities approach has moved at least some distance along the spectrum in the direction of perfectionism.

Is that a problem for Nussbaum? I contend that it is not. I do not think *any* normative political theory can be developed without some degree of perfectionism. Because Nussbaum's capabilities are at a high level of generality, and because whether or to what degree one translates them into functioning is optional, and because they seem (to me, at any rate) to form a highly plausible account of basic goods that are universally valued, I do not think Nussbaum has moved very far along the continuum. She is still closer to Rawls's political liberalism than to Raz's perfectionist liberalism.

Is Preference Utilitarianism a Viable Alternative?

A key argument in favour of the capabilities approach is that it avoids the problem of adaptive preferences – that is, when a person's preferences are deformed by the sub-optimal options available to them. This can be a difficult problem for utilitarian accounts which aim at preference-satisfaction. However, Heather Baber (2007) offers a preference utilitarian view which claims to be able to surmount the problem; she argues that in the kind of cases Nussbaum cites, people whose options are limited do not have distorted preferences but simply prefer the best they are able to get in the circumstances.

The preference utilitarianism that Baber offers is an advance on earlier forms. In classical utilitarianism as formulated by Bentham, utility was measured in terms of pain and pleasure: the greater the preponderance of pleasure over pain, the greater the utility. This, however, has been widely regarded as a simplistic account; are all pleasures of equal value? Is 'push-pin as good as poetry', as Bentham claimed? John Stuart Mill proposed a refined version in which the higher pleasures (i.e. pleasures of the intellect) were of greater value than the lower pleasures (pleasures of the body). A problem with Mill's account, however, is that it raises the spectre of a superior judge who decides which pleasures we should most value, thus overriding the autonomy of the individual. Preference utilitarianism, on the other hand, respects autonomy because it aims to satisfy the preferences that people actually have, rather than the preferences they ought to have.

Baber argues that in the case studies of Vasanti and Jayamma, neither woman's preferences are adaptive in the sense Nussbaum intends. Nussbaum, Baber claims, 'confuses the absence of occurrent frustration with preference satisfaction' (2007: 3). Baber says that Nussbaum's account offers no reason to suppose that Jayamma would turn down a promotion at the brick-kiln if one were offered. But she has taught herself not to feel frustrated by the fact that she is not going to be offered one. As Baber puts it, 'Extinguishing felt frustration does not mean extinguishing preference' (2007: 5).

On Baber's account, the kind of cases Nussbaum cites do not pose a problem for preference utilitarians. Preference utilitarians do not lack motivation for improving the lot of uncomplaining individuals: 'Where an individual prefers options that are not on offer [the preference utilitarian] holds that it would be better for him if they were' (2007: 12).

The scope of this chapter does not allow for a full-scale assessment of whether preference utilitarianism or the capabilities approach offers the best theory for international development and women's rights. There may well be considerable merit in both and indeed there are points of agreement between them; both provide ethical grounds for improving the lot of disadvantaged and unfairly treated individuals. However, two considerations seem to favour Nussbaum's side of the argument. One is that even if Baber is correct that women like Vasanti and Jayamma have not had their preferences deformed but are merely keeping their true preferences quiet, that could cause difficulties for her project of providing the preferred options. Since the preferred options are not expressed, still less agitated for, it might be hard to know what options should be provided. The other consideration is that since Baber wants more options available so that people can satisfy their preferences, the capabilities approach could supply exactly that menu of options. In practice, even though Baber disagrees with Nussbaum's account of adaptive preferences, she could find much to agree with in the ten capabilities, since they provide opportunities for preference-satisfaction across the most important areas of human life.

Summary

Women and Human Development offers a cogent development of the capability approach pioneered by Sen. Nussbaum's ten capabilities seem to capture the most important possibilities needed for human flourishing. They are transcultural goods. Historically they have not been made available to everyone; in the ancient world only kings or emperors would have had the full range of capabilities, and even today many people, especially women, lack them. What is characteristically liberal about Nussbaum's approach is that she argues that everyone should have them – not only those who are powerful enough to get them for themselves. Nussbaum also offers further arguments against cultural relativism and puts forward a sophisticated defence of universalism. No doubt that debate will continue, but proponents of cultural relativism do need to take account of Nussbaum's arguments.

The capabilities approach has been influential in political theory and has been applied in many areas: development, public health ethics, environmental ethics and educational justice (see Robeyns and Fibieger Byskov 2021). It has also continued to be important in Nussbaum's own work – informing, for example, her work on animal rights.

Chapter 5

Nussbaum and Animal Rights

Capabilities for Animals

The status of other animals and our relationship with them is a
thread that runs through much of Nussbaum's writing. It can be
traced back to her engagement with Aristotle, a natural historian
who wrote extensively about biology and who conceived of human
beings as animals, with our own distinctive nature and function in
nature. Nussbaum's ten capabilities that should be made available
for all humans included, as we saw in Chapter 4, the opportunity to
relate to other species (Nussbaum 2000). She explores animal emotions in her book *Upheavals of Thought*, published in 2001. Also
in 2001, Nussbaum reviewed a book by the legal theorist Steven
Wise, *Rattling the Cage*. Nussbaum supported Wise's programme
of greater legal rights for non-human animals – she wrote that the
book made 'an important contribution to progress on one of the
most urgent moral issues of our time' – but thought his case needed
a more secure philosophical foundation: '*Rattling the Cage*, while
provocative, is more of a work of activism than of scholarship. Its
powerful rhetoric and compelling social message are marred by historical and theoretical shortcomings' (Nussbaum 2001b: 1513).

In 2004, she and Cass Sunstein (a Harvard professor of law and
behavioural economist) co-edited and contributed to the book *Animal Rights: Current Debates and New Directions* (which included an
essay by Wise). Nussbaum and Sunstein were in a relationship for ten
years and the book is another example of Nussbaum's fruitful intellectual collaborations. It reflected a growing international concern
with our treatment of animals: as Sunstein states in his introduction,
'since the early 1990s, the animal rights question has moved from
the periphery and toward the center of political and legal debate'
(Sunstein in Sunstein and Nussbaum 2004: 4).

This focus on a pressing contemporary issue is typical of Nussbaum,
who has always sought to apply her considerable knowledge of classical and early modern philosophy to problems in the here and now. The

book is noteworthy in Nussbaum's oeuvre for two reasons. First, she takes on the role of curator, with Sunstein, of a range of contemporary positions on animal rights, by some of the most influential theorists in the field. Second, in her own contribution she extends the capabilities approach to the question of animal rights. She goes on to develop this approach further in *Frontiers of Justice* (2006).

The appearance of *Animal Rights* in 2004 was prescient. Throughout the twenty-first century, the issue of animal rights has become ever more urgent, with growing numbers of vegetarians and vegans who are motivated not only by respect for the moral status of non-human animals but also by a concern for the ecological consequences of intensively raising livestock for meat. *Animal Rights* focuses on the former, but the more recent consciousness of the environmental effects adds additional and compatible arguments for sensitivity about our treatment of other animals.

It is characteristic of Nussbaum's commitment to pluralism and rational, open debate that *Animal Rights* is not propaganda for a single viewpoint but juxtaposes a range of different positions, which, often explicitly, conflict with one another. It does, however, have an overall agenda – it is a book that takes the question of animal rights seriously and all the contributors agree that our treatment of animals ought to be improved, if to different extents, in different ways and for different reasons. This focus on the practical – what actually needs to be done – is again characteristic of Nussbaum, as is the fact that as a result of her work on animal rights she changed her own practice and became a vegetarian.

The book is divided into two parts, 'Current Debates' and 'New Directions', which we will explore now.

Current Debates

This section consists of eight essays, covering a range of diverse and often opposed positions. The contributors are Steven M. Wise, Richard A. Posner, Peter Singer, Cora Diamond, Gary L. Francione, Richard A. Epstein, James Rachels, and co-authors Lesley J. Rogers and Gisela Kaplan. I focus here on Peter Singer's contribution – partly because he is the doyen of the animal rights movement and partly because his preference utilitarianism is one of the main competitors to Nussbaum's capabilities approach.

Singer's chapter is a response to the essay by Richard Posner (2004), in which Posner critiques Singer's utilitarian position (see below), and urges instead what he calls a 'humancentric' approach – one based on the fact that human beings have sympathetic sentiments towards other animals, and we can make these sentiments more effectual by increasing our knowledge of the animal world, by better information about the way animals are treated in farms, abattoirs and laboratories, and by enforcing already-existing laws against cruelty to animals. Thus in Posner's view no change in either the legal or the ethical status of animals is necessary.

Singer in turn responds directly to Posner. He begins with a re-statement of his own preference utilitarian position: what should matter is not what species an organism belongs to, but the extent to which it can experience pleasure and pain and so have preferences. For this reason,

> pigs are objects of moral concern, but lettuces are not. Pigs can feel pleasure and pain, they can enjoy their lives, or want to escape from distressing conditions. To the best of our knowledge, lettuces can't. We should give the same weight to the pain and distress of pigs as we would give to a similar amount of pain and distress suffered by a human being. (Singer in Sunstein and Nussbaum 2004: 80)

Singer then turns directly to Posner's claim that 'ethical argument is and should be powerless against tenacious moral instincts', which is given as an epigraph, providing a target to shoot at, at the head of Singer's essay. What does Posner mean by moral instincts? Presumably those which are *universalisable* – that at least is the most venerable as well as the most widely accepted criterion of morality. But now Posner needs a way of determining which instincts are universalisable ones, which would seem to require the ethical arguments he eschews. Moreover: even if we leave aside the normative claim that ethical argument *should* be powerless against moral instincts, Posner has also made the factual claim that ethical argument *is* powerless against moral instincts. As Singer shows with a wealth of examples, ethical arguments have frequently been influential, throughout history, in changing deep-seated moral instincts. The abolition of slavery is a salient example. Singer concludes that Posner's humancentric stance does not afford justification for Posner's own opposition to cruelty to animals. As Singer says, 'We need to look elsewhere for an ethic that will provide a basis for improving [animals'] position' (in Sunstein and Nussbaum 2004: 90).

Singer's own candidate for that ethic is, as stated, preference utilitarianism. I will compare this with Nussbaum's rival candidate, the capabilities approach, below.

New Directions

'Current Debates', then, is a survey of the main existing positions in debates over animal rights, as of 2004. The second section, 'New Directions', consists of new theoretical departures and new developments in law and policy, in six essays. The essays are by Daniel J. Wolfson and Mariann Sullivan, David Favre, Cass R. Sunstein, Catharine A. MacKinnon, Elizabeth Anderson, and Martha Nussbaum. I'll briefly summarise Sunstein's contribution, but it's Nussbaum's essay I focus on.

In his essay 'Can Animals Sue?' Sunstein points out that there are two ways of extending rights, for any group. The more radical course is to call for more rights. The more modest but perhaps more pragmatic course is to ensure that existing rights are respected. It is this latter course that Sunstein discusses. He argues that mistreated animals can and should sue – that is, they can be the plaintiffs in legal actions, though of course the suit has to be pursued by a human representative on their behalf.

Martha Nussbaum's chapter, 'Beyond "Compassion and Humanity": Justice for Nonhuman Animals', is the last in the book and it brings together approaches discussed earlier in the book, looking at the limitations of contractarianism and utilitarianism when applied to other animals, before making a cogent case that the capabilities approach is the best theoretical underpinning for improving the lives of our fellow creatures.

Nussbaum begins with an account by Cicero of Roman games staged by Pompey, in which there were combats between men and elephants. The evident misery and despair of the animals, who saw no hope of escape, aroused the compassion of the crowd, who rose as one to curse Pompey. Cicero writes that the crowd felt a sense of commonality – *societas* – with the doomed animals. The anecdote shows that it is possible for humans – even humans who were accustomed to enjoying the spectacle of the violent deaths of men and animals – to extend sympathy and consideration to other species. But on what footing does this consideration stand?

The Contractarian View

On a contractarian view, we owe duties of justice to those we have formed (real or hypothetical) contracts with, each agreeing to duties and responsibilities. Nussbaum first considers Kant's contractarian position as applied to animals, which is, as she says, 'very unpromising'. Kant argued that we have no direct duties to animals. We ought to treat them kindly, not cruelly, but only because 'cruel or kind treatment of animals strengthens tendencies to behave in similar fashion to humans' (Nussbaum 2004b: 300). Nussbaum claims that this is a 'fragile empirical claim about psychology' (2004b: 300). For if upon investigation it were to turn out that cruel treatment of animals did *not* as a rule lead to cruel treatment of humans, then there would be no reason at all to treat animals decently. For Kant, duties cannot be owed directly to animals because they lack rationality. They cannot be parties to any sort of contract, even a hypothetical one, as they lack 'moral reciprocity'.

Nussbaum allows, however, that a contractarian approach of a more accommodating nature than Kant's could allow for direct duties to animals. Rawls excludes animals from claims about *justice*, but he claims that we have 'duties of compassion and humanity' (cited in Nussbaum 2004b: 300). Rawls's famous Original Position has no place for animals. Not only do they lack rationality – at least the kind of rationality necessary for settling on principles of justice – but there is too great an asymmetry of power between humans and other animals for any sort of bargain to be struck. And therefore 'Rawls's omission of animals from the theory of justice is deeply woven into the very idea of grounding principles of justice on a bargain struck for mutual advantage (on fair terms) out of a situation of rough equality' (Nussbaum 2004b: 301).

The duties we owe to animals, then, are in Rawls's view based not on justice but compassion. Compassion generates duties in the following way: a feeling of compassion imposes a duty 'to refrain from acts that cause the suffering that occasions the compassion' (2004b: 302). (This is similar to David Hume's view that moral obligations are generated from sentiment.) Although Rawls does not spell this out, Nussbaum believes he would accept that duties from compassion are formed in this way.

However, for Nussbaum that is still inadequate. An approach grounded in duties of *justice* is necessary to take account of animals as subjects, with their own lives to lead and goals to pursue. As Nussbaum puts it:

> When I say that the mistreatment of animals is unjust, I mean to say not only that it is wrong *of us* to treat them in that way, but also that they have a right, a moral entitlement, not to be treated in that way. It is

unfair *to them*. I believe that thinking of animals as active beings who[1] have a good and who are entitled to pursue it naturally leads us to see important damages done to them as unjust.

Note that *rationality*, so central to contractarian accounts, is not required to do any work here. Nussbaum contends that her own capabilities approach is the most appropriate foundation for claims of justice towards other animals. But first she considers another rival theory, utilitarianism.

The Utilitarian Position

Nussbaum starts by acknowledging the substantial contribution that utilitarian theory has made in recognising moral entitlements for animals. Bentham and Mill in the nineteenth century and Peter Singer in our own time have used utilitarian arguments very effectively to further the cause of animal liberation. Nussbaum identifies one general virtue of utilitarianism and one that is specific to animals. The general virtue is the willingness of utilitarians to challenge moral conventions and follow the arguments wherever they lead. The more specific virtue is that for utilitarians it is not necessary to take real or hypothetical part in the rational deliberations that create principles of justice in order to be covered by them (as it is under contractarian theories). Rationality is not required. As Bentham famously said: 'The question is not, Can they *reason*?, nor Can they *talk*? but, Can they *suffer*?' (Bentham [1789] 1961: 381, n.331).

Nussbaum goes on, however, to identify a number of problems for utilitarianism. First, there is the problem of *sum-ranking*. That is, the utilities (whether defined hedonistically or in terms of preference-satisfaction) of different individuals are aggregated to form a total – the higher the better. But how those utilities are *distributed* does not form part of the calculation. Sum-ranking could allow 'some people's extremely high well-being to be purchased, so to speak, through other people's disadvantage'[2] (Nussbaum 2004b: 303). Therefore it could also allow ill-treatment of animals if this led to increased well-being for a sufficient number of humans.

A further problem is what type of utility is to be pursued. For Bentham it was pleasure; for Singer (and Baber) it is the satisfaction of preferences. But both of these come with difficulties. Pleasure is, as Nussbaum points out, 'an elusive notion' (2004b: 304). Moreover, pleasure is fungible in a way that, for example, basic political entitlements

[1] It is significant that Nussbaum uses *who* rather than *which* here.
[2] I am reminded here of Ursula K. Le Guin's short story, 'The Ones Who Walk Away from Omelas'.

are not. Basic political entitlements cannot be traded off against each other; it makes no sense to deny somebody free speech on Tuesday afternoons and compensate by giving them extra health care for the rest of the week. We must also ask whether pleasure, however defined, really is the only valuable thing in life. Recalling the argument made in *The Fragility of Goodness* (1986), Nussbaum points out: 'The grief of an animal for a dead child or parent, or the suffering of a human friend . . . seem to be valuable, a sign of attachments that are intrinsically good' (2004b: 304). There is also the problem of 'bad pleasures' – pleasures that involve the suffering of other creatures, such as the pleasure of a circus audience when animals are made to perform tricks. Are these, too, to count positively? If not, why not?

Preference utilitarianism escapes some of these problems but has its own attendant difficulties. There is the general problem, already discussed, of adaptive preferences. Moreover, preference utilitarianism 'has no room for deprivations that never register in the animal's consciousness' (Nussbaum 2004b: 304). The utilitarian view can of course consider suffering felt by a deprived animal, but it cannot consider deprivations that the animal does not feel.

Finally, there is the problem of numbers. The meat industry causes suffering to animals on an enormous scale, but it also brings into being billions of animals who would not otherwise have existed. It's at least possible that this might result in just a little bit more utility than if those animals had never been born – in which case utilitarianism could be used to *justify* the meat industry.

Nussbaum also mentions Mill's refined version of hedonistic utilitarianism, which recognises different *qualities* of pleasure, valuing intellectual pleasures more highly than bodily ones. But this, Nussbaum argues, is a move away from standard utilitarianism and towards the Aristotelian ideal of *eudaimonia* – that is, all-round flourishing in dimensions appropriate to the animal, rather than a sum total of homogeneous pleasures. Nussbaum makes this case at greater length in a 2004 paper, 'Mill between Aristotle and Bentham'. Here she argues that Mill was torn between Bentham's conception of happiness as pleasure and Aristotle's conception of happiness as flourishing and although he does not spell out that conflict – in fact *Utilitarianism* (1859) is nominally a defence of Bentham – he achieves, albeit in an inexplicit and unsystematic way, a kind of synthesis of the two:

> despite Mill's unfortunate lack of clarity about how he combined the two conceptions, he really did have a more or less coherent idea of how

to integrate them – giving richness of life and complexity a place they do not have in Bentham, and the absence of pain and of depression a role that Aristotle never sufficiently mapped out. The result is the basis, at least, for a conception of happiness that is richer than both its sources – more capable of doing justice to all the elements that thoughtful people have associated with that elusive idea. (Nussbaum 2004c: 62)

Mill's theory, or adumbration of a theory, thus points the way towards a more fleshed-out ideal of flourishing rather than maximal pleasure (though it does not exclude pleasure) – that is to say, a capabilities approach.

The Capabilities Approach Applied to Other Animals

Nussbaum holds that the capabilities approach can be 'extended to provide a more adequate basis for animal entitlements than the other two theories under consideration [contractarianism and utilitarianism]' (2004b: 305–6). The goal of the approach is 'to address the need for a rich plurality of life activities' (2004b: 305). Nussbaum calls in Aristotle and Marx to support the claim that it is a tragic waste when a person never has opportunities to perform functions essential to their nature. If this is so in the case of human beings, then it is so for all life forms. Of course, other species do not have the same functions as *Homo sapiens*. They do not (for the most part and in most senses) have rationality. But unlike Kant, Nussbaum does not regard reasoning as the sole function worthy of respect. She takes the side of the biologist Aristotle, who judged 'that there is something wonderful and wonder-inspiring in all the complex forms of animal life' (2004b: 306). The aim of the capabilities approach, then, is that 'no animal should be cut off from the chance at a flourishing life and that all animals should enjoy certain positive opportunities to flourish' (2004b: 307).

If we apply this to, say, the treatment of battery-farmed hens, it has an immediate plausibility. To flourish, hens need to live according to their natures, which means moving around freely, foraging for food, scratching the ground to look for seeds or insects, living in a social group with a pecking order, being followed around by their chicks and so on. It is obvious that a hen imprisoned in a tiny cage can do none of these things. The capabilities approach offers an intuitively appealing reason why this is wrong.

A utilitarian approach also gives us a reason why this is wrong: caged hens *suffer*. But that answer takes little account of specific species-needs. Indeed, for the utilitarian, species is morally irrelevant. But in the capabilities approach, 'the species-norm ... tells us what the appropriate benchmark is for judging whether a given creature has decent opportunities for flourishing' (Nussbaum 2004b: 310). The capabilities approach can serve as a *diagnostic* tool – encouraging us to think about the natural functions of a particular species and whether human intervention is preventing them from performing those functions.

It would be impossible to draw up separate capability lists for every species, of course. But Nussbaum aims to show that the ten basic capabilities she set out for human flourishing can be applied to other animals, with species-specific modifications. Here is the list again, with a summary of how each one could be tailored according to species:

1. *Life.* Animals should not be killed gratuitously, for sport or for luxury items such as fur. Killing for food is more problematic, as this happens to prey species in the wild anyway. Killing very young animals would be wrong, as would killing them after a painful, miserable confined life (see Capabilities 2, 3 and 4). If animals die painlessly after healthy, free-range lives, then killing them for food might not be unjust.

2. *Bodily Health.* All animals are entitled to a healthy life according to their nature. Pets already have some legal protection; so, too, do working animals and zoo animals, although these laws are not always well enforced. But the health of farmed animals is much less well protected, an asymmetry that needs to be remedied.

3. *Bodily Integrity.* Violence and abuse against animals should be banned. This includes docking of body parts: the de-clawing of cats, for example, should be banned even if it causes no pain, as it prevents the cat performing natural functions.

4. *Senses, Imagination and Thought.* Clearly animals have more limited functions in this capability than humans do; nevertheless all animals should have 'free movement in an environment that pleases the senses'. The precise areas of freedom will depend on the species.

5. *Emotions.* Animals are entitled to lives in which they can form emotional attachments and be free from fear, loneliness and boredom.

6. *Practical Reason.* Again this capability is more limited than in the case of human beings, but we should ask 'to what extent the

creature has a capacity to frame goals and projects' and allow or enable it to do so.

7. *Affiliation.* As in the human case, Nussbaum separates this into two parts – A: the capability to form relationships with same-species members and also with humans; B: being able to live in a culture which respects them and treats them as dignified beings (as Nussbaum points out, there is no equivalent to this requirement in a utilitarian approach, since animals would not consciously suffer from the lack of such a capability).

8. *Other Species.* Like humans, other animals should be able to live in relation with the rest of the natural world.

9. *Play.* This capability is central to all sentient animals (it would not apply to insects or sponges). It requires many of the same policies outlined in the other capabilities: space, freedom, presence of other species-members to interact with.

10. *Control Over One's Environment.* Other animals cannot directly control their environment as humans do, so here the emphasis switches to what humans should *provide* for animals under this capability. Under the political part, animals should be part of a political conception that respects them and will treat them justly; humans will have to act on their behalf to ensure this. Under the material part, animals do not have property rights but their habitats should be protected. (See Nussbaum 2004b: 314–17)

Frontiers of Justice

In *Frontiers of Justice* (2006) Nussbaum returns to the issue of justice for animals. Her discussion is longer and fuller than the chapter in *Animal Rights* and occurs in the context of a book-length exploration of how the capabilities approach can cover three disadvantaged groups who tend to fall through the net of contractarian theories: people with disabilities, citizens of poorer countries, and non-human animals. I focus here on the last of these.

The section devoted to animals has the same title as the chapter in *Animal Rights*, 'Beyond Compassion and Humanity', and recycles some of the material there, albeit at slightly greater length. The upshot is the same: Nussbaum argues that neither contractarianism nor utilitarianism offer an entirely adequate basis for thinking about justice for animals, and the capabilities approach does better. However, she then proceeds to go deeper into the implications of the capabilities approach, developing ideas about the role of the imagination, about the dignity of animals, about the problem of how much human intervention in the lives is appropriate, and about the ethics of eating meat. Interestingly, she raises a number of problems to which she does not have the solution – and this is characteristic of Nussbaum, for whom philosophy is always a work in progress.

The Role of the Imagination

Nussbaum wrote about the importance of imagination in *Cultivating Humanity* (1997) and she returns to it in *Frontiers of Justice*. Imagination is, of course, a central human power for Nussbaum and the capacity to exercise it is fourth on her list of capabilities, 'Senses, Imagination and Thought' – being able to use senses, imagination and thought in a 'truly human' way, cultivated by education. Imagination is necessary for following the method of what Nussbaum, following Rawls (who himself follows Aristotle and Sidgwick), calls 'reflective equilibrium' (2006: 352). This method involves examining our own moral beliefs, asking which are the deepest in cases of conflict, revising as necessary, seeking consistency. As Nussbaum stresses, the method relies on the use of the imagination: 'we inform ourselves about alternative possibilities by imagining the form of life that these possibilities would construct, asking ourselves what suffering or flourishing there would be in lives governed by these political principles' (2006: 353). Using the imagination in this way is more difficult, of course, when investigating ethical claims of non-human animals. We can't imagine ourselves into the lives of other species as completely or as confidently as we do with fellow humans. As Thomas Nagel (1985) reminds us (albeit in a different context and for a different purpose), we cannot *really* imagine what it is like to be a bat.

For this reason, utilitarians prefer 'a pure reliance on principle' (Nussbaum 2006: 353); the question is kept simply to whether an animal is suffering or not, and imagination is not needed. In practice, though, Nussbaum points out that utilitarians who are filled with generous wrath at the ill-treatment of animals *are* using their imaginations: 'Peter Singer's writing contains some of the most powerful invitations to imagine animal suffering ever written' (2006: 354). What is more, good imaginative writing is a vital instrument in alerting people to animal suffering and convincing them of its importance. Storytelling is one way to direct the imagination towards the

109

lives of animals. We might note here that in *Cultivating Humanity*, seven years earlier, Nussbaum was already urging the use of stories and literature to enlarge human sympathies towards each other – an example of the thematic consistency of her writing.

The capabilities approach uses sympathetic imagination to develop our moral judgements about animal lives, to 'make them real to us in a primary way' (Nussbaum 2006: 354). But it cannot do that work alone; imagination needs to be supplemented by 'theoretical insights about dignity to correct, refine and extend both judgments and imaginings' (Nussbaum 2006: 354).

Dignity

The value of dignity is a frequent theme in Nussbaum's writing. In *Women and Human Development* it is presented as a concomitant of human flourishing. If you are prevented from performing central human functions, the result is loss of dignity. If you have the capability to perform those functions – and decide for yourself how you are going to do so – the result is dignity.

That is all very well, but can this ideal be extended to non-human animals? There might seem to be a difficulty in regarding a chicken or rabbit as having dignity. There are two reasons for this difficulty. The first is an ambiguity in the word 'dignity'. It can mean being worthy of respect. Or it can mean the quality of being solemn, serious, important, impressive. If we interpret dignity in the latter way, then it's true that chickens and rabbits don't seem to have it. But this, of course, is not the sense Nussbaum has in mind. She has in mind the first meaning: being worthy of respect.

But here the second and more serious objection comes in. Can a creature which lacks *rationality* be worthy of respect? There is a long tradition in Western thought which answers in the negative. Nussbaum traces it back to the Stoics, who saw a 'sharp split' between humans and other animals (and also between pre-rational children and rational adults). Immanuel Kant, Nussbaum says, further widened this split. Kant believed that human beings inhabited two realms: a deterministic world where we are governed by the laws of nature; and a world of rationality and moral freedom. Non-human animals inhabit only the deterministic world. And so, for Kant, 'human dignity and our moral capacity, dignity's source, are radically separate from the natural world' (Nussbaum 2006: 131). For this reason, human beings are ends in themselves, but animals could never be ends in themselves, on Kant's view, only means (which is why we do not owe direct moral duties to them).

Nussbaum contests the Kantian view. She points out that 'dignity just is the dignity of a certain sort of animal' (2006: 132). The kind of dignity that we humans have is rooted in certain natural facts about us: our rationality, certainly, but also our mortality and fragility. Angels, gods or super-beings from science fiction who were immortal and invulnerable would have a very different kind of dignity from ours. Our dignity does depend on our being able to exercise our powers, including rationality, but it is also connected to our animal nature and our knowledge of the inevitability of sickness, aging, loss and death. Since human dignity is of the kind that it's appropriate for humans to have, it follows that other animals can have the kind of dignity that is appropriate for them – a dignity rooted in their *nature*.

Besides, it is over-simplifying to draw a sharp line between rational beings (humans) and irrational beings (all other animals). In fact, as Nussbaum says, 'in nature we find a rich continuum of types of intelligence, and practical capacities of many types' (2006: 133).

Ought we, then, to make a claim of equal dignity among all species? Nussbaum clearly thinks so. She states: 'It seems there is no respectable way to deny the equal dignity of animals across species' (Nussbaum 2006: 383). I think it might be worth inserting a proviso here, that the species should be *sentient* to be a candidate for equal dignity. I find it impossible to take seriously the dignity-claims of a mosquito or an amoeba. Nussbaum, I think, would agree; she writes: 'it seems plausible to consider the possession of sentience as a threshold condition for membership in the community of beings who have entitlements based on justice' (2006: 362). With that qualification made, Nussbaum sees no reason to deny the equal dignity of all animals. Yet, for strategic reasons, she refrains from making this a necessary principle for the capabilities approach to animal entitlement. She wants to create an *overlapping consensus* (note the Rawlsian term) whereby people with different ideologies and principles can agree on the goal of securing basic capabilities for non-human animals. But many, especially those who hold religious doctrines, will find the idea of equal dignity for all animals hard to accept. Therefore, although Nussbaum herself upholds the principle of equal dignity, she opts 'to treat the question of equal dignity as a metaphysical question on which citizens may hold different positions while accepting the basic substantive claims about animal entitlements' (Nussbaum 2006: 383). Note that this differs from the capabilities approach as applied to humans, where the principle of equal dignity is non-negotiable.

The Tiger and the Gazelle

There is a traditional moral distinction between positive and negative duties: that is, things we should do and things we must not do. It has often been held that negative duties are stronger – so that while it is culpable to harm others, *allowing* harm by not intervening to prevent it is either not culpable or is less culpable. This moral distinction has been challenged by a number of modern philosophers (see for example James Rachels' 'Killing and Letting Die', 2001) and Nussbaum too rejects it. Under the capabilities approach, at least as applied to human beings, moral duties are not limited to refraining from actively harming others but include providing them with the necessary conditions to flourish.

But can this distinction be applied more fittingly in the case of non-human animals? Nussbaum begins by conceding that it is 'at least coherent' to say that we should not actively harm animals but that we have no duty to support their flourishing. Their flourishing is a matter for the species itself. There's a plausible case that we should not interfere, because 'the sovereignty of species, like the sovereignty of nations, has moral weight' (Nussbaum 2006: 373).

Nevertheless, although Nussbaum acknowledges that there is 'much truth' in this argument, she cannot fully accept it. In the first place, huge numbers of animals are already living under the control of humans and we have duties of care which follow from that. But even where wild animals are concerned, sometimes human intervention is necessary to preserve habitats, protect endangered species, or to save animals from the consequences of natural disasters. What she recommends is a form of respectful, sensitive paternalism, which aims to strike a balance between supporting the welfare of a species and allowing it to flourish for itself. Paternalist acts which aim at securing animal autonomy are therefore justifiable, indeed morally required.

So far so good. Details of just how and when to intervene may be dismayingly complicated but at least the principle justifying intervention is clear. However, Nussbaum then moves on to the trickier question of harms that animals do to *each other*, and what humans should or could do about it. Tigers eat gazelles, without showing any regard for their capabilities. Ought we, then, to try to police animals in the wild, protecting prey from predators? Nussbaum concedes that this sounds absurd; and yet,

> to the capabilities approach, as to Utilitarianism, what happens to the victim is the key issue, not who does the bad thing. The death of a gazelle after painful torture is just as bad for the gazelle when torture is inflicted by a tiger as when it is done by a human being. That does not mean that death by tiger is as blameworthy; obviously it is not. But it does suggest we have similar reasons to prevent it, if we can do so without doing greater harms. (2006: 379)

It is that last proviso that seems to doom the project of protecting vulnerable animals in the wild. Nussbaum says that we should protect gazelles if we can do so 'without the type of massive intervention that would be harm-producing' (2006: 379) – but it seems extremely likely that it *always* would be harm-producing. Are we to remove gazelles from their habitat? Attend them with armed guards? But then what happens to the tigers? Indeed Nussbaum points out that 'the needs of the predatory animal must also be considered' (2006: 379). Intervention would disrupt the local ecology and would not satisfy the principle of allowing animals to flourish – that is, live the natural lives they evolved to live.

Nussbaum acknowledges that cases like this are complicated and difficult. In my view, such a goal is not just complicated and difficult to achieve but intrinsically undesirable. Intervention in the wild to protect prey species from predators would always bring bad consequences. As Anders Schinkel objects, 'If the relations between predators and prey animals must be made just, or else controlled so as to stay within the limits set by justice, that would be the end of the natural world as we know it' (2008: 50).

It is, however, hard to disagree with Nussbaum's open-ended conclusion to the discussion: 'Humans are intervening in animals' lives all the time, and the question can be only be what form this intervention should take' (Nussbaum 2006: 380).

Can We Eat Meat?

In *Animal Rights* (Sunstein and Nussbaum 2004), Nussbaum did not claim that the capabilities approach necessarily committed one to vegetarianism. With certain important provisos in place (that the animals were not killed when very young, and that they were treated humanely during their lives), a proponent of the capabilities approach could accept meat-eating (although a *New Yorker* interview of 2016, by Rachel Aviv, states that Nussbaum herself no longer eats meat).

Nussbaum returns to the question in *Frontiers of Justice* (2006) and again does not rule out meat-eating. This time the focus is more on what is realistically achievable. She refers to the painless killing of animals for food as 'one of the very difficult cases' and states: 'It seems wise to focus initially on banning all forms of cruelty and then moving gradually towards a consensus against killing at least the more complexly sentient animals for food' (Nussbaum 2006: 393). The strategy is a gradualist one, and even in the long run does not rule out the killing of species of relatively low sentience. Moreover, aiming for this long-term goal must depend on practical realities:

> The use of animals for food in general is a much more difficult case [than banning the killing of animals for their fur] since nobody really knows what the impact on the world environment would be of a total switch to vegetarian sources of protein, or the extent to which such a diet would be compatible with the health of all the world's children. (2006: 402)

Nussbaum again makes use of the idea of *thresholds* here. If we can achieve suffering-free lives and pain-free deaths for animals, that is a reasonable threshold for the delivery of the capabilities – and a more realistically achievable one than banning all killing of animals for food.

A Critique from Anders Schinkel

In the paper in the journal *Ethics and the Environment* (2008) quoted above, Anders Schinkel argues that Nussbaum does not follow through the logic of her own capabilities approach. In his view it ought to commit her to opposing the killing of animals for food (as well as the use of animals in scientific research). An animal-welfare approach, based on compassion and humanity, could sanction the farming of animals for food, as long as they are treated humanely. But Nussbaum claims to have gone *beyond* compassion and humanity with her theory, and Schinkel agrees that she is right to do so. Schinkel also states that a moderate form of a rights-based position – one that gave animals rights that could be trumped by human interests – could also sanction the killing of animals for food (Schinkel 2008). But the capabilities approach is more demanding.

The most basic capability is being able to live a full lifespan. Schinkel quotes Nussbaum's 2004 essay 'Beyond Compassion and Humanity': 'If animals were really killed in a painless fashion, *after* a healthy and a free-ranging life, what then?' (Nussbaum 2004b: 315, my italics). As Schinkel points out, however, the killing does not occur after the animal's life, but in the middle of it, if not near the beginning. All the other capabilities are thus compromised. As Schinkel puts it, the rest of the list would have to run like this: 'capability 2 would read, in abbreviated form, "entitlement to a healthy life . . . until we eat them"; 3 would read, "entitlements against violations of bodily integrity . . . until we eat them"; 4, "access to sources of pleasure . . . until we eat them . . . and so on' (2008: 53–4). Schinkel argues that Nussbaum is therefore inconsistent in her application of the capabilities approach with regard to non-human animals, and says there are just two routes out of the inconsistency:

1. She can remove the utilitarian element from her thinking, which places importance only on whether the animal suffers. The approach would then be more consistently capabilities-based and would entail opposition to killing animals for food.
2. She can tone down the capabilities approach into a more modest-rights based approach, which gives animals rights that are *defeasible* when human interests are concerned. Meat-eating would then be allowed, but much of what is distinctive and appealing about the capabilities approach would be lost.

Schinkel's preference would be for the former (Schinkel 2008). Or indeed there might be some further refinement of the capabilities approach that would offer a third way. But it does seem clear that some adjustment is required to remove the inconsistency that Schinkel points to.

Summary

- Nussbaum's work on animal rights demonstrates how powerful and adaptable the capabilities approach is. It shows the theory's applicability to other species, and forms the basis for principled interventions in the way we treat animals.
- *Animal Rights: Current Debates and New Directions* (2004) showcases Nussbaum's commitment to pluralism and dialogue, in that it gives room to competing points of view.

115

- Both *Animal Rights* and *Frontiers of Justice* are continuations of Nussbaum's ongoing engagement with, and critical differentiation from, other ethical and normative perspectives.
- As is always the case with Nussbaum, her work addresses ethical and political problems in the real world and seeks practical solutions.

Chapter 6

Nussbaum and Religion

Liberty of Conscience, Accommodation
and Burqa Bans

The value and significance of religion in people's lives is a consistent theme throughout Nussbaum's work. In *Cultivating Humanity* (1997) she proposed that all humanities students should learn something about the major world religions. In *Sex and Social Justice* (1999) she balances the rights of women against religious freedom. Her ten capabilities include a commitment to the protection of free exercise of religion, under capabilities 6 (Practical Reason) and 7 (Affiliation). Nussbaum herself, born into a Protestant family, converted to Judaism when she married Alan Nussbaum, and after their divorce in 1987 continued to practise that faith, having her *bat mitzvah* in 2008.

It is not, of course, a surprise that a liberal should take an interest in religious freedom. Liberalism has always entailed a strong commitment to religious tolerance. Indeed this is where the whole tradition of Western liberalism begins. As Russell Blackford puts it (citing Rex Ahdar and Ian Leigh in support), religious freedom 'is the prototypical liberal freedom, a cornerstone of modern political rights' (2012: 1). One of the foundational texts of liberalism is John Locke's *Letter Concerning Toleration* of 1689 (Locke: 2013), which argues that the practice of religion should not be under the control of the state but a matter for individual conscience. It is true that Locke entertains certain exceptions to his principle, doubting whether it should apply fully to Roman Catholics or Muslims, for reasons of state security. To a modern reader this strikes one as distinctly illiberal. It is an example of the kind of inconsistency (or hypocrisy) of which anti-liberals frequently accuse liberals. But one cannot really use Locke's inconsistency as a criticism of liberalism; rather, it suggests he was not being liberal *enough*. Liberals after him (and, in the case of Roger Williams, before him) have interpreted the principle of religious liberty more fairly and generously.

Indeed, since Locke the idea of individual freedom has widened in liberal states to include *non*-religious beliefs and practices: freedom of expression of political dissent and of unpopular or controversial views, freedom to make experiments in living, freedom to pursue different forms of sexuality, and so on. Nevertheless, religious freedom, as well as being the foundation of all those other freedoms, is still a cornerstone of political rights and liberals are bound to take it seriously.

In 2008, Nussbaum published *Liberty of Conscience,* a defence of the American tradition of religious equality. She followed it up in 2012 with *The New Religious Intolerance*, a trenchant attack on what she sees as growing religious intolerance in Europe, especially towards Muslims. These two books are the focus of this chapter.

Religious Fairness

Liberty of Conscience is a work of political philosophy. But as is often the case with Nussbaum, it includes elements of other disciplines too, in this case drawing on history and law, as well as analysis of contemporary American politics and some autobiographical material. Nussbaum writes: 'I am a committed Jew whose membership in a Reform Jewish congregation is an important part of my life and my search for meaning' (Nussbaum 2008: 9). As is also characteristic of Nussbaum, the book has a clear and urgent message: that liberty of conscience is a rare and valuable thing, and that it is currently under threat.

Nussbaum begins by invoking the tradition of the Pilgrim Fathers, describing the thousands of American children who dress up as seventeenth-century Puritans every Thanksgiving. They commemorate the settlers who fled England in 1620 to freely practise their religion in the New World. The story is significant for three reasons. First, those who fled were not treated as equals in England; their form of Christianity was not that of the established Church and they did not have the same rights as the majority. Religious freedom is often *distributed unequally*, as this example indicates. Second, religious freedom is *precious*: so precious that people will undertake a perilous ocean voyage to get it.

The story has a special relevance for Nussbaum, whose mother's ancestors sailed to America on the *Mayflower*. But, she notes, the Pilgrim Fathers did not always honour the religious liberty they had secured for themselves in the case of others; indeed 'they established their own repressive orthodoxy from which others fled in turn' (Nussbaum 2008: 2), and centuries later, having come over to America on the *Mayflower* became a badge of social superiority and an excuse to discriminate against more recent immigrants, such as Jews and Roman Catholics. This is the third significant point illustrated by the story: that equal religious liberty is *precarious*.

As Nussbaum notes, 'People love in-groups that give their members special rights', but, she says, '[t]he dominant American tradition repudiates this style of thinking' (2008: 2). She quotes Justice Jackson in a legal judgment of 1943 (in the context of upholding the right of Jehovah's Witnesses not to recite the pledge of allegiance):

> If there is any fixed star in our constitutional constellation, it is that no official, high or petty, can prescribe what shall be orthodox in politics, nationalism, religion or other matters of opinion or force citizens to confess by word or act their faith therein. (Jackson quoted in Nussbaum 2008: 3)

So the dominant American tradition rejects a two-tiered system where rights are conceded to the unorthodox on unequal terms. Nussbaum often subsequently refers to this principle as the 'fixed star' (a term from navigation, possibly taken from Shakespeare's Sonnet 116). The principle is based on the First Amendment to the American Constitution, which states that 'Congress shall make no law respecting the establishment of religion, or prohibiting the free exercise thereof'.

Nussbaum contends that America is better at dealing with the needs of a religiously diverse population than are the European nations. America, a nation whose population is largely formed of immigrants and their descendants, had to pay attention to religious diversity from the beginning (nor, incidentally, was it torn apart by wars of religion as Europe was in the sixteenth and seventeenth centuries). European nations had until not too long ago religiously homogeneous populations and, Nussbaum argues, recent immigration, especially from Muslim countries, has presented them with challenges they are ill equipped to deal with. She holds that Europe could learn much from the American constitutional tradition, and says she feels 'considerable pride in the U.S. tradition, which seems to me to have struck basically the right balance between need for neutral institutions and the needs of people of faith' (2008: 14).

The purpose of *Liberty of Conscience* is twofold. Nussbaum wants to explain and defend the principle of religious fairness (i.e. equal religious liberty for all). But another part of her purpose is to warn that it is under threat: 'Without vigilance, our "fixed star" may not be fixed for much longer' (Nussbaum 2008: 4).

Nussbaum identifies threats from two directions. Right-wing evangelical Christians have made frequent attempts to identify the United States with their brand of Christianity. She lists a slew of right-wing politicians who have used religious rhetoric in patriotic contexts, suggesting that failure to share these religious values is un-American. At the same time, Nussbaum is on guard against the misuse (as she sees it) by the left of the term 'separation of church and state'. She states that in the period after the Second World War, many left-wing Americans used the idea to denigrate Roman Catholics and to seek to deny religious schools protection from the state. She also claims that many contemporary intellectuals seem motivated by an aversion to religion (she cites Daniel Dennett as an example), and says that many liberals (in the American sense of the word – i.e. progressives) use 'the rhetoric of separation [of church and state] without asking how much separation is really good or fair' (2008: 11).

Nussbaum does not deny the need for *some* separation of church and state. But a total cleavage would be both impractical and undesirable. The modern state is implicated in just about every aspect of people's lives. As she says, it would be 'horribly unfair' if the state fire department refused to put out a blaze in a church, or if clergy were barred from running for state office. What Nussbaum is calling for is the right *degree* of separation of church and state, always with the aim of treating all religions fairly. As she puts it:

> Seen in its right relation to the idea of fairness, the idea of separation of church and state does not express what the left sometime uses it to express, namely contempt for, and desire to marginalize, religion. Our tradition has sought to put religion in a place apart from government, in some ways and with some limits, *not* because we think it has no importance for the conduct of our lives or the choices we make as citizens, but for a very different reason ... separation of church and state is, fundamentally, about equality, about the idea that no religion will be set up as *the* religion of our nation, an act that immediately makes outsiders unequal. (Nussbaum 2008: 11–12)

Concepts and Principles

Nussbaum argues that eight distinct though related concepts are present in the tradition of religious equality. (This, incidentally, is a characteristic of her clear, analytical style of philosophising; she is a committed list-maker.) The concepts are:

- Liberty
- Equality and Equal Respect
- Conscience
- Protection of Minorities
- Neutrality
- Establishment
- Separation
- Accommodation

There is a certain lexical priority to these concepts. The most important is *equality* – this is the 'key thread holding all the others together' (Nussbaum 2008: 21). But equality alone is not enough; after all, citizens might be equal by all having the same *lack* of religious liberty. So equality needs to be supplemented by *liberty*. Liberty is important because it allows us to follow the dictates of our *conscience*, which Nussbaum says is a precious and vulnerable thing. These three govern how we should apply all the other concepts – how much separation is fair, how much accommodation is required, and so on.

Nussbaum raises an important question in relation to neutrality, to which I shall return: 'Why is it "free exercise of *religion*" that gets the breaks, when citizens have so many things to care about, and so many ways, both religious and non-religious, of arranging their most fundamental conscientious commitments?' (2008: 22). The tradition of religious equality, Nussbaum says, has combined these concepts to form 'six normative principles' (further evidence of her liking for list-making). The principles (with my summary of Nussbaum's comments on each) are as follows:

- *The Equality Principle*: citizens must have equal rights, and equal respect from the state.
- *The Respect-Conscience Principle*: the state must respect different religious commitments and guarantee protected spaces for religious observance, as well as ensuring that all citizens enter the public square on equal terms.
- *The Liberty Principle*: the state must guarantee liberty of belief and speech, liberty of religious practice (consistent with the rights of others) and allow religious bodies to organise their own affairs.
- *The Accommodation Principle*: sometimes citizens are entitled to exemptions from laws because of their religious beliefs.

121

- *The Non-establishment Principle*: the state must not endorse one religion over others.
- *The Separation Principle*: a certain degree of separation is required between church(es) and state. (Nussbaum 2008: 25)

It will be noticed that there is no principle of religious tolerance, which, considering that liberalism has its origins in that principle, might seem odd. The explanation is that Nussbaum prefers the principle of *respect* to that of tolerance, which seems 'too grudging and weak' (2008: 24). This seems close to the conception of tolerance as *recognition*, as argued for by Charles Taylor (1994) and Anna Galeotti (2002) among others. Influential in recent multicultural theory, the idea of recognition is that beliefs and practices of minority cultures should not just be permitted but should be acknowledged and respected. Lack of recognition, or mis-recognition, is said to cause psychological damage and alienation. Liberals who uphold recognition regard it as necessary for an inclusive and pluralistic society. Although Nussbaum does not use the *word* 'recognition', she seems to endorse that view.

Nussbaum claims that the combination of six normative principles is 'distinctively American', a contrast to the European tradition where minorities are generally expected to assimilate and conform. She traces the origins of the tradition to the work of Roger Williams, the seventeenth-century founder of the Rhode Island Colony and writer of *The Bloudy Tenent of Persecution* (1644), a plea for religious liberty and freedom of conscience which pre-dates Locke by half a century.

Life and Work of Roger Williams

It is not an insignificant part of Nussbaum's achievement in *Liberty of Conscience* (2008) that she revived interest in an almost forgotten figure of considerable importance in the tradition of religious liberty. Roger Williams seems to have been a remarkable person and in many ways a man ahead of his time. Born around 1603 in England, he grew up to attract the attention of some significant intellectual figures: the Lord Chief Justice Sir Edward Coke took an interest in him, arranging for his education at Pembroke College, Cambridge, where Williams took a degree in classics. He was a talented linguist and quickly mastered Latin, Greek, Hebrew, French and Dutch. (Later, he used this talent to learn several Native American languages.) He also made friends with the poet John Milton, teaching him Dutch in exchange for Hebrew lessons. Williams became an ordained priest in the Church of England, but was not happy with the stern Anglican orthodoxy of the time. In 1630, having witnessed the cruel treatment of a Puritan dissenter (who was pilloried, mutilated and imprisoned for life) Williams left England and set sail for Massachusetts.

There he upset the Massachusetts Bay colony by writing a pamphlet which attacked their claims to Native American property. This concern for the rights of Native Americans was unusual and unpopular among the colonists at the time. The authorities ordered his arrest, but Williams fled before they could capture him, and proceeded to set up his own colony on Rhode Island. He had many friendships with Native Americans, learning a number of native languages well enough to be able to debate in them, and wrote a book on the Narragansetts language. The Rhode Island colony under his leadership was also the first state in North America to ban slavery (in 1652).

Nussbaum recounts how Williams set sail for England in 1643 to secure a charter for his new colony; on this voyage he wrote his book about Native American languages, and while in England he wrote *The Bloudy Tenent of Persecution* (*tenent* meaning 'principle'). He later wrote a longer, more comprehensive version in reply to criticism. He also renegotiated the royal charter after the English Restoration. The revised charter includes a specific commitment to the religious liberty which he had argued for in *The Bloudy Tenent*:

> [N]oe person within the sayd colonye, at tyme herafter, shall bee any wise molested, punished, disquieted, or call in question, for any differences in opinion in matters of religion, and doe not actually disturb the civill peace of sayd colony; but that all and every person and persons may . . . freely and fully have and enjoye his and theire owne judgments and consciences. (Williams quoted in Nussbaum 2008: 49)

This commitment to religious freedom is echoed over a century later in the First Amendment to the American Constitution, which guarantees religious freedom for the individual and forbids state-established religion. It also anticipates Article 10 of the 1789 French Declaration of *Les Droits de l'Homme*:

> *Nul ne doit être inquiété pour ses opinions, même religieuses, pourvu que leur manifestation ne trouble pas l'ordre public établi par la Loi* (Nobody is to be disturbed on account of their opinions, even religious ones, provided that their manifestation does not trouble the public order established by the Law).

But there is a significant difference between the American formulation and the French formulation, which supports Nussbaum's contention that the American tradition is a better guarantor of religious freedom than the European one. Article 10 does not single out religious opinions as especially deserving of protection as compared to other types of opinion; indeed the use of the word *même* (even) suggests that religion only just sneaks into the protected zone.

Nussbaum argues that Williams's defence of religious liberty in *The Bloudy Tenent* is as rich as John Locke's, 'and considerably more perceptive concerning the psychology of both persecutor and victim' (2008: 51). She identifies six key differences (another list) between Locke's theory of religious liberty and that of Williams:

- Locke never attacks the idea of a state-established church. Provided the established church does not persecute other religions, he sees it as compatible with religious freedom. Williams, on the other hand, argues against an established church, which increases the *risk* of persecution and implies that citizens who do not belong to it are less than equal with those who do. Williams's opposition to an established church was eventually enshrined, via James Madison, in the First Amendment to the US Constitution.
- Locke has little to say about the preciousness of individual conscience. For Williams, it forms the moral basis for his theory of religious liberty. He described forcing somebody to say or do something against their conscience as 'soul-rape'. Nussbaum sees this view of conscience, as something both precious and vulnerable, as one of his most important contributions to the justification of religious liberty. (It also fits well with her own view, presented in *The Fragility of Goodness* [1986], that the most valuable things in human life are also the most vulnerable.)
- The third difference is (to my mind) the most important as regards its implications for actual government policies. Locke does not emphasise the idea of *accommodation*: that is, allowing exemptions to laws for people with special religious requirements. (A familiar example of accommodation is the exemption, in the UK, of motorcycling Sikhs from the compulsory wearing of crash-helmets, which would not fit over their turbans.) Locke assumes that if laws are framed neutrally in the first place then accommodations are not likely to be required. Williams, on the other hand, 'allows exceptions to general laws for conscience's sake (Nussbaum 2008: 67), provided public safety is not threatened.

- Nussbaum states that Locke tends to argue from Protestant premises. She claims that Locke 'even relies on skepticism about religious truth' (2008: 67–8) which she says many religious believers could never endorse. A further point, which Nussbaum does not mention but which supports her case, is that Locke often deploys arguments which would only have force for a Christian; he claims, for example, that religious toleration is 'so agreeable to the Gospel of Jesus Christ . . . that it seems monstrous for Men to be so blind, as not to perceive the Necessity and Advantage of it'. Williams, on the other hand, 'tries to develop an independent ethical argument for his political principles, based on the dignity and vulnerability of conscience' (2008: 68). Thus his arguments have a more universal appeal.
- Fifth, Locke sees no overlap between politics and religion; he conceives of them as entirely separate spheres. Williams, by contrast, sees them as meeting and overlapping 'in a shared moral space' (Nussbaum 2008: 68). (Nussbaum's use of the word 'overlap' here is deliberate; she wants to show that Williams anticipates John Rawls's idea of the overlapping consensus, whereby citizens with differing comprehensive doctrines can nevertheless agree on political principles.)
- Finally, Nussbaum says Locke offers no psychological explanation for *why* people should want to persecute others for their religious beliefs. But Williams does. He explains the psychology of persecution as stemming from anxious fear and a desire for security.

Nussbaum could also have added the reservations that Locke expresses about Roman Catholics and Muslims; he fears that they might owe allegiance to a foreign authority rather than to the nation of which they are citizens. There are no equivalent reservations in Williams's work.

Accommodation in Action

For Nussbaum, developing a theory is not an end in itself, but is only of use as an explanation of and guide to practice. Much of *Liberty of Conscience*, therefore, is taken up with practical, real-life cases where religious liberty clashes with the law and how these cases can be solved by accommodation. I shall take one of her case studies from the mid-twentieth century as exemplary of her method. The case concerns Adell Sherbert, who worked in a textile mill in South Carolina. In 1959, all the mills in the locality moved to a six-day week and the extra day worked was Saturday. But Sherbert was a Seventh-day Adventist, for whom Saturday is the Sabbath, when church attendance is required. She refused to work on Saturdays and as a result was fired. Moreover, she was not eligible for unemployment compensation, since it was ruled that she had turned down available work. Mrs Sherbert appealed, complaining that she had been unfairly burdened. The state at first rejected her case, 'saying that they were simply treating everyone the same' (Nussbaum 2008: 136). In 1963, however, the US Supreme Court found in Sherbert's favour, in what Nussbaum calls a 'landmark opinion by Justice Brennan which still shapes legal analysis today' (2008: 136).

This case is a significant one since it highlights the fact that treating everybody the same (the State of South Carolina's line of initial defence) may result in unfair burdens – or, as other multicultural theorists have put it, *unequal impact* (see e.g. Kymlicka 1995). For Mrs Sherbert's co-workers, the extra day worked on a Saturday did not prevent them going to church, since they attended on Sundays. Therefore the same ruling impacted more harshly on Sherbert than on her co-workers – which is prima facie unfair.

The unfair burden/unequal impact argument has been challenged. Brian Barry points out that *all* laws have unequal impact and this is not by itself evidence that they are unfair:

> If we consider virtually any law, we shall find that it is much more burdensome to some people than to others. Speed limits inhibit only those who like to drive fast. Laws prohibiting drunk driving have no impact on teetotallers. Only smokers are stopped by prohibitions on smoking in public places. Only those who want to own a handgun are affected by a ban on them, and so *ad infinitum*. (Barry 2011: 34)

However, in most cases the unequal impact is intentional: laws against speeding are *supposed* to impact on those who wish to drive fast, not on those who do not. But the effect on Mrs Sherbert of South Carolina's employment laws was an *unintended* side effect. The six-day week was not imposed with the aim of preventing Mrs Sherbert going to church, and the rule about not granting compensation to those who had left work of their own volition was never intended to penalise religious observance. If we accept Williams's claims for the preciousness of conscience – how wounding it is to be forced to act in opposition to it – then Sherbert's case is very strong.

Contemporary Controversies

Nussbaum concludes the book by considering a number of current controversies where religious liberty is at stake. These don't all have clear-cut answers, as Nussbaum acknowledges, but she proposes that the analytical framework she has developed 'has the potential to help us further, as we confront some of our time's most divisive question' (2008: 307). One of the controversies she discusses is the Pledge of Allegiance, a daily ritual in many American schools where children recite a pledge of loyalty to 'one nation under God'. As Nussbaum points out, this formulation (which was introduced in the 1950s, to distinguish Americans from 'godless communists') excludes not only atheists and agnostics but also large numbers of religious people – polytheists, Buddhists, and those of monotheist faiths who do not believe that God has a special interest in looking out for America. It is true that reciting the Pledge is not compulsory. One may be excused on grounds of conscience. Still, in practice peer pressure and the fear of being thought unpatriotic might make children reluctant to opt out.

It's clear that Nussbaum regards the Pledge in its current form as unconstitutional; however, she says, '[g]iven public feeling on the issue, it would cause a national crisis' (2008: 314) if the Supreme Court were to rule it unconstitutional. However, Nussbaum hopes that greater public understanding of other religions, as well as of atheism and agnosticism, will help people realise that opponents of the Pledge are not dangerous subversives (though she cautions that strident atheism which shows contempt for religion will not assist this process). In 2006, the US House removed jurisdiction from the Supreme Court over the use of the words 'under God', which Nussbaum finds 'deeply regrettable' (2008: 3125). Her proposed remedy is that the issue should be talked about more, with minority viewpoints represented, and the history of the current form of the pledge needs to be better known. Only in this way can we expect views to change.

Another issue Nussbaum discusses is the teaching of evolution in schools. There is a complex history of controversy around this issue, but the most pressing contemporary concern is whether intelligent design (ID) should be taught alongside evolution as an alternative theory. ID claims that certain features of organisms show 'irreducible complexity' – features which could not have come into existence gradually because they contain too many interdependent moving

127

parts. Therefore at least some features of organisms must have had an intelligent designer. As Nussbaum emphasises, this is not a respectable scientific theory and has no defenders within the scientific community. In 2006 Judge John Jones ruled that it was unconstitutional to teach ID on the grounds that it is a 'thinly disguised religious viewpoint' (Nussbaum 2008: 324) and thus it would be unconstitutional for a federal state to endorse it. Nussbaum strongly approves of this verdict. She regards this as a clear case of where church and state really do need to be separate:

> Our children need to learn science undiluted, and the incursion of religious viewpoints into this sphere is unfortunate. It seems fine, and in fact valuable, for children to learn about religious viewpoints in courses on history and culture. To substitute a religious viewpoint for science is to jeopardize our future. (2008: 327)

Nussbaum urges more public discussion of evolution, so that misguided objections to it diminish. Here (as in her proposal for more debate about the 'under God' phrase in the Pledge) she shows her trust in the Rawlsian idea of *public reason*.

The last contemporary controversy Nussbaum discusses is burqa-wearing by Wahhabist women. This is a topic she explores in greater depth in her next book on religion, *The New Religious Intolerance* (2012).

The New Religious Intolerance

In her preface, Nussbaum describes the genesis of the book. She wrote a piece for the *New York Times* 'Opinionator' column in 2010 (a development of views she had already put forward in her 2008 book *Liberty of Conscience*), arguing trenchantly against the proposed burqa bans in a number of European countries at that time. (The French government banned public wearing of the burqa and niqab in 2010; Belgium did the same in 2011, Bulgaria in 2016, Denmark in 2018.)

In response to the Opinionator piece, she received a huge postbag of comments from readers, representing a wide variety of strongly argued views, and she began to think of devoting a whole book to the topic. Thus was *The New Religious Intolerance* born. The story offers yet more evidence of Nussbaum's role as a public intellectual – she wants to connect with people and make them think philosophically about ethical and political issues, and uses popular media as well as academic books and papers to do so.

Anxiety and Suspicion

Nussbaum claims that Europe and the USA, despite bloody pasts where religion is concerned (more so in the case of Europe), today pride themselves on religious tolerance; but in fact there is a resurgence of intolerance: 'Our situation calls urgently for searching critical self-examination, as we try to uncover the roots of ugly fears and suspicions that currently disfigure all Western societies' (Nussbaum 2012b: 2).

Religious intolerance is not confined to Western societies, of course. One might equally cite persecution of Christians in the parts of the Middle East and Africa (see Rupert Shortt's 2012 book, *Christianophobia*) or, more recently, the persecution of Uyghur Muslims in China. But Nussbaum focuses only on Western countries. Perhaps that is because they are supposedly liberal societies and Nussbaum wants liberal societies to live up to their principles. Perhaps it is simply because she doesn't care to tackle too many problems at once.

Nussbaum lists a number of recent developments that, she says, indicate a rise in Western religious intolerance: in Europe, burqa bans, laws against the Muslim hijab, a ban on the construction of minarets in Switzerland, attacks on kebab shops, and Anders Breivik's terrorist attacks in Oslo; in the USA, cases of discrimination against hijab-wearers, planning permission being denied to mosques and Islamic community centres, and moves in Oklahoma and Tennessee to outlaw sharia law, even though it is *already* the case that sharia law could not be imposed in US courts. Nussbaum finds the situation in Europe to be worse – perhaps because of the USA's stronger tradition of religious liberty – but warns that both Europe and America are travelling down the road of religious intolerance, especially with regard to Muslims.

In response, Nussbaum recommends that three things are urgently needed – and they are three virtues that she has already passionately argued for in other contexts:

- political principles expressing equal respect for all citizens, and an understanding of what these principles entail for today's confrontation with religious difference . . .
- rigorous critical thinking that ferrets out and criticizes inconsistencies . . .

129

- a systematic cultivation of the 'inner eyes', the imaginative capacity that makes it possible for us to see how the world looks from the point of view of a person different in religion or ethnicity. (Nussbaum 2012b: 2–3)

Fear, Disgust and Respect

Nussbaum spends some time analysing the psychology of fear, which she characterises as a 'primitive emotion' which is evolutionarily hardwired (2012b: 25). But 'what helped humans survive in evolutionary prehistory is not always helpful today' (2012b: 27). Nussbaum blends together evolutionary theory, philosophy and modern psychology to present her picture of the role fear plays in our decisions and behaviour (2012b: 33–5). She also links fear to another primitive emotion, disgust. I shall not discuss her ideas about emotion in any detail here, since that forms the subject of the next chapter; but the thrust of the argument is that, rather than nourish our biological tendencies to fear and disgust with rhetoric, we should seek to tame them by reason and better understanding of facts. Drawing on John Stuart Mill, Nussbaum says fear should be 'moralized' by sympathy (2008: 28).

What is needed in place of fear (in place of *irrational* fear, that is; Nussbaum is clear that rational fears do serve useful purposes) are the three virtues cited earlier: (1) a political principle of equal respect; (2) ethical consistency; and (3) a sympathetic imagination. Not much more needs to be said about the principle of equal respect; it underlies Nussbaum's capabilities approach and her political liberalism, as must already be clear by now. With specific regard to equal respect in the case of religion, Nussbaum turns again to the two traditions she identified in *Liberty of Conscience*: Lockean neutrality and Williamsian accommodation. Of the two she favours Williams's tradition of respect for conscience, and accommodation; but she is clear that even the less demanding neutrality favoured by Locke would be a big improvement on the current situation. Nussbaum's second principle, of *ethical consistency* and its application, needs a little more discussion.

Ethical Consistency

By ethical consistency, Nussbaum means that one must not make exceptions to ethical rules in order to favour the group which one belongs to or feels sympathy with, or to discriminate against other groups which one does not belong to or feel sympathy with. That is, rules must apply equally across the board. This is, of course, in line with the ethical universalism that Nussbaum argued for in *Sex and Social Justice* (1999).

One might object that Nussbaum's own policy of religious accommodation runs counter to ethical consistency. After all, if we allow exemptions (e.g. allowing Sikh motorcyclists not to wear helmets) are we not saying that rules *don't* apply across the board? The answer to that objection, of course, is that (justified) exemptions *are* ethically consistent, for they are based on a universal principle: that *nobody* should be forced to act against their conscience.

The kind of ethical inconsistency Nussbaum has in her sights is very different. She is talking about cases where the same action is unremarked when performed by one group yet condemned when performed by another – and the *only reason* for the difference is group-membership. Nussbaum argues that opposition to burqa-wearing rests on ethical inconsistency. People in Europe and America do not worry about face-covering in most cases. It is only when *Muslims* cover their faces, she says, that it is perceived as a problem. Nussbaum identifies five of the most frequently heard arguments against the burqa and critiques them one by one.

Five Arguments Against the Burqa

1. Security. This argument holds that 'security requires people to show their faces when appearing in public places' (Nussbaum 2012b: 105). Nussbaum denies that this is the case. She writes:

> It gets very cold in Chicago – as, indeed, in many parts of Europe. Along the streets we walk, hats pulled down over ears and brows, scarves wound tightly around noses and mouths. No problem of either transparency or security is thought to exist, nor are we forbidden to enter public buildings so insulated . . . Moreover, many beloved and trusted professionals cover their faces all year round: surgeons, dentists, (American) football players, skiers and skaters . . . In general, what inspires fear and mistrust in Europe, and, to some extent, in the United States, is not covering per se, but Muslim covering. (2012b: 106–7)

This section of the book is almost identical to the piece Nussbaum wrote for the *New York Times* Opinionator column in 2010, but there is one perhaps significant change. In the original piece she said that it was 'clearly' Muslim face covering which inspired fear and distrust, and she has now removed that word and replaced it with the phrase 'in general'. That is a slight concession, but the charge in substance still stands. The only factor she is able to find to account for the difference between reactions to the kind of everyday face coverings she describes, and to the burqa, is fear and mistrust of Muslims.

There are, however, other relevant factors which she does not consider. An obvious one is that hats, scarves, surgeons' masks and so on are removed when the occasion requires: we would think it objectionable if someone persisted in wearing a scarf wound around their face, or a surgeon's mask, in a bank, a classroom or a court of law, for example. A burqa is worn *all the time* in public; and, because it is thought of as a religious symbol, people are aware that asking for its removal might cause offence. Having a different reaction to the burqa than to a scarf wound around the face on a cold day is no evidence of a double standard, but of a consistent standard. I wholly endorse Nussbaum's principle of seeking consistency. But it does not seem to do the work she requires of it here.

That said, it is of course possible or even likely that some of the opposition to burqa-wearing does stem from Islamophobia. But it does not seem to me very effective, philosophically, to challenge the *agenda* of those urging burqa bans. One may have bad reasons for advancing arguments, but the arguments still need to be evaluated on their merits. It seems to me that Nussbaum could counter this argument without impugning the motives of those who advance it. She could say that it would be ethically consistent to require *temporary removal* of the burqa in situations where other face coverings would be removed; but that in at least some of these situations, an accommodation could be reached, exempting the burqa-wearer from removal and employing other means of identification. The accommodation would be justified because face covering for the burqa-wearer is a religious requirement, whereas for the other face-coverers (with their scarves, surgeons' masks etc.) it is not. Asking everyone alike to uncover would have an *unequal impact* on Wahhabist women.

The other part of the Security argument does not focus on everyday transparency or identification but is concerned with the specific threat posed by terrorism – in other words, the burqa could be used as a *disguise* by terrorists. Some countries have indeed taken action against burqa-wearing on these grounds. For example, Chad banned the full-face veil in 2015, following a bombing attack by burqa-wearing Boko Haram militants, in which twenty people were killed;

Congo Brazzaville also banned the full-face veil in 2015 'to counter terrorism'; Cameroon banned it later the same year following two suicide bomb attacks by burqa-wearers.

Nussbaum accepts that '[in] the Middle East it might possibly be a clever strategy for a terrorist to don a *burqa*' (2012b: 107) and would presumably concede the same for areas of Africa where there is an appreciable Muslim population of the burqa-wearing persuasion. However, she argues that it would be a stupid strategy for a terrorist to wear a burqa in North America or Europe as this would be more likely to attract attention than escape it.

I am not sure that this is true. A burqa-clad person boarding a bus in, say, east London would attract no attention whatsoever. Still, it is an empirical question whether a burqa would be an effective disguise in North America or Europe, and it doesn't have to be decided in advance. We can simply say that *if* no or hardly any terrorists in those countries ever adopt such camouflage – and that seems to be the case so far – then Nussbaum is right that a ban is unnecessary.

2. Transparency and civic friendship. The argument here is that face-covering hinders communication and civility among citizens. This, incidentally, was the argument accepted by the European Court of Human Rights in upholding the French ban of 2010. Nussbaum's first response is that burqas and niqabs do not (usually) cover the eyes, and the eyes are the 'windows of the soul' (2012b: 110). Therefore the burqa does not hinder communication as much as is claimed. Nussbaum supports this point with an anecdote about how she had to cover her own face, bar the eyes, over a period of several weeks while there was a construction project going on near her office and the air was dusty; her students at first found it weird but soon adapted and did not feel unable to relate to her. In fact, some decided to wear similar masks themselves. (We might note, additionally, that during the Covid-19 pandemic when public face-covering was widespread and, in some countries, including the UK, obligatory, communication did not seem to be a serious problem.)

More generally, Nussbaum argues that difficulties in communicating with someone who looks odd usually come not from the odd-looking person, but from oneself. Disabled people are often victims of this form of prejudice. But it can and should be overcome; we should exercise the virtue of sympathetic imagination that Nussbaum urges. If we find it hard to talk to someone who looks different, we should blame ourselves, not them, and try to do better. Nussbaum says: 'I think talking to someone wearing a *burqa* is about as difficult, for the unhabituated, as talking with someone who is blind or who has Tourette's, and less difficult than talking with someone who has mental illness' (2012b: 113). It might be objected that the person who is blind, has Tourette's or is suffering from a mental illness cannot help it; whereas the burqa-wearer *can* help covering her face. She could make things less difficult by uncovering. But the burqa is regarded as a religious requirement – at least by those who wear it – and so, in Nussbaum's view, removing it would do violence to one's conscience (unlike the simple removal of a scarf).

3. Objectification. The third argument identified by Nussbaum is that 'the *burqa* is a sign of male domination that symbolizes the objectification of women' (2012b: 114). Nussbaum's reply is that even if this is true, there are many other examples of male domination and objectification of women in modern societies, such as pornography, revealing women's clothing, and plastic surgery undergone by women to try to achieve beauty norms that cast women as sex objects. If we were being ethically consistent, we should seek to ban those things too. Nussbaum also claims that those who criticise the burqa on these grounds typically know little about the practice and what it symbolises within Wahhabist Islam, and she says that ill-informed critique of others' religious customs is 'nosy and rude' (2012b: 119).

4. Coercion. Nussbaum states:

> A fourth argument holds that many women wear the *burqa* because they are coerced. This is a rather implausible argument to make across the board, and it is typically made by people who have no idea of the circumstances of this or that individual woman. We should reply that of course all forms of violence and physical coercion in the home are illegal already, and laws against all forms of violence and physical coercion should be enforced much more zealously than they are. Do the arguers really believe that domestic violence is a peculiarly Muslim problem? If so they are dead wrong. (Nussbaum 2012b: 122)

Unusually for Nussbaum, she does not exercise here the principle of charity towards a view with which she disagrees. She briskly brushes it aside. There seem to me to be two points at which her confident line of argument is questionable. First, with regard to Nussbaum's claim that the argument from coercion is implausible 'across the board', I take it she means that it is implausible to assert that burqa-wearing actually is coerced in many cases; the evidence is lacking, we do not know what kind of numbers are involved. This interpretation is supported by Nussbaum's follow-up statement that those who make the claim are ignorant of the circumstances of individual burqa-wearers. Nussbaum's objection seems open to a *tu quoque*, though. Is she in possession of data which show that no or very little burqa-wearing is coerced? If so, she should produce the data; but if not, then like those she criticises she is speaking from a position of ignorance.

The second point is that Nussbaum here responds to the accusation of coercion as though it were merely an accusation of violence. That is, she concentrates on the coercive measures but not on the blocking of interests which is their end. Nussbaum might respond that if you take care of the first the second will take care of itself. I lack her confidence about this. It may be harder to enforce the laws against violence than she assumes. A woman who is subject to physical abuse may well be too scared to report it. What is more, the coerced wearing of the burqa may itself conceal signs of violence which would otherwise arouse suspicion. Yasmin Alibhai-Brown writes, in a *Guardian* article: 'A fully burqaed woman once turned up at my house, a graduate, covered in cuts, burns, bruises and bites. Do we know how many wounded, veiled women walk around hidden among us?' (2015). This is not to make any claims about the *extent* of violence against Muslim women. Contrary to what Nussbaum appears to assume, claiming that in many cases burqa-wearing may be coerced does not commit one to any claim that violence against women is greater amongst Muslim families than the rest of the population.

Besides, actual physical violence is not the most important issue here. It is the credible *threat* of violence that makes for coercion. Or the threat of sustained hostility or ostracism. In such cases it is no good appealing to laws against physical violence and demanding their enforcement.

Coerced burqa-wearing *relies on the legality* of burqa-wearing, in two senses. There is the obvious sense that there would be no point in forcing a woman to wear a garment which she would then be obliged to remove by the authorities (and penalised for wearing). Furthermore, coerced burqa-wearing is *facilitated* by the fact that other women can be seen to be wearing burqas. A husband who wishes to make his wife cover up can say, 'Why don't you wear a burqa, like Mrs X?' Note also that once a woman has been coerced into wearing a burqa she, too, can be presented as an example that non-burqa-wearing women should follow. The more Mrs Xs there are, the more force this manipulative appeal has.

I am not, of course, making the claim that much or most burqa-wearing *is* coerced. Perhaps coerced burqa-wearing in Western societies is rare or non-existent. Without evidence that it is widespread there are no grounds for a ban. Moreover, even if it were widespread, a ban might be too crude and insensitive a response, giving rise to unintended consequences. A more subtle, sympathetic and flexible approach to the problem, if there is a problem, would probably yield better results. But Nussbaum does not need to impugn the good faith of those who raise this concern. Her own argument does not require that. After all, if one is concerned about coercion against women in general, it is ethically consistent to include Muslim women in that concern.

5. Health. Finally, Nussbaum turns to the argument from health: 'the *burqa* is per se unhealthy, because it is hot and uncomfortable', a *paternalist* argument which she describes as 'perhaps the silliest of the arguments' (2012b: 129). Certainly, as she presents it, it is less than compelling. As she points out, 'Clothing that covers the body can be comfortable or uncomfortable, depending on the fabric' (Nussbaum 2012b: 129). In hot weather, covering the body may be healthier than not, diminishing the risk of skin cancer. Moreover, being hot and uncomfortable is not a risk to health in any case. It is simply being hot and uncomfortable, which is certainly not a major enough harm to justify paternalist intervention.

There are stronger forms of the argument, however, not considered by Nussbaum. Direct skin contact with the sun's rays is our main source of vitamin D, and habitual all-body covering leads to vitamin D deficiency, a condition that causes bone abnormalities, rickets and muscle weakness. This fact might suffice to make a case for a paternalist burqa ban, if a ban were the only way to remedy the matter.

But it is not the only way. Burqa-wearers could remove the burqa in their own gardens or other private spaces and soak up some sunshine. Vitamin D supplements in tablet form are available. A government concerned about vitamin D deficiency in burqa-wearers could publicise the condition and its causes and consequences, and make supplements available to correct it, without recourse to the blunt instrument of a ban, which has many other effects besides counteracting vitamin D Deficiency.

This chapter of the book is passionately argued and stimulating to read, but it is somewhat uncharacteristic of Nussbaum in its polemical tone and its focus on the arguer's presumed agenda rather than the details of their arguments.

Is Religion Special?

In both *Liberty of Conscience* and *The New Religious Intolerance*, Nussbaum argues that religious beliefs and practices deserve special protection, in the form of accommodations, in virtue of the fact that they are *religious*. As I have argued elsewhere (Robshaw 2020), a possible objection would be that religious beliefs are not more special than other deeply held beliefs and they do not require a category of their own. The liberal commitment to individual liberty should be enough, alone, to protect religious beliefs and practices along with other beliefs and practices. Nussbaum is concerned to protect freedom of conscience. But religion is just one example – a salient one, certainly – of freedom of conscience, and Nussbaum's argument would apply equally to other, non-religious beliefs where moral conscience is at stake – such as pacifism, vegetarianism, feminism or political ideologies. Moreover, religious practices must be subject to the same constraints as non-religious practices. They must not be such as would cause harm to others, as Nussbaum herself has already argued in the case of FGM (1999).

Cécile Laborde, in her book *Liberalism's Religion* (2017), makes the case that liberalism should work with a 'disaggregated' notion of religion; that is to say, that religion should not be considered a single category for the purposes of political/legal decisions, but should be disaggregated 'into a plurality of different interpretive dimensions' (2017: 2). This reworking of the role of religion in liberal theory 'implies that religion is not uniquely special: whatever treatment it receives from the law, it receives in virtue of features that it shares with nonreligious beliefs, conceptions and identities' (Laborde 2017: 3). No doubt Nussbaum could come back with a response to Laborde. It's not possible to settle the question categorically here. It is sufficient to note that the place of religion within liberal theory is still a matter of debate, and Nussbaum has made important contributions to that debate.

Summary

- Both *Liberty of Conscience* and *The New Religious Intolerance* offer powerful pleas for religious freedom, combining reasoned argument with emotional commitment. These are two of Nussbaum's most deeply felt books.

- Nussbaum's work on religion demonstrates her deep knowledge of the liberal tradition and her use of the foundational liberal ideals of liberty and equality.
- Both books, but *Liberty of Conscience* in particular, show her skills as a narrative historian.
- Nussbaum has performed a valuable service in bringing the important but neglected figure of Roger Williams back into the debate around religious freedom.
- Both *Liberty of Conscience* and *The New Religious Intolerance* focus on controversial contemporary issues.

Chapter 7

Nussbaum and the Emotions

Emotions as Cognitive Judgements – and a Normative Critique of Anger

One of Nussbaum's key achievements has been to bring the study of the emotions to centre stage in moral and political philosophy. For a long time, emotions were neglected by moral philosophers. Writing in 1973, Bernard Williams (who was to become Nussbaum's friend and mentor) noted:

> Recent moral philosophy in Britain has not had much to say about the emotions. Its descriptions of the moral agent, its analyses of moral choice and moral judgement, have made free use of such notions as attitude, principle and policy, but have found no essential place for the agent's emotions, except perhaps for recognising them in one of their traditional roles as possible motives for backsliding, and thus potentially destructive of moral rationality and consistency. (Williams 1973: 207)

Williams ascribes this state of affairs partly to the influence of Kant. Kant's theory of morality in *The Groundwork of the Metaphysics of Morals* (1785) states that it is one's *duty* to act morally, and one knows what is the moral thing to do by the use of *reason*. Clearly emotion has no part to play here, either as a motivator (in fact Kant famously argued that it is more morally admirable to act dutifully *against* one's inclinations than in line with them) or as a means to ascertain what the right thing to do is.

Kant's *deontological* theory, as it is called, has had a profound and lasting influence. Its only serious rival in moral philosophy until quite recently was utilitarianism – but this, with its emphasis on calculating and weighing the consequences of acts with a view to determining which produce the greatest amount of pleasure, welfare or preference-satisfaction, also left little room for the emotions.

Towards the end of the twentieth century, the wind changed. Philosophers (such as Williams in the essay quoted above) began to argue for a return of the emotions to moral philosophy; and Nussbaum played a significant role in adding momentum to this change of direction.

From her first book, *The Fragility of Goodness* (1986), Nussbaum has been interested in the role emotion has to play in ethics and politics, and her views have developed throughout her career. She writes about the emotions of fear and disgust in *The New Religious Intolerance* (2012), as noted in the last chapter. But her first full-length book to take the emotions as its main theme was the earlier *Upheavals of Thought* (2001). This was followed by further work on the emotions in *Hiding from Humanity* (2004) and again in *Anger and Forgiveness* (2016). To put the matter simply: *Upheavals of Thought* builds and defends a theory in which the emotions play a vital role in moral and political philosophy, while *Hiding from Humanity* and *Anger and Forgiveness* set limits to that role. This chapter will mainly focus on the last of these books, as the most recent statement of Nussbaum's position – which contains some changes from earlier formulations – and as the book with the most direct relevance to her political philosophy. But first, a summary of the two earlier books.

Upheavals of Thought

The title is taken from Marcel Proust's *Remembrance of Things Past*. In a passage that Nussbaum uses as an epigraph, Proust writes that M. de Charlus' falling in love with Charlie Morel produces 'real geological upheavals of thought', causing a sudden mountain landscape of 'Rage, Jealousy, Curiosity, Envy, Hate, Suffering, Pride, Astonishment, and Love' (Proust quoted in Nussbaum 2001a). In the Proustian view, then, as in Nussbaum's, emotions are not separate from thought but are a *form* of thought, which projects outwards to objects in the world. Nussbaum states in her introduction that emotions are 'intelligent responses to the perception of value' (2001a: 1). And this has consequences for ethics:

> Instead of viewing morality as a system of principles to be grasped by the detached intellect, and emotions as motivations that either support or subvert our choice to act according to principle, we will have to consider emotions as part and parcel of the system of ethical reasoning. (Nussbaum 2001a: 1)

The 'system of principles to be grasped by the detached intellect' looks like a glance at Kant's theory, which Nussbaum of course rejects (as she rejects utilitarianism). But note that she does not *exclude* the intellect from her account of emotions. Her position is that emotions are not mere prompts to action but are themselves moral judgements – which have the possibility to be either true or false.

Emotions are therefore *cognitive judgements*. But, Nussbaum says, we need a broad definition of 'cognitive' which does not entail that the emotion can always be formulated as a linguistic proposition by the entity experiencing it. That would rule out infants and non-human animals as having emotions. But to have an emotion, in Nussbaum's theory, does entail 'thought of an object combined with thought of the object's salience or importance' (2001a: 23), even where this isn't or cannot be put into words by the thinker.

In Nussbaum's theory, then, we cannot rely solely on the straightforward rationality required by deontological ethics or by utilitarianism. To make moral judgements we must also take account of 'the messy material of grief and love, anger and fear' (Nussbaum 2001a: 1–2).

The book begins with an account of Nussbaum's own grief at her mother's death – neither the first nor the last time that Nussbaum uses autobiography in her writing. But the purpose of it is not to focus the reader's attention on the personal emotions of Martha Nussbaum; it is there because grief is a universal emotion and the reader will be able to relate her narrative to their own experience. Nussbaum's grief ascribes three roles to her mother:

> as a person of intrinsic worth in her own right; as *my* mother, and an important constituent of my life's goals and plans; and as *a mother*, that is, a type of person that it would be good for every human being who has one to cherish. (2001a: 53)

For Nussbaum, emotions are *eudaimonistic* – that is, bound up with one's goals and projects in life, goals and projects on which one's flourishing depends. Emotions are cognitive responses to objects and events that are important in an individual's life but which do not lie within the individual's control. Some might perhaps find it hard to accept that emotions have a cognitive component. It might seem as if an emotion as primal as grief has nothing to do with cognition. After all, a cow separated from her calf feels grief; are we to ascribe a cognitive component to her moos of distress? Nussbaum would simply answer, yes. The cow cannot of course express her grief in the form of a proposition. Nevertheless, her grief arises from *knowledge*. She knows her calf is important to her, she knows her calf is missing, and she knows this is outside her control (that is why she grieves).

Because of this lack of control, emotions are 'acknowledgements of neediness and lack of self-sufficiency' (2001a: 22). For this reason, the Stoics urged that one should try to eliminate emotions as far as possible – otherwise one is constantly vulnerable to the shocks that life delivers. Nussbaum, however, while accepting the Stoic analysis of emotions, disagrees that we would get on better without them. On the contrary, emotions are bound up with what is most valuable in our lives, which we must continue to value if we are to flourish; and so we must accept some degree of vulnerability (a line of argument which echoes that in *Fragility*). Nussbaum therefore describes herself as a 'neo-Stoic' (2001a: 5).

Nussbaum emphasises throughout that emotions are not separate from the intellect: the traditional split between reason and emotion has no place in her account. She emphasises, too, that there is a continuum between the emotions of humans and non-human animals, and between childhood emotions and adult emotions. But the fact that emotions have deep roots does not mean we are at their mercy: 'cognitive views of emotion entail that emotions can be modified by a change in the way one evaluates objects' (Nussbaum 2001a: 232). Instead of the Kantian story of a rational will forcibly suppressing unruly passions, 'we can imagine reason extending all the way down into the personality, enlightening it through and through' (2001a: 232). So such emotions as anger and hatred can be changed through changes in thought – and this has consequences for politics:

> Clearly this view has important implications for moral education, in the area, for example, of emotions towards other races and religions: we can hope to foster good ways of seeing that will simply prevent hatred from arising, and we don't have to rely on the idea that we must at all times suppress an innate aggressive tendency. (2001a: 233)

The most valuable method of moral education is imaginative art and literature, as Nussbaum has argued throughout her career. Emotions can be altered cognitively by imagining different objects for them, or moderating the intensity of one's own emotions through cultivating sympathy for the other. The book goes on to consider the moral lessons we can learn from such works as Proust's *Remembrance of Things Past*, Dante's *Divine Comedy*, Emily Brontë's *Wuthering Heights*, Mahler's Second Symphony, Walt Whitman's poetry and James Joyce's modernist masterpiece *Ulysses*. Nussbaum takes a progressive view of the emotions: that is to say, she believes that destructive emotions, based on incomplete knowledge or faulty reasoning, can be transcended; we can teach ourselves to *ascend* from them to compassion and love (not that she claims this is easy; on the contrary it is a life's work). Concluding her analysis of Molly Bloom's final, silent, stream-of-consciousness soliloquy in *Ulysses*, Nussbaum writes:

> By ending with Poldy and Molly, who both endorse and tenderly mock the spirit of ascent, I have tried to indicate that even in their real-life imperfect form, indeed especially in that real form, in which the incompleteness of human life is accepted rather than hated, love and its allies among the emotions (compassion, grief) can provide guidance towards social justice, the basis for a politics that addresses the needs of other groups and nations, rather than spawning the various forms of hatred that our texts have identified. (2001a: 713)

Upheavals of Thought is a big (751 pages), complex and closely reasoned book – though like all Nussbaum's work it is very clear and readable. It's far too rich to do justice to in this brief summary; I would strongly recommend reading it in full. For our purposes here, it provides the theoretical framework which underlies the specific emotions Nussbaum goes on to explore in *Hiding from Humanity* and *Anger and Forgiveness*.

Hiding from Humanity

Hiding from Humanity, published three years after *Upheavals of Thought*, continues Nussbaum's exploration of the emotions. It is a shorter book, focused on two specific emotions, disgust and shame, and is more directly related to public policy. Nussbaum's contention is that disgust and shame should be used neither as a basis for framing laws nor for making legal decisions. She does not contend that law should be emotion-free. On the contrary, she thinks that emotions are necessary foundations of laws. We make certain acts illegal because they (justifiably) anger us or make us scared and we decide on appropriate penalties according to the level of anger or fear the illegal act causes. Recall Nussbaum's cognitive theory of emotion. Anger and/or fear can be *reasonable* responses to an act, if we are correct in our assessment of its threat or harmfulness. (Later, Nussbaum changes her mind about anger, as we shall see.) Nussbaum also stakes a claim for compassion as an emotion that should guide law-making and sentencing – though like anger and fear this can sometimes misfire (see 2004a: 55–6). But all these emotions can be and often are cognitively well founded. That is, they can involve beliefs that are reasonable and true. But, Nussbaum argues, disgust and shame are not cognitively well founded in this way and should have no place in law. (She notes in passing that the emotion of jealousy should be excluded from laws and legal judgments, too.)

The roles played by disgust and anger in law are not the same. Disgust features as a *reason* why certain acts are made illegal in the first place: they make people feel disgusted, an unpleasant emotion, and therefore should not be tolerated by law. Shame comes in at the *sentencing* stage: shaming penalties are inflicted in order to demonstrate disapproval and enforce social norms. For example, it was suggested by Amitai Etzioni that first-offence drug dealers should have their heads shaved and be sent home without any pants (Nussbaum 2004a: 4).

Shame and disgust are of course connected. One normally feels shame if one knows one has disgusted others. Disgust also plays a role in sentencing: the more disgusting the act is perceived to be, the more shameful the sentence ought to be (in the minds of shaming-penalty proponents).

Nussbaum has no truck with any of this. Neither emotion should have anything to do with framing laws or deciding on penalties. In fact she suggests we might be better off without disgust altogether. Disgust was useful in our evolutionary history, she concedes; but the thought content of disgust is 'typically unreasonable, embodying magical ideas of contamination, and embodying impossible aspirations to purity, immortality and non-animality' (2004a: 14). As for shame, it is more complicated, arrives earlier in life, and does have some positive aspects. The desire to avoid it may push one towards 'valuable ideals and aspirations' (Nussbaum 2004a: 15). But what Nussbaum calls 'primitive' shame – that is, 'shame connected to an infantile demand for omnipotence and the unwillingness to accept neediness' (2004a: 15) – is, like disgust, a way of *hiding from our humanity.*

It is in this book that Nussbaum explicitly connects her theory of emotions to her political liberalism. Political liberalism has its basis in equal human dignity and mutual respect among citizens.

But disgust and shame repudiate this dignity and respect. Moreover, thinking about disgust and shame illuminates political liberalism: we realise that its ideals are undermined by 'the narcissism, the shrinking from animality and mortality, and the anxious obsession with the "normal"' (2004a: 321) which underlie both disgust and shame.

Nussbaum argues that disgust and shame are especially inimical to a liberal conception of justice, for both are typically heaped on minority groups. But a politically liberal state is committed to equal respect for *all* persons and groups, and for ways of life and comprehensive doctrines not shared by the majority. This is always subject to the harm principle, of course; practices that harm others should not be respected but prevented. But Nussbaum's whole point is that disgust and shame are not related to any reasonable judgement of what is harmful. That is why they are irrational, and normatively problematic.

Anger and Forgiveness

Nussbaum's 2016 *Anger and Forgiveness* (dedicated to the memory of Bernard Williams) is in my view one of her best books. Full of penetrating psychological insights, it is a significant advance on Nussbaum's previous work on the emotions. It argues, counter-intuitively, that anger and forgiveness as customarily understood are *not* good things and we need to rethink how we approach them. It is cogently argued and a pleasure to read. And it provides valuable new terminology to help us think about the emotions in relation to ethics and politics: terms such as *the road of payback, the road of status, the transition,* and the three realms of human interaction, the *Personal Realm*, the *Middle Realm* and the *Political Realm*. Nussbaum begins her study, as is her wont, with the ancient Greeks.

The Kindly Ones

In Aeschylus's play *The Eumenides*, Orestes is pursued by the *Erinyes* (Furies) for the crime of matricide. Orestes killed his mother, Clytemnestra, at the behest of Apollo, because she had killed her husband, and Orestes' father, Agamemnon (and she killed him because he had sacrificed their daughter, Iphigenia, as discussed by Nussbaum in *Fragility* – see Chapter 1). With the Furies in hot pursuit, Orestes reaches Athens where he is tried by a jury, presided over by the goddess Athena. Orestes is acquitted.

The vengeful Furies, baulked of their prey, burst into a furious outcry. But Athena renames them the Eumenides (the Kindly Ones) and says that they will forever be honoured in Athens.

Nussbaum interprets the story as a symbol for the transformative effects of law on the community. Vengefulness is to be changed into justice, and justice is to be tempered with mercy. But Nussbaum goes further than Aeschylus, arguing that the emotion of anger is *always* 'normatively problematic' (2016: 5).

This represents a significant change in her position. In *Hiding from Humanity* she had argued that anger, like fear and compassion, and unlike disgust, shame and jealousy, had a part to play in law-making and sentencing. It is interesting to note that her first version of the ten capabilities did not mention anger; but in the version put forward in *Women and Human Development* (2000) Nussbaum includes, under Capability 5 (Emotions) the capacity to feel 'justified anger' – this at the instigation of Marilyn Friedman. By 2016 her position has changed and anger is no longer endorsed. This offers a good example of Nussbaum's flexibility. She is not a dogmatist. She is always prepared to re-examine her position.

Where Three Roads Meet: the Road of Payback, the Road of Status and the Transition

The Road of Payback

Anger, says Nussbaum, involves a 'double-movement' (2016: 20). There is a backward-looking part which focuses on the pain, harm or offence received; and a forward-looking part which thirsts to make the offender suffer. Nussbaum calls this the *road of payback*. Aristotle held this view; he thought the forward-looking part, the desire to pay back the offender, was pleasant, a form of *hope*. Nussbaum calls in support from other thinkers too for the view that looking forward to payback is an intrinsic part of anger: the Stoics, Joseph Butler, Adam Smith and contemporary empirical psychologists such as Richard Lazarus and James Averill (2016: 22).

Nussbaum acknowledges that other emotions can also involve this double-movement; compassion, for example, looks back at misery suffered and forward to alleviating the misery. However, Nussbaum says that forward-lookingness is not intrinsic to compassion, but dependent on the situation; compassion prompts one to lend a helping hand if one can, but often this is impossible. We can feel compassion for people we have no possibility of helping – people who are already dead, for instance. In such cases, the forward-lookingness is missing. Yet we would still identify the emotion as compassion. So, Nussbaum argues, forward-lookingness is not an essential constituent of compassion; but of anger, it is.

I am not sure this distinction holds up. When the object of one's compassion is unreachable, still one feels that one *would help if one could*. It seems that it is equally possible to feel anger at an unreachable object – one might feel angry at Caligula for his many cruelties and feel that *one would make him suffer if one could*.

This, however, is not really the essential point. Nussbaum could easily concede that anger is not the only emotion in which the forward-looking element is intrinsic and it would not damage her overall argument. For with compassion, when it's possible to act on the forward-looking impulse – to actually help the person who is suffering – then this *works*. The person's suffering really is relieved. The forward-looking part, we might say, takes care of the backward-looking part. But this is not the case with anger. The road of payback does not really achieve its aim. If I were to travel in a time-machine to ancient Rome and pay back Caligula as I feel he deserves, this would not in any way alleviate the suffering of his victims or bring them back to life.

As Nussbaum says, if we had a non-cognitive account of the emotions, this would not be a problem. We might simply reply, 'Well, that's the way it is. When we are hurt, or those we care about are hurt, we want to lash out. That's the way we're constituted; that's how we evolved.' But Nussbaum's cognitive account does not allow this simple response. Anger depends on a *belief* – and the belief involved in the road of payback is a false one. As Nussbaum puts it, 'Doing something to the offender does not bring dead people back to life, heal a broken limb or undo a sexual violation. So why do people somehow believe that it does?' (Nussbaum 2016: 22). A little later she puts the same point more forcefully: 'The question now is, Why? Why would an intelligent person think that inflicting pain on the offender assuages or cancels her own pain? There seems to be some kind of magical thinking going on' (2016: 24).

Nussbaum does not fail to acknowledge the attraction of the idea of payback. She says it has 'deep roots in the imaginations of most of us' and that it probably derives from 'metaphysical ideas of cosmic balance' (2016: 24). She notes, too, that in literary works 'ideas of "comeuppance" . . . give us intense aesthetic pleasure' (2016: 25).

Nevertheless, she says, aesthetics can be misleading. For the fact remains that however painfully we make the offender suffer, this does precisely nothing to wipe away the original harm.

Nussbaum's argument, then, supports her earlier-stated conclusion that the road of payback is normatively problematic because 'the beliefs involved are false and incoherent, ubiquitous though they are' (2016: 5).

Of course, punishment of offenders could serve a useful purpose in deterring them from repeating the offence, or others from following suit. But that is a different kind of justification for punishment, and it does not deliver what those who take the road of payback seek.

The Road of Status

The road of payback is dismissed because it depends on incoherent beliefs. But there remains another justification for payback: what Nussbaum calls *the road of status*. This, Nussbaum argues, does at least make sense, but is normatively problematic for different reasons.

Suppose we think of injury in terms of personal status (as indeed many people do). Somebody does me an injury. I feel humiliated, downgraded. I have lost status. But if I can retaliate, injuring my aggressor as severely as – or, better, more severely than – they injured me, now *their* status is lowered and mine is back up where it was, or even a little higher. As Nussbaum emphasises, this does actually work. Unlike the road of payback, the road of status does take me where I want to go.

But this road, too, is normatively problematic. It is true that '[m]any societies do encourage people to think of injuries as essentially about them and their own relative ranking' (Nussbaum 2016: 28). But Nussbaum does not agree that this is either admirable or helpful:

the tendency to see everything that happens as about oneself and one's own rank seems very narcissistic, and ill-suited to a society in which reciprocity and justice are important values. It loses the sense that actions have intrinsic moral worth . . . If wrongful injuries were primarily downrankings, they could be rectified by the humiliation of the offender, and many people, certainly, believe something like this. But isn't this thought a red herring, diverting us from the reality of the victim's pain and trauma, which needs to be constructively addressed? (2016: 28)

The road of status, then, also fails to lead us anywhere useful. Nevertheless, we do feel anger when somebody injures us or those we care about. What are we to do with this anger? The third road supplies the answer.

The Transition

What Nussbaum calls 'the Transition' is also forward-looking, but in a more constructive sense. The move is towards 'forward-looking thoughts of welfare, and, accordingly, from anger into compassionate hope' (Nussbaum 2016: 31). Nussbaum presents Martin Luther King's famous 'I have a dream' speech as an example of the Transition in action. Motivated by anger at the injustices suffered by Black Americans, King takes neither the road of payback (by seeking punishment of white Americans) nor the road of status (by seeking to humiliate white Americans) but instead sets out a vision for a better future – 'reshaping retributivism to work and hope', as Nussbaum puts it (2016: 33).

Transition anger takes the form of thinking: 'How outrageous! Something must be done about this!' (2016: 35). It pivots swiftly from the painful feeling of anger to practical planning to make things better. It is welfarist. Securing improved welfare may indeed happen to involve punishment for reasons of deterrence, or to incapacitate dangerous people and keep the public safe, or to reform offenders – but the *goal* is not to make offenders suffer, nor should harsher suffering be inflicted than is necessary to achieve deterrence, incapacitation or rehabilitation. Nussbaum allows that the emotion of anger can have some limited utility – as a signal that something is wrong, as motivation to put things right, and as a deterrent to warn others not to overstep the mark. But 'beneficent forward-looking systems of justice have to a great extent made this emotion unnecessary, and we are free to attend to its irrationality and destructiveness' (2016: 40).

And here it is worth noting that although this analysis of the role of anger from Nussbaum is new – in earlier writings she assigns much stronger value and usefulness to anger – it is nevertheless entirely consistent with the meliorist approach she has taken throughout her career. Her aim is always to seek practical ways to improve matters, rather than luxuriate in how dreadful they are.

Nussbaum goes on to make some interesting distinctions between anger and other reactive emotions. Anger differs from gratitude, not merely because gratitude wishes good rather than ill, but also because gratitude is part of a reciprocal system which is beneficial to society (2016: 47). Anger and grief have certain points in common: both are focused on a damage to the self and both are painful. But grief is focused on the *loss* rather than on the perpetrator of the damage. What is more, grief has a crucial part to play in the story of one's life, in a way that anger does not: 'deep pangs of longing for the lost are ways of registering the immense importance of that lost person, and thus important ways of making wholeness and sense out of the narrative of one's life' (2016: 48).

Nussbaum also explores the relationship of anger to other negative emotions such as disgust; in fact, she suggests that disgust is really quite close to status-focused anger and often mingled with it.

Anger's Gatekeepers

In the final section of her chapter on anger, Nussbaum considers what steps we can take to keep anger within reasonable bounds (note again the characteristic practical turn). She identifies three useful strategies:

1. *Smith's judicious spectator*. Nussbaum takes the idea of the 'judicious spectator' from Adam Smith's *The Theory of Moral Sentiments* (1759). Smith proposes that we should establish the degree of anger appropriate to any dispute by imagining oneself as a neutral spectator of events. The spectator, he says, will still feel sympathetic anger at seeing another person treated injuriously; but the anger will be tempered, partly by the spectator's non-involvement, but also, and more interestingly, because the judicious spectator will consider the situation of the other party as well as the injured one. This approach suggests a *movement* of emotion congenial to Martha Nussbaum's philosophy; it 'moves from concern for the ranking of fragile ego toward more general and constructive social concern' (2016: 53).

2. *Aristotle's gentle temper*. Nussbaum endorses Aristotle's suggestion that we cultivate a gentle temper and attempt a sympathetic understanding of the person who has offended us. Although Aristotle does not share Nussbaum's view that non-transitional anger is always inappropriate, he does think that we are more likely to fall into the vice of excess anger than the vice of deficient anger. Cultivating a gentle temper corrects this excess, making it less likely that anger will arise and, if it does, making the gentle-tempered person

less likely to desire retribution or humiliation of the offender. The road to transition is thus unimpeded.

3. *Aristotle's playful disposition.* Aristotle also observes (in the *Rhetoric*) that those who are laughing or at play are less likely to get angry. So, too, are those who feel secure and free from pain. In all these conditions, the ego is unthreatened – and Nussbaum holds that cultivating a playful disposition is the best way to feel relaxed and secure: 'play is a set of stratagems by which the ego grows strong enough to live in a world with others'.

Nussbaum's overall position, then, is that although anger is evolutionarily hard-wired and we would not be human if we didn't feel it, we are justified in taking a normative view. We are not at anger's mercy. Both in terms of our personal emotions and in terms of public policy, we can manage anger and turn it to constructive purposes.

It's important here to note that Nussbaum's theory, while rooted in evolutionary psychology, does not fall into evolutionary determinism. Much knee-jerk opposition to evolutionary psychology comes from a failure to appreciate that the one does not entail the other.

Nussbaum on Forgiveness

Transactional Forgiveness

Nussbaum's analysis of forgiveness is original and insightful and might well cause the reader to re-examine everything they thought they knew about it. She begins by identifying the traditional or classic conception of forgiveness, which she illuminatingly terms *transactional forgiveness*. Transactional forgiveness is just that: a transaction, a deal. One can obtain forgiveness, but only by paying for it. As a model account of this type of forgiveness, Nussbaum takes that offered by Charles Griswold in his 2007 book, *Forgiveness: A Philosophical Exploration*. In Griswold's account forgiveness has six stages. To earn forgiveness, a person must: (a) acknowledge responsibility; (b) repudiate their deeds; (c) express regret to the injured party; (d) commit to changing; (e) show understanding of the damage done to the injured person; and (f) offer a narrative explaining how they came to do wrong and an assurance that they are becoming a better person (Nussbaum 2016: 57). Only when all these stages are in place can the injured party forgive.

Nussbaum traces this classic account through a genealogy of Jewish and Christian scriptures and commentaries. But though this conception of forgiveness has such a venerable ancestry, Nussbaum finds it contains elements of 'aggressiveness, control and joylessness' (2016: 58). She might also have added that since it demands a *performance* from the candidate for forgiveness it is likely to lead to hypocrisy.

Transactional forgiveness, then, is ruled out as a model.

Unconditional Forgiveness

Unconditional forgiveness is a better, though, in Nussbaum's view, still imperfect model. Here the wronged party forgives freely without compelling the wrongdoer to go through all of Griswold's six stages. This clearly has advantages over the transactional model but is still 'not free of moral danger' (Nussbaum 2016: 77). As Nussbaum puts it:

> The minute one sets oneself up as morally superior to another, the minute one in effect asserts that payback was a legitimate aim – but one that I graciously waive – one courts the dangers of both the road of status (inflicting a status-lowering on the offender) and the road of payback ('coals of fire'). (2016: 77)

What is more, unconditional forgiveness does not clearly point towards the *transition*, because it looks back, not forward: it wipes the slate clean, but writes nothing on it.

Unconditional Love

The third and best possibility – though no doubt also the hardest to achieve – is *unconditional love*. Although the Judaeo-Christian tradition has always emphasised transactional forgiveness, there is also a counter-tradition, to be found in the Gospels, which 'departs altogether from judgement, confession, contrition and consequent waiving of anger' (Nussbaum 2016: 78). Love is felt immediately, before forgiveness even gets out of the blocks; there is no anger to be waived. Nussbaum gives the example of the Prodigal Son story from the Gospel of Luke. Here, the father does not first feel anger when his wayward, wasteful son returns home, and *then* decide to forgive. He simply feels intense love and rushes to embrace his son.

Unconditional love also points *forward*, not back: 'The direction of [the father's] love is Transitional; his love points to a future, and that future will almost certainly contain advice' (2016: 81).

An objection at this point might be that we do not always or indeed usually have a parent–child relationship with those who wrong us, so that unconditional love is far harder to achieve. Nussbaum would no doubt accept this and perhaps would say that this is why we need the transition – to move us from anger towards love, and the more swiftly the better. She goes on to explore how this movement of emotion works in three realms: the *intimate* realm, the *middle* realm and the *political* realm.

The Intimate Realm

The intimate realm is the realm of family relationships, parent/child, spouses, partners and lovers (it is in this realm, of course, that the immediate unconditional love of the Prodigal Son's father is most likely to occur). An important point about this realm is that much of it is inaccessible to law. We must navigate it alone, or sometimes with the help of therapists and counsellors. Nussbaum identifies four key features of this realm:

1. It is central to *eudaimonia* (human flourishing) – as Nussbaum was already emphasising in her first book, *Fragility* (1986).
2. Relationships in the intimate realm involve *trust*.
3. The damage caused by breakdown of relationships is personal and internal and cannot be addressed legally.
4. We usually have intimate relationships with people we *like*. (2016: 93–5)

Nussbaum argues, with much supporting evidence, that the road of status and the road of payback do not work at all well in intimate relationships. They simply make matters worse. Unconditional love is therefore recommended, and a moving forward rather than dwelling on past wrongs. As is often Nussbaum's way, she turns to literature for examples, citing the moving scene in George Eliot's *Middlemarch* where Harriet Bulstrode shows unconditional love for her husband Nicholas after he is disgraced. Nussbaum compares this with Medea's murderously vengeful behaviour in Euripides' tragedy; the contrast could hardly be starker or the lesson clearer.

Nussbaum does not neglect to include one's relationship with oneself as part of the intimate realm. One can be angry at oneself for past misdeeds and inflict self-punishment (the road of payback); and one can belittle and downgrade certain aspects of one's personality to elevate others (the road of status). But this is futile, painful and does not look forward. We should have love and compassion for ourselves just as for others. And here Nussbaum notes that her views on guilt (as expressed in *Upheavals of Thought* [2001] and *Hiding from Humanity* [2004]) have changed. She used to think that guilt could be a positive force, motivating us to improve our moral behaviour. She now sees guilt as a 'self-punishing anger' (Nussbaum 2016: 134) and an emotion we should transition away from. We should cultivate 'a more generous and constructive attitude toward [our own] imperfections' (2016: 134), just as we should for those of others. This is a further example of how Nussbaum's thinking develops throughout her career, and how she is unafraid to own past mistakes. She notes that her changed views on ethics owe a lot to her former teacher Bernard Williams – which no doubt is why the book is dedicated to his memory.

The Middle Realm

What Nussbaum terms the 'middle realm' is the area between intimate relationships and the forces of law and the state, that is, 'dealings with strangers, business associates, employers and employees, casual acquaintances' (2016: 138). It is the life we lead as we go about our daily business. It is, of course, a realm replete with possibilities for annoyance, frustration and the experience of (real or imagined) slights and insults. On rare occasions it can also be a realm where serious harms occur. For the vast majority of encounters in the middle realm, Nussbaum agrees with the Stoics – most of these annoyances are not worth getting angry about. (Serious harms require a different response.) Nussbaum does not agree with the Stoic disvaluing of 'external goods', but she does agree with the arguments Seneca advances against anger in *De Ira*: that it is often occasioned by trivialities, that it is an unpleasant feeling, that it is often counterproductive and that far from adding to one's dignity it detracts from it (see Nussbaum 2016: 143).

Insults or slights in the middle realm (when real) should always be met with the Transition: 'This is outrageous, and it should not happen again.' Nussbaum differs slightly from Seneca in holding that sometimes a *performance* of anger can achieve useful results (e.g. when making a complaint), but the performance has to be judiciously calculated and probably won't be very effective if one is genuinely ablaze with anger. She disarmingly admits, however, that she is not very good at following her own advice. She recounts an anecdote in which she became disproportionately furious at a large man on an airline flight who – showing off his masculine strength under the guise of being helpful – patronisingly heaved her case out of the overhead locker after she had asked him not to. Nussbaum could not resist delivering a stinging put-down and obsessing about the incident for days afterwards. Further anecdotes concern an alter ego, 'Louise', who has to deal with various infuriating colleagues. All these stories are entertaining and told with humour but they reinforce the serious point that in none of these situations is getting angry of the slightest use. It is always better to move swiftly to the Transition.

Unlike in the intimate realm, Nussbaum does not seem to urge a role for unconditional forgiveness or unconditional love when it comes to the middle realm. Perhaps there might be a place for those qualities in an abstracted, attenuated sense. Annoying people could be forgiven or loved in virtue of their humanity, rather than as individuals. But in general, the emphasis is more on protecting *oneself* from unnecessary anger and its consequences, rather than forgiving or loving others.

Nussbaum also considers the question of 'gratuitous gratitude'. Sometimes people in the middle realm are unexpectedly friendly, helpful or competent. If it is a mistake to feel anger when people do their jobs badly, would it not also be a mistake to feel gratitude when they do them well? Nussbaum says no. After all, kind or thoughtful behaviour can be an unexpected windfall, and feeling gratitude for it is *pleasant* – unlike anger. What is more, expressing gratitude 'enhances future cooperation' (Nussbaum 2016: 164).

The whole section on the middle realm is as entertaining as it is wise. Nussbaum concludes that 'Seneca's advice is easy to state, difficult to follow' (2016: 167). But it's important to follow it as far as one is able – and a sense of humour helps.

However, not all bad experiences in the middle realm can be laughed away. Serious wrongs can occur: 'life, health, bodily integrity, work and employment, major aspects of one's property' could all be threatened or damaged (2016: 164). Unlike the intimate realm, in these cases it is not helpful to focus on the perpetrator (they are not emotionally important to us, after all); we should instead focus on the *act*. And it is here that we must call in the Eumenides – that is, the law. Which leads us on to the political realm.

The Political Realm: Everyday Justice

Nussbaum divides the political domain into two: *everyday justice* and *revolutionary justice*. The first of these is concerned with policing and the criminal law – how to deal with 'wrongful acts against groups or individuals within an ongoing legal framework that is not itself based . . . upon fundamental injustice' (Nussbaum 2016: 172). This is contrasted with *revolutionary justice*, where the whole system needs to be overhauled – which is addressed in Nussbaum's chapter 7.

Nussbaum's position derives from her critique of anger and her argument that retribution is an incoherent policy based on magical thinking. The justice of the state should be forward-looking, not obsessed with payback. And just as intimate relationships thrive where there is trust, so too do political communities. The political realm thus requires 'the proper combination of impartial justice, acknowledgement of wrongs, and empathetic generosity' (2016: 173).

In line with her earlier political theory, Nussbaum's approach is welfarist and capabilities-based. It is consequentialist, but not in the simple utilitarian sense. The goal is not growth or wealth, nor can capabilities be traded off against each other. Her aim is a society where each citizen has the opportunity to flourish in their own way – an ideal which she describes as 'Millian in spirit' (2016: 174). But alongside her consequentialism Nussbaum allows a deontological element: denying or impairing any of the capabilities doesn't only produce bad consequences but is *unjust*. Nussbaum has already argued for this position on philosophical grounds but in this context it also has strategic value, for it helps produce that trust in the state necessary for a healthy political community.

Nussbaum's aim is that this welfarist, non-retributivist basis for criminal justice should be the subject of a Rawlsian overlapping consensus: people from different traditions and different comprehensive doctrines could all agree on it despite their disagreements on other matters. But herein lies a challenge: how to sell this ideal of 'nonangry justice' to the public. After all, as Nussbaum acknowledges, many people do hold harsh views on retribution, and such views are popular politically.

Nussbaum suggests two answers. One is that there are precedents. Gandhi, Martin Luther King and Nelson Mandela all succeeded in winning converts to their peaceful programmes for change; and they did so by tapping into pre-existing religious ideas and popularising them. So, part of the answer is to work with what we have. Nussbaum also recommends a focus on the *efficacy* of a less retributive approach. We should, she says, try to change the popular slogan from 'tough on crime' to 'smart on crime' (Nussbaum 2016: 177).

Note, though, that for Nussbaum 'public acknowledgement of wrongdoing' remains important. We should not treat victims of crime exactly as we'd treat victims of a natural disaster: 'institutions should not treat murder as like being mauled by a tiger' (2016: 178). The acknowledgement of wrongdoing helps form and strengthen trust in state institutions of justice.

Following Bentham (and here it is once again worth noting that Nussbaum, though not a utilitarian, uses good ideas wherever she finds them), she argues that the best justice system should be based on *ex ante* policies rather than *ex post*. That is to say, it should pursue policies which seek to reduce crime, rather than coming down hard on it after it has happened. She uses an illuminating analogy to reinforce the point. Imagine visiting a country where elevators were unregulated and badly maintained, with the result that they often broke down, causing inconvenience, injuries and fatalities. A visitor to such a country would be appalled and would demand to know why this problem wasn't fixed. If a citizen of that country replied that they didn't choose to spend time and money on the problem, but they did punish elevator-owners very severely when mishaps occurred, the traveller would be entitled to think that the state did not take safety very seriously. And that, Nussbaum says, is pretty much the situation most states are in with regard to dealing with crime (2016: 180).

Of course, if *ex ante* policies have been put in place and some, if fewer, crimes are still committed (as is inevitable) then *ex post* measures will be needed. Nussbaum considers a number of theories of punishment and rejects those with a strong retributive element. She is somewhat more approving of the theories of R. A. Duff and Dan Markel which, though nominally within a retributivist framework, actually focus on 'communication and reform' (Nussbaum 2016: 190). She is most approving of Jean Hampton's expressive theory of punishment, which dispenses altogether with the retributivist element and justifies punishment only in terms of promoting social welfare, because it can 'teach both wrongdoers and the public at large the moral reasons for *choosing* not to perform an offence' (Hampton [1984] quoted in Nussbaum 2016: 191). Both Hampton and Nussbaum are open to empirical findings about *what works* – a thread which runs throughout Nussbaum's work.

The required conditions, then, for state coercion (note that Nussbaum eschews the word 'punishment') are:

> it must be compatible with equal dignity and non-humiliation, it must be accompanied by public acknowledgement of the seriousness of the wrongdoing, and it must be justified to the person involved as only one part of a much more comprehensive project in which we reasonably aim to promote social welfare. (Nussbaum 2016: 192)

Nussbaum notes that a multidisciplinary approach to the question of state justice is necessary (2016: 194). It requires contributions from legal and educational theory and the social sciences. This again highlights her belief that philosophy should not be practised in isolation from other disciplines.

Nussbaum is against victim impact testimony about the effects the crime has had on them or their family: this is 'bringing the Furies into the courtroom' (2016: 194). Anger and the desire for vengeance should have no place in the law. Reprising arguments made in *Hiding from Humanity* (2004a), Nussbaum rejects the use of 'shame penalties'. The arguments against are both *normative* (they are wrong, for they undermine dignity and invite vindictiveness) and *empirical* (they don't work, for they do not deter crime).

Nussbaum does, however, show sympathy for John Braithwaite's system of community 'conferences' where predatory wrongdoers face their victims and their own families, managed by a coordinator, who helps the offender recognise their own wrongdoing and assists them in reintegrating into the community. The aim is to view the crime as the bad act of a good person. Nussbaum records a similar approach used with troubled teenagers in a Chicago high school. Note that she visited this programme for herself to see how it worked, which is typical of her personal involvement and engagement with the issues she explores.

Two Conceptions of Mercy

Nussbaum identifies two competing concepts of mercy: the *monarchical* and the *egalitarian*.

The monarchical form of mercy has much in common with Judaeo-Christian traditions of forgiveness: forgiveness is bestowed from on high by a superior power. Nussbaum cites Portia's famous speech in *The Merchant of Venice* ('The quality of mercy is not strained / It droppeth as the gentle rain from Heaven') as an example.

The egalitarian conception of mercy comes from the Greco-Roman tradition. It holds that mercy is needed because 'we are all in this together, we understand human life because we are in its midst and burdened by its difficulties' (Nussbaum 2016: 206). Nussbaum uses another Shakespeare play to exemplify this conception: *Measure for Measure*, in which the Duke shows mercy to all the wrongdoers, including the unmerciful Angelo, looking on human frailty with a tolerant eye.

Nussbaum, of course, strongly favours the egalitarian form. She finds this form of mercy preferable to forgiveness as traditionally conceived, because it does not demand apology or abasement, it focuses on facts, and it is not hierarchical. It is close to the virtue of 'unconditional love' (2016: 209).

The Political Realm: Revolutionary Justice

In her earlier work, Nussbaum discussed the problem of *adaptive preferences* (see Nussbaum 1999): that is, when people become so accustomed to living under oppressive conditions that they cease to see change as possible and acquiesce in their lot. Now, it might be advanced as an objection to Nussbaum that, far from being normatively problematic, anger is actually a very good thing for those who are oppressed: it blows adaptive preferences away. Nussbaum acknowledges this point and says that anger might be thought to have three valuable things going for it: it is a sign that the oppressed understand their condition; it is a motivator for change; and anger at oppression is *justified* (recall that Nussbaum herself, in an early formulation of her capabilities list, included 'justified anger' under the capability of Emotions).

Nevertheless, Nussbaum argues that 'noble anger' is an unreliable guide to action (2016: 211). And here Nussbaum hints at an important psychological truth, in my view insufficiently remarked upon: that feeling angry usually makes one feel *righteous*. (Indeed, people who have an uneasy sense that they might be in the wrong often get angry – at times, it seems, on purpose – and then their doubts disappear.) It is therefore not a good idea to pursue justice under the influence of anger, because the measures one takes – however unwise, disproportionate or violent – will feel justified.

159

Nussbaum as usual supports her argument with empirical findings from the real world. Over the last century or so, she says, the three most successful revolutionary struggles – Gandhi's campaign of non-violent resistance to the British Raj, the struggle against apartheid in South Africa, and the civil rights movement in the USA – were all conducted in a spirit of non-anger. The repudiation of anger does not mean acquiescence to injustice, as those successful campaigns show. Nelson Mandela's establishment of the Truth and Reconciliation Commission is a prime example of Nussbaum's Transition: 'a statement of outrage, followed by generous forward-looking thoughts' (Nussbaum 2016: 240).

Nussbaum's overall conclusion is a radical one: we need to stop thinking of anger as a good thing. We need a compete reorientation, so that we learn to see 'the irrationality and stupidity of anger' (2016: 249). Of course, we are human and battling against anger is hard. But the first step is to accept that it is a battle we ought to fight.

Responses

Anger and Forgiveness was well received. The South African activist and lawyer Albie Sachs, quoted on the back of the 2016 Oxford University Press hardback edition, professed himself 'astonished and delighted' at the way Nussbaum, 'using intuitions drawn from classical Greek and Roman literature and modern philosophy, explains better than most historians and political scientists how in South Africa we converted the sword of apartheid into the ploughshare of constitutional democracy'. Gregory R. Peterson, reviewing it in the *Journal of Moral Philosophy*, described it as 'an outstanding work, one that manages to build on many threads of Nussbaum's previous scholarship while breaking new ground', and commended its 'insightful and nuanced phenomenology of anger' (2021). Timothy P. Jackson wrote that Nussbaum 'offers a magisterial brief' against retribution and anger and states that 'there is much for a Christian ethicist to admire in her learned and creative treatment of moral emotion' – although he does also take Nussbaum to task for not sufficiently distinguishing between love and justice, anger and hatred, retribution and revenge and sanctity and utility (2018).

Not all Nussbaum's work on the emotions has been equally praised. John Kekes wrote a stinging review of *Hiding from Humanity* for the journal *Mind*: one central strand of his criticism is that Nussbaum fails to distinguish justifiable instances of disgust from non-justifiable ones; similarly, she gives no criteria for differentiating 'good' shame from 'bad' shame. That is a reasonable criticism to make, opening up a fertile area of debate; but Kekes's critique goes much further than that: he accuses Nussbaum of producing 'absurd pronouncements, blatant inconsistencies, unreliable references and prolix purple prose in place of argument' (2005: 441). Perhaps a clue to the vehemence of his attack can be found in his claim that 'The psychological foundations of liberalism, Nussbaum's public myth, rests on the stories she tells about the human condition' (2005: 439). Kekes is a long-time foe of liberalism – his book *Against Liberalism* was published in 1997 – and perhaps seized the opportunity to take a tilt at one of liberalism's most prominent proponents. Clearly, if one is not a liberal one will find much to disagree with in Nussbaum's work – but I would still contend that even if you reject Nussbaum's ideology, *Hiding from Humanity* contains many penetrating psychological insights.

The Monarchy of Fear

In 2018, Nussbaum published a further book in which emotions are central. In this case, it is *fear* that is put under the lens. The use of the word *monarchy* is significant: for an American rooted in the republican tradition, monarchy represents tyranny, and throwing off its shackles represents liberty and democracy. Subtitled 'A Philosopher Looks at Our Political Crisis', the book was triggered by the 2016 election of Donald Trump, and the political polarisation, and fear (on both sides), that this caused. Nussbaum argues that fear is a driver of extremism and we should do our best not to be influenced by it when it comes to political decision-making. Nussbaum, of course, had already argued that fear was an important factor in anti-Muslim sentiment and legislation in her 2012 book, *The New Religious Intolerance*, and this book represents a further development of that view.

She argues that fear is in fact anterior to anger and has a toxic role to play in other negative emotions, such as disgust and envy. Fear is 'both chronologically and causally primary, getting its teeth into us early and then coloring the rest of our lives to a greater or lesser degree' (Nussbaum 2018: 14–15). It poisons political life and is an underlying cause of misogyny. (Incidentally, Nussbaum makes a psychologically acute distinction between sexism and misogyny: sexism is a belief that women are inferior to men; misogyny is hatred and intimidation designed to keep women in that inferior place.)

161

Fear can be defused, Nussbaum argues, with 'hope, love and work' (2018: 15). Nussbaum does not claim that it is easy to eliminate fear (any more than it is easy to eliminate disgust or anger); but she never confuses the difficult with the impossible. She retains her characteristic meliorist approach. Despite her concerns about the political climate in America in 2018, she is very clear that the lives of most people, especially women and ethnic minorities, are much better than they were fifty years ago. Nussbaum is a progressive in the true sense of that word: that is, she believes that progress in human affairs is both desirable and possible – and has, albeit unevenly and insufficiently, already been achieved in many ways. The task is to keep striving for further progress, encouraged by gains already made.

Summary

- Both *Anger and Forgiveness* and *The Monarchy of Fear* display the characteristically important role of the emotions and human psychology in Nussbaum's moral and political theory, an importance that we can track right back to her earlier work on the Greeks and Romans.
- Both books offer further testimony to Nussbaum's interdisciplinary approach: human psychology, criminology, history and literature are all used illuminatingly in the philosophical arguments she builds.
- *Anger and Forgiveness* in particular represents an important new direction in Nussbaum's thought: a rejection of anger and the increasing role it plays in social and political life, offering in its place a forward-looking approach that differs significantly from traditional notions of forgiveness.
- Her work on the emotions highlights the positive, meliorist tenor of her thought. Nussbaum's approach to problems is always to try to solve them rather than take refuge in anger or despair.

Chapter 8

Nussbaum and Global Justice
Cosmopolitanism, Material Aid and Immigration

Nussbaum is and always has been a universalist. She holds that there is such a thing as human nature and that – although plastic and alterable – it is pretty much the same everywhere. She proposed a cosmopolitan theory of education in *Cultivating Humanity* (1997). Her capabilities approach is predicated on the claims that we all have a need to flourish; that what counts as flourishing is essentially the same across cultures; and that we all have an equal right to be given the opportunities to do so. Throughout her career she has argued for the principle of equal human worth and dignity – and she has put in practical efforts to achieve this in her position as a research adviser at the World Institute for Development Economics Research and in her development work in India.

Nussbaum wrote about global justice explicitly in *Frontiers of Justice* (2006). Much of that book is concerned with bringing disabled people and non-human animals, who, Nussbaum argues, are neglected by a contractarian approach, fully into the moral fold. But the problem of economic inequalities among nations is addressed too. She argues that neither a contractarian nor a utilitarian approach is a satisfactory framework for eliminating unjust global economic inequalities. Instead, she recommends application of her and Sen's capabilities approach. To put this into practice she suggests ten principles. They include the principle that each nation-state has its own responsibility to provide the capabilities, at least at threshold level – but this, Nussbaum, argues, does not obviate the need for richer nations to provide economic aid to poorer ones. And so another, important, principle states that '*Prosperous nations have a responsibility to give a substantial portion of their GDP to poorer nations*' (Nussbaum 2006: 316, italics in original). The figure she suggests is 2 per cent of GDP (gross domestic product). There is little on how these principles are to be implemented. The role of philosophy is to determine what the principles should be; when it comes to implementation, 'philosophy must turn the job over to other disciplines' (2006: 323). Nussbaum concludes the book by saying: 'Here I have offered only a sketch of what this approach might ultimately say. But even a sketch is a step forward, on the way to a fully global theory of justice' (2006: 407).

The Cosmopolitan Tradition

The Cosmopolitan Tradition (2019) is Nussbaum's first book-length exploration of the cosmopolitan ideal – that is, the claim that we are all 'citizens of the world'. In this chapter, I explore her exploration. The book is subtitled 'A Noble but Flawed Ideal', which already gives a clear sense of her position: she finds much to value in cosmopolitanism but much to object to as well – at least, in the form the tradition has developed historically. She aims to show that her capabilities approach preserves what is valuable in the cosmopolitan tradition while avoiding its deficiencies.

I focus in turn on her discussions of the following:

- cosmopolitanism in the ancient world;
- cosmopolitanism in the work of Grotius;
- cosmopolitanism in the work of Adam Smith;
- global issues today;
- the capabilities approach as an alternative to cosmopolitanism.

and end with a challenge for Nussbaum: can the capabilities approach meet the duty of material aid to disadvantaged nations?

Cosmopolitanism in the Ancient World

The book begins with the well-known anecdote about the ancient Greek Cynic, Diogenes. Asked where he came from, he replied with a single word: *kosmopolitês* – a citizen of the world. He does not define himself by country of origin, nor by class, status or gender. In Nussbaum's view this is where the cosmopolitan tradition begins. It focuses on what we share – we are *all* citizens of the world – rather than what divides us:

> Cynic-Stoic cosmopolitanism urges us to recognize the equal, and uncon-
> ditional, worth of all human beings, a worth grounded in moral choice-
> capacity (or perhaps even this is too restrictive?), rather than on traits

that depend on fortuitous natural or social arrangements. (Nussbaum 2019: 2)

Nussbaum notes that this ideal has egalitarianism at its heart. It is non-hierarchical in its very essence – apart from two exceptions she notes and addresses later in the book. These are the omission of people not fully capable of making informed choices (i.e. those with severe cognitive impairments) and non-human animals. Nussbaum wants to bring these, too, into the cosmopolitan fold. But with those omissions repaired, Nussbaum finds much to approve in the cosmopolitan tradition. Although she focuses on its origins in the Western classical world, especially from the Stoics, she points out that it is by no means exclusively a Western tradition; Buddhism as well as the African concept of *ubuntu* embody the idea (2019: 3–4).

The cosmopolitan ideal is a moral one but it generates political obligations. However, Nussbaum argues that the founders of the Western tradition effected a 'bifurcation' of the obligations thus generated. The bifurcation is between the duties of *respect* or *justice* owed to others as moral agents – recognising their dignity and their right to liberty – and the duties of *material aid* owed to others. Nussbaum says the classical or Stoic tradition concentrates solely on the first branch of the bifurcation, neglecting the second. For the Stoics, 'The dignity of moral capacity is complete in itself' (Nussbaum 2019: 5) and therefore money, social position and decent living conditions are irrelevant. The truly free person has no need of external aids. Not even adequate shelter; Diogenes apparently lived in a barrel.

Now, focusing on the first branch of the bifurcation – duties of *respect* (or justice) – in this way does generate some important duties: it would require 'an end to aggressive war, support for people who have been unjustly attacked, and a ban on crimes against humanity' (Nussbaum 2019: 5), which is all to the good. However, the second branch of the bifurcation, material aid, should not be neglected either. We are not all Diogenes and most people need more to flourish than a barrel to live in. Nussbaum lists some of the most glaring effects of material inequality throughout the world in 2019. A newborn American baby could expect to live to 79, while a Somalian baby would on average die at 49. Literacy levels in the United States, Europe and some other parts of the world are close to 100 per cent, while in Ethiopia they are at 39 per cent and in Niger only 15.5 per cent. And other goods such as clean water, access to health care and adequate food are distributed very unevenly indeed.

The Stoic version of cosmopolitanism neglects such material inequalities. It is as though they accept John Rawls's First Principle of Justice (equal basic rights and liberties for all) but ignore his Second Principle (the so-called Difference Principle, that material inequalities should only be allowed when they benefit the worst-off). Nussbaum does not explicitly make this comparison with Rawls but it seems to parallel her position: instead she formulates it in terms of 'first-generation' rights (political liberties) and 'second-generation' rights (economic conditions), a distinction which seems to allude to Karel Vašák's theory of human rights (see Vašák 1977). Nussbaum believes that the legacy of Stoic cosmopolitanism has influenced international politics and caused a neglect of second-generation rights:

> We have a fairly well worked-out set of doctrines about duties of justice, which command wide assent and have become the basis for widely agreed accounts of 'first-generation rights.' We have no equally worked-out doctrines on the other duties, those in the 'second-generation,' and we do not seem even to know where to begin, once we step outside of national boundaries. (Nussbaum 2019: 7–8)

The Legacy of Cicero

The Roman statesman and philosopher Cicero was not a member of a Stoic community but his ethical views are in some ways close to those of the Stoics. In *De Officiis* (*On Duties*), written in 44 BCE, Cicero identifies two kinds of justice: not harming others, and respecting property rights. Nussbaum notes that *how* property came to be distributed in the first place is not a consideration for Cicero – he starts from the existing distribution and argues that any expropriation is unjust.

Cicero regards these duties of justice as stringent, to be observed without exception. Moreover, they are fully global, to be extended to citizens of all nations and 'form the basis for a truly transnational law of humanity' (Nussbaum 2019: 28). Nussbaum states that this conception of international justice became extremely well known in subsequent centuries, influencing the work of Grotius, Kant and Adam Smith.

However, the other kind of duties that Cicero recognises – duties of material aid – are less stringent. Cicero does regard them as basic to human nature, but there are many constraints as to how, when and to what extent they should be fulfilled. In general, he thinks it is better to bestow material aid on those to whom you have close ties. Duties of beneficence are most strongly owed to family, friends and fellow citizens. Strangers can be helped if this does not cause any personal loss for the giver: you can help a stranger by giving them advice, directions or water. But for bestowals that *cost* the giver, strangers are right at the back of the queue. As Nussbaum puts it:

> Cicero proposes a flexible account that recognizes many criteria as pertinent to duties of aid: gratitude, need and dependency, thick association – but also preserves a role for flexible judgement in adjudicating the claims when they might conflict . . . What is clear, however, is that people outside our nation always lose out. (Nussbaum 2019: 33)

This distinction, between duties of justice and duties of material aid, has been extremely influential and Nussbaum claims it influences thinking about human rights even today. But she argues that it does not stand up. She presents three distinct arguments against it:

1. *Justice is also an external good.* Suppose we accepted the Stoic view (although Nussbaum does not) that external goods are of no importance: that to be happy we must not fuss about things outside our control, be content with what we have, and achieve *ataraxia* (a state of mental serenity). If this were so, material deprivation would not be an evil. But then neither would unjust or disrespectful treatment. Within the Stoic worldview there seems to be no room to say that one kind of external good (justice on the part of others) is more to be valued than another (material aid from others) – for they are *both* external goods and therefore we ought to be able to do without either of them.
2. *The interdependence of justice and material aid.* But suppose, again, that we accepted in principle that duties of justice were called for but duties of material aid were not. We would quickly find that attending to the duties of justice *costs money* – police, lawyers, a judiciary, courts and a penal system all have to be paid for, presumably through taxation. In states where government is weak, few taxes are collected so the infrastructure is not well supported: travel is unsafe, policing unreliable, the legal system inefficient. To fix these problems of justice, material resources will be needed; so we *cannot* attend to duties of justice without material aid. The problem is even more acute when we consider *global* justice – without (yet) considering any redistribution of

resources, preventing torture, cruelty, unjust war and genocides requires large-scale military expenditure as well as the funding of the required international institutions. The bifurcation converges.

3. *There is no clear distinction between positive and negative duties.* There is a distinction in moral philosophy, commonly invoked but equally commonly disputed, between positive and negative duties (as earlier discussed in Chapter 5). Negative duties are things we must not do. Nussbaum says that Cicero's duties of justice look very like this: we must refrain from unjust acts such as 'aggressive war, torture, rape and so on' (2019: 42). Positive duties demand action, and tend to be regarded as less binding: it is *good* to per-form acts of beneficence, but not demanded in the way that, say, not assaulting or murdering people is demanded. If one takes this line, then, one could uphold the Ciceronian distinction between duties of justice (negative duties) which we must fulfil absolutely, and duties of material aid (positive duties) which we can fulfil according to our own taste and judgement. So, as Nussbaum puts it: 'If we refrain from cruelty and torture, and so on, then we are doing no wrong, even if we are unwilling to spend our money on people at a distance, even where justice issues themselves are in play' (Nussbaum 2019: 42).

However, this convenient distinction has been questioned, not least, as Nussbaum points out, by Cicero himself. In *De Officiis* he argues that standing by and allowing injustice is as blameworthy as actually committing it. But Cicero places this argument within his section on justice, so he seems to limit its scope – not extending it to the question of material aid. He thinks we have a duty to prevent others being assaulted, but no such duty to relieve hunger or poverty. But Nussbaum takes Cicero's own reasoning further than he did. Since he is right that you can't claim to have done nothing wrong if you stand by and watch somebody being assaulted when you could have prevented it, then neither can you make that claim of innocence if you stand by and watch somebody starve. In both cases, you have knowingly allowed harm to occur.

In her usual style, Nussbaum considers what might be said in defence of a position she disagrees with. An upholder of Cicero's view might argue that the duties *are* different – for in defending innocent people against acts of assault or aggression we are defending them against a wrongdoer, but there is no such wrongdoer in the frame for cases of hunger and poverty. To this Nussbaum has a twofold answer:

in the first place, from the point of view of the victim it scarcely matters whether their plight is caused by a wrongdoer or by brute bad luck. They need help either way. But in any case, Nussbaum does not agree that hunger and poverty are never caused by wrongdoers:

> we cannot assume that . . . hunger and poverty are not caused by the wrongful act of another person or persons. Given that hunger is typically caused not so much by food shortage as by lack of entitlement to food, it is a thoroughly human business, in which the arrangements of society are profoundly implicated. (Nussbaum 2019: 50)

Nussbaum's overall position on Cicero, then, is that he was right to argue for the universality of the duties of justice, and his influence in that regard has been positive. But he was wrong (a) to separate duties of justice from duties of material aid, and (b) to represent the duties of material aid as less stringent. Nussbaum's analysis and critique of his arguments move towards a position where 'we' – that is, citizens of wealthy, developed nations – have much stronger transnational duties to alleviate material deprivation than we currently suppose.

Early Modern Cosmopolitanism

The Stoic cosmopolitan tradition, founded on a belief in equal human worth and dignity (which Diogenes anticipated or inaugurated, and which Cicero drew upon), was taken up by a number of thinkers in the early modern world. By then the shape of the world had changed fundamentally. The ancient Greeks lived in a relatively small world of competing city-states, the Romans in an expanding empire outside of which (and sometimes within which) lay hostile tribes requiring to be subdued. By the early modern era – that is, the sixteenth century onwards – the nation-state was beginning to emerge. The cosmopolitan ideal required adaptation to the changed conditions. Nussbaum considers the work of two thinkers from early modern Europe who made important contributions: Hugo Grotius (1583–1645) and Adam Smith (1723–90).

Grotius

Hugo Grotius (the form of the name is Latinised – his birth name was de Groot) was a Dutch scholar, humanist and lawyer who still today is regarded as the father of international law. Nussbaum credits him with three major contributions to the updating of the cosmopolitan tradition:

1. Grotius gives a *systematic* account of cosmopolitanism. He bases it on universal moral norms which should govern the relationships of nation-states, and applies his theory to specific issues such as the laws of war and property rights.
2. He makes a start on the problem of material aid, offering a theoretical justification for at least some redistribution across national boundaries – an advance on the Stoic neglect of that issue.
3. Most importantly for Nussbaum, Grotius adapts the cosmopolitan tradition to a world of nation-states. For Grotius, the individual person is the fundamental subject of moral and political justice, as for the Stoics; but this in turn generates a recognition of national sovereignty, as an expression of the autonomy of the individuals living there; and over and above the nation-state he has a vision of an international society, governed by universally accepted moral norms.

Grotius's writings laid the foundations for the Peace of Westphalia (which ended the wars of religion between Catholic and Protestant nations and is often held to have established the principle of national sovereignty) in 1648, three years after his death. Nussbaum states that his work marked 'the dawning of the Enlightenment' (2019: 100) and was an influence on such thinkers as Hobbes, Locke and Kant. One statement in his *De Iuri Belli ac Paci* (*On the Laws of War and Peace*) was particularly daring and influential: 'What we have been saying would have a degree of validity even if we should concede (*etiamsi daremus*) that which cannot be conceded without the utmost wickedness, that there is no God . . .' (Grotius quoted in Nussbaum 2019: 103–4).

This dictum (known simply as the *etiamsi daremus*) represents a significant move which was taken up by later Enlightenment philosophers: a commitment to the idea that morality is justified by human reason, independently of God. Grotius also argued for the principle that no nation should interfere with the religious practices of another (although he did not have anything to say about religious persecution *within* nation-states). Grotius himself was a religious man, a Protestant who had to flee the Netherlands because of his commitment to the Arminian heresy, but religion has no role to play in his conception of international law.

Nussbaum explores three areas of tension in Grotius's thought which are still unresolved today: the problem of humanitarian intervention; duties of material aid; and the question of a world government. Let's take them one by one.

Is Humanitarian Intervention Ever Justified?

Grotius believes in individual autonomy. Individuals have the right to form their own political communities and make their own laws. From this basis emerges the doctrine of national sovereignty. So far so good. But then, it does happen sometimes that nation-states oppress their own citizens. What then are other states obliged to do? It looks as if one must either fail to respect the autonomy of the oppressed individuals (if one does not intervene) or fail to respect national sovereignty (if one does). This is a dilemma for Grotius and, as Nussbaum says, it leads him to a 'complex and indeterminate position on humanitarian intervention' (2019: 107).

Nussbaum notes two weaknesses in Grotius's discussion of the problem. First, he fails to give an account of what makes a state legitimate in the first place and would recognise the legitimacy of slave-owning tyrannies. Second, he has nothing to say about political inclusiveness, although in his own day women and many others were excluded from the political sphere. These are perhaps understandable omissions for a seventeenth-century writer. And certainly, if a modern-minded theorist narrows what counts as a legitimate state, excluding tyrannies and states where large numbers of inhabitants lack citizens' rights, intervention might in some cases be easier to justify. Still, it remains a tricky question even so.

Grotius does give a list of crimes which *could* justify foreign intervention, taken mainly from classical literature: killing one's parents, cannibalism, piracy, incest and homosexuality. Not all of these are equally grave or even crimes at all today. At the same time, Nussbaum notes that Grotius misses out many other types of crime that today *are* regarded as grave, such as slavery and genocide – which, as Nussbaum points out, just shows how hard it is to separate universal moral principles from local customs.

Still, despite her reservations about his examples, Nussbaum is in agreement with Grotius's overall position, which she summarises as follows:

moral respect for national sovereignty, combined with knowledge of both the greediness and the fallibility of human judgment, should make us very reluctant to intervene forcibly in the affairs of another nation. Yet in some grave and extreme instances it is both permissible and praiseworthy to come to the defence of the oppressed. (Nussbaum, 2019: 127)

Decisions about when intervention is or isn't justifiable cannot be made in advance. They have to be made on a case-by-case basis. But Nussbaum contends that Grotius's discussion of the problem, despite its seventeenth-century blind spots, is still helpful as a guide to thinking through this complicated issue.

Duties of Material Aid to Other Nations

The Stoic form of cosmopolitanism was deficient in one important respect, as Nussbaum argued earlier in the book: it fails to provide a moral basis for duties of material aid. Grotius repaired this omission by supplying two key ideas: 'common goods, and claims of need' (Nussbaum 2019: 128). Common goods include such things as water, air and uncultivated land. So there should be right of passage over sea, rivers and land; and goods transported through countries shouldn't be taxed, unless the country incurs expenses in the passing through. Claims of need offers a more far-reaching principle of a right to material goods: nobody should be denied the necessities of life, such as 'food, clothing and medicine' (Grotius quoted in Nussbaum 2019: 129). This applies to foreigners and refugees too.

As Nussbaum notes, however, the details of how this would work remain unclear. Grotius does not specify 'what mechanisms of redistribution he envisages, either within or between nations' (2019: 130).

There is thus a good deal of working out to do before Grotius's principles could be put into practice; and it is fair to say that this question has still not been settled today. But Grotius does allow room for duties of intra- and international material aid in principle – which is an advance on Cicero.

A World Government?

The logical conclusion of the cosmopolitan ideal would seem to be a world government. If, as Grotius and Nussbaum agree, the individual person is the moral unit and all persons have equal worth and dignity, why have national boundaries within which different laws obtain? Since we are all citizens of the world, it might seem to follow that one government is enough for all of us.

Neither Grotius nor Nussbaum takes this step, however. What Grotius proposes, on Nussbaum's interpretation, is a kind of halfway house, where citizens have universal rights but nations are sovereign, and there is a constant tension between these moral commitments. This is, in Nussbaum's view, better than the current arrangement, which she describes (attributing the description to the international relations scholar Hedley Bull) as 'a world consisting of atomic nation states whose relations among themselves are those of self-interest and security only' (2019: 135–6).

Nussbaum rejects the call for a world government (which she had already argued against in *Frontiers of Justice*). If established by force it would probably be a tyranny (Nussbaum 2019: 136). Even if it were established by agreement between nations, or evolved gradually, there would still be the problem that, once established, it would, Nussbaum believes, lack checks and balances, and it would lack accountability, too (2019: 137). Moreover, a one-size-fits-all government for the whole world would tend to smooth away regional differences and alternative ways of doing things: it would instantiate *perfectionism*, rather than the political liberalism espoused by Nussbaum.

Nussbaum goes on to consider two other models for international society. One would be the Kantian ideal, developed by John Rawls in *The Law of Peoples* (1999), according to which sovereign nations 'connect only in a compact regarding their (peaceful) international relations' (Nussbaum 2019: 137). But Nussbaum sees this model as too thin; it doesn't generate duties of material aid among nations, or granting asylum for refugees, or cooperating to protect the environment. (Still, Rawls might reply, it doesn't *preclude* those duties either.)

The second model she considers is what Bull called 'the New Medievalism'. On this model, there are *layers* of authority rather than sovereign states, with regional authorities, national authorities and supranational bodies all having decision-making powers of different scope – just as in mediaeval Europe there were vassal-states, kings and over-arching authorities such as the Pope or Holy Roman Emperor. Nussbaum accepts that something like this model is taking shape as a result of globalisation, but decries it, since the supranational powers are multinational corporations rather than accountable bodies.

What we need, Nussbaum concludes, is a return to Grotius's strong defence of national sovereignty. The nation-state, Nussbaum argues, is 'still the primary locus of human self-expression and human autonomy' (Nussbaum 2019: 140).

One detects a sense of unfinished business here. Exactly where the rights of the individual citizen end and the rights of the sovereign state begin is unclear. Nor is it clear what should govern relations between states. Later in the book Nussbaum returns to these questions and argues that her capabilities approach is a preferable alternative to the cosmopolitan tradition that she has discussed. I shall argue that that, too, raises some questions that need answering.

Adam Smith

Adam Smith was an important figure of the eighteenth-century Scottish Enlightenment, whose two main works, *The Theory of Moral Sentiments* and *The Wealth of Nations*, have been influential in both ethics and economics. He knew the works of the Stoic and Stoic-influenced philosophers – Cicero, Seneca, Epictetus and Marcus Aurelius – extremely well, and Nussbaum represents him as, like Grotius, taking their cosmopolitan ideal and improving on it. She argues that his work is a crucial step on the road that leads from the Stoic tradition of cosmopolitanism to her own capabilities approach.

Smith is sometimes presented as a callous advocate for capitalism who explained human motivation entirely in terms of self-interest. But this caricature is unfair. Although Nussbaum acknowledges that his ideas about free markets might be controversial, his argument rests on 'a keenly observed sympathy for the working man and a respect for that person's human potential' (2019: 144). Smith agrees with the cosmopolitan tradition's insight about the value of human dignity. But he disagrees with their disregard for externalities. On the contrary, he argues that many human beings, as a result of externalities such as poverty, unemployment, exploitation and lack of education, lead lives that are 'mutilated and deformed' (quoted in Nussbaum 2019: 143).

Smith holds that such mutilations and deformations are both unjust and inefficient. We now begin to see how this thought prepares the way for the capabilities approach. For to allow people to lead lives of dignity, injustices must be addressed:

> Smith sees that institutions matter for a life worthy of human dignity and that slavery, colonial domination and certain forms of domination

174

by the rich over the poor are violations of basic justice. Smith's argument thus strikingly anticipates similar arguments made by proponents of the Capabilities Approach today. (Nussbaum 2019: 159)

In particular, Smith argues strongly for the importance of education. He points out that natural differences in ability are much smaller than we think; that a philosopher and a street porter may well be of the same ability at birth and up to the age of six or eight – but the gap widens as they go on to pursue different occupations, until 'the vanity of the philosopher is willing to acknowledge scarcely any resemblance' (Smith quoted in Nussbaum 2019: 150). He goes on to argue that the state should therefore provide 'the most essential parts of education' (quoted in Nussbaum 2019: 164), compulsorily, for all, before they begin paid work. Nussbaum notes that he was a pioneer in this regard in Britain. She claims his argument anticipates that of Marx in his discussion of human functioning in his *Economic and Philosophic Manuscript of 1844*, but that Smith places more emphasis on the importance of education, where Marx concentrates more on material conditions (Nussbaum 2019: 166).

Smith's other important contribution to the cosmopolitan tradition is his internationalist outlook. He (famously) supports free trade between nations; he denounces colonialism and argues for the right of national self-determination; and he is critical of aggressive patriotism. The major gap in his account, Nussbaum says, is that though he is in favour of free trade he has nothing to say about freedom of movement. Nevertheless, his work does provide 'a sketch of a transnational politics of human capability' (2019: 167).

Global Issues Today

The post-Grotian cosmopolitan tradition casts individuals as *both* members of a global moral community *and* citizens of sovereign states. In Nussbaum's view, our duties as members of the global moral community are more acute today than they were in the time of Grotius, let alone the Stoics, because we live in a far more interconnected world. As a result of economic globalisation, our consumer choices have effects on workers on the other side of the world; our use of energy affects the environment for all; and one country's health policies can influence the global spread of diseases – a fact made starkly evident by the Covid-19 pandemic, which hit the world a year after *The Cosmopolitan Tradition* was published.

175

At the same time, since we can communicate with other people all over the globe, instantaneously, at the touch of a button, we have better opportunities to share ideas and knowledge and to collaborate on projects. This presents us with new responsibilities and new opportunities. It might also increase the tension between our duties as members of a global moral community and citizens of a sovereign state.

Nussbaum identifies five current problem areas to work on. I select just two for discussion here, as they seem among the most pressing in today's world: material aid for nations in need, and migration.

Material Aid

Throughout *The Cosmopolitan Tradition* Nussbaum has stressed that material aid to those in need should be as stringent a duty as the duty of justice, and has argued that, although recognition of this was lacking in Cicero and other Stoic philosophers, Grotius and Smith went a long way to repairing this deficiency. Yet when she comes to discuss how this duty can be fulfilled in today's world, she is cautious and tentative. Indeed, the section devoted to this question is entitled 'The Inefficacy and Moral Difficulty of Foreign Aid' (2019: 222).

As we have seen, Nussbaum had previously proposed in *Frontiers of Justice* (2006) that richer nations should devote at least 2 per cent of GDP to help developing nations. To put this in perspective, the year that *The Cosmopolitan Tradition* was published, the USA contributed 0.2 per cent of the federal budget to foreign aid (Ingram 2019). The UK parliament recently voted to drop British foreign aid from 0.7 per cent of GDP to 0.5 – and even with this cut remains in the top eight donors in the world (Luk 2021). One might think, therefore, that by 2019 Nussbaum would have been urging nation-states to meet their obligations to the global moral community and strive harder to reach that 2 per cent.

However, since *Frontiers of Justice* Nussbaum has changed her position. She is now of the view that benevolent paternalism is 'morally problematic' (2019: 223), and is moreover sceptical about whether foreign aid actually works in any case. As she puts it: there is 'mounting evidence that foreign aid not only does little to no good, but can often be detrimental' (2019: 224). She cites the work of the health economist Angus Deaton, who argues that even when aid reaches the intended recipients (and where autocratic, corrupt or inefficient governments are in power, it doesn't), it weakens the political will of a people to create their own stable and efficient institutions (Deaton cited in Nussbaum 2019: 225).

This is a difficulty for Nussbaum. She has spent over two hundred pages arguing that the early versions of cosmopolitanism bifurcated our duties to others and neglected the material aid side of the bifurcation. But now she finds herself in the position of having (however reluctantly) to neglect it herself. Nussbaum points out that her position is not exactly the same as the Stoic cosmopolitans; they didn't even see the importance of material aid for the distant needy, whereas she sees it but feels powerless to do much about it. But that is an awkward position, as Nussbaum acknowledges: 'Believing that we have moral duties, but also that actually acting on those duties may well be counterproductive, is not a comfortable place to be for morally sensitive people' (2109: 227).

Nussbaum does think there are other things we can do to work towards global material justice. One can write reports, books or articles to draw attention to global problems and to help those in need work towards their own solutions; richer nations can 'share technological advances and pool knowledge in other ways' (2019: 228). And one of the ideas we can share is, of course, Nussbaum's capabilities approach (to be discussed below).

Asylum and Migration

Nussbaum identifies the issue of asylum and migration as one of the most acute and politically inflammatory global problems of today. The basic insight of the cosmopolitan tradition, she says, is that 'respect for humanity requires us to furnish the basic wherewithal of human life, somehow, to those in desperate need' (Nussabum 2019: 230). Allowing asylum or immigration is not the first measure to which a wealthy nation should have recourse, in Nussbaum's view. First, they should look at the possibility of delivering overseas aid to provide the basic wherewithal of human life. If *that* fails (and as we have seen, Nussbaum thinks it is very likely to) then those forced by need or persecution to leave their home country should have 'at the very least a right of temporary sojourn in another land' (2019: 230).

Stated in such general terms, such a position would probably command wide agreement. But as Nussbaum goes on to say, the position fails to deal with a number of key distinctions: 'Between formal or legal migrants and undocumented migrants; between permanent residency and citizenship, and between both of these and temporary guest-worker status; and finally, between political asylum and economic migration' (2019: 230).

However, Nussbaum herself does not state where she stands on those distinctions. She states that there is already 'an impressive and diverse philosophical literature' on the subject, and a footnote directs the reader to Wellman (2015), Blake (2003, 2013), Carens (2013), Hosein (2013, 2104), Miller (2014) and Walzer (1983). But she says that to make her own contribution to the debate would be beyond the scope of the chapter, so we are left wondering what exactly, in Nussbaum's view, the wealthier nations ought to do about asylum and migration. It is clear that she is not an advocate of open borders: she states that 'nations have the right to defend both their security and their national political culture' (2019: 231) and to this end they are entitled to limit the number of immigrants admitted in order to preserve economic stability, and to require immigrants to 'express the willingness to live under the rule of law and in accordance with the nation's basic constitutional principles' (2019: 231). In addition, Nussbaum says that migrants must not be denied entry 'for reasons of ethnicity or religion' (2019: 231).

This may all be easy enough to agree with in principle, but it offers considerable scope for disagreement in practice. There are no case studies here, no facts and figures, no examples of good practice. How many migrants and asylum-seekers does the United States take in each year, for example? Does Nussbaum think that number should be higher? If so, by how much? Or more generally, what variables should be taken into account in fixing an optimal level of immigration for any particular state? Candidates might include the wealth of the state, the level of infrastructure, its population density, its colonial history. What weighting should be given to each variable? And if a figure were arrived at, what kind of events or developments would justify changing that figure? It is unlike Nussbaum to neglect the practicalities of a problem, but there is very little guidance as to how to apply the principles of cosmopolitanism. But perhaps the capabilities approach will do better?

Capabilities in Place of Cosmopolitanism

Nussbaum sees her capabilities approach as the true heir to the cosmopolitan tradition. It preserves that tradition's emphasis on equal human worth and dignity and its (Grotian) commitment to the moral importance of the nation.

One major difference is that the cosmopolitan tradition was always firmly anthropomorphic, ruling out non-human animals as objects of moral concern. Nussbaum argues for a clear break from this element of the tradition; her version of the capabilities approach demands that 'non-human animals have intrinsic importance as end' (Nussbaum 2019: 238). Nussbaum has, of course, argued extensively for that view in 'Animal Rights' (2001b) and *Frontiers of Justice* (2006).

Taking that difference as a given, though, in what ways can the capabilities approach make good on the duties of justice to *humans* that the cosmopolitan tradition enjoins?

The capabilities approach makes no 'bifurcation' between duties of justice and duties of material aid. Nussbaum's list of ten capabilities (see Chapter 4) mingles both kinds of duty. Indeed, Nussbaum argues that they cannot be separated, since 'all entitlements cost money to convey and protect' (2019: 245). For example, Capability 2 (Bodily Integrity), which stipulates that the individual must be secure against violent assault, requires an efficient police service and judiciary – which need to be funded. Or Capability 6 (Practical Reason), which involves being able to engage in critical reflection about the planning of one's life, requires education, and that costs money. Nussbaum argues that nation-states must levy taxes to pay for these capabilities.

Nussbaum sees the capabilities approach as a recipe for constitution-making. She argues that 'every single nation has a reason to implement the list in some form' (Nussbaum 2019: 246) because the capabilities are universal. But because they are at quite a high level of generality, there is room for filling in the details of implementation differently in different nations; and, Nussbaum says, individual nations can 'add things that are not on the list' (2019: 246) according to local requirements. But the capabilities are not to be imposed; rather, they should be made prominent in international forums so that they can have an *influence* on national constitutions, laws and policies.

Nussbaum is a political liberal in the Rawlsian tradition, and it's important that the capabilities are seen in terms of political liberalism: that is, they are a broad set of principles based on a conception of what makes for a flourishing human life (and where applied to other animals, to flourishing non-human lives), but they are not a comprehensive doctrine. They leave plenty of room for flourishing in different ways, and so they can't be termed either paternalist or perfectionist. Just as Rawls argued that an overlapping consensus on a core set of laws and political principles would develop *within* a nation-state, shared by citizens of different religions and political ideologies, so Nussbaum argues that the same kind of overlapping consensus on the capabilities can be reached *among* nation-states, despite differences in culture, religion and political traditions.

Criticisms of The Cosmopolitan Tradition

The Cosmopolitan Tradition is, by Nussbaum's standards, rather a short book and it leaves certain important areas under-explored. It was based on a set of lectures Nussbaum gave at Yale University in 2000, with additional material, such as that on Grotius and Smith, subsequently added; as Nussbaum says, it is 'unabashedly a book of connected essays, not a continuous historical narrative' (2019: 8). There is nothing wrong with that in principle; Nussbaum used the same approach to good effect in *Sex and Social Justice*. But here it's not quite as effective; the book feels somewhat unbalanced, as most of the essays deal with ancient and early modern conceptions of cosmopolitanism, while contemporary issues are discussed comparatively briefly in the last two chapters (which total only forty-six pages together). Matt MacManus, reviewing the book for *Human Rights Review*, wrote: 'it . . . lacks the focus and sweep of her best work' and 'spends a lot of time engaged in analysis that has only a tangential link to contemporary debates' (MacManus 2021: 243).

I focus here on three (interconnected) areas which might usefully be developed further: (a) the problems of material aid and migration; (b) cashing out the capabilities approach; and (c) engagement with contemporary theorists.

The Problems of Material Aid and Migration

From the very first chapter of the book, Nussbaum takes Cicero and the Stoics to task for the bifurcation of duties which led to the duty of material aid to others being neglected. She welcomes the work of Grotius, Smith and her own capabilities approach as remedying that neglect. Yet, when it comes to addressing the duty of material aid in the modern world, she more or less throws her hands up in despair: aid to foreign countries doesn't work, indeed it makes things worse. What are we then to do? There seems to be an imbalance here. Nussbaum has spent over two hundred pages arguing that duties of material aid are as stringent as those of justice and indeed cannot be separated from them. Yet in just a few pages she reveals that those duties of material aid cannot, after all, be met. One feels that this is an area that desperately needs further work – and there are contemporary political philosophers who have written extensively about it, but whose ideas Nussbaum does not discuss (see 'Engagement with Contemporary Theorists' below).

The problem of asylum and migration, too, is discussed briefly (seven pages) and the discussion does not come to any firm conclusions. Usually, a meliorist attitude and the determination to apply theoretical insights to real-world policy-making are defining features of Nussbaum's work. Here, they seem less in evidence than one would expect.

Cashing Out the Capabilities Approach

Nussbaum presents the capabilities approach as a new, improved version of the cosmopolitan tradition, which preserves its important insights about equal human worth and dignity but is more suited to the modern world. Yet when we attempt to cash out exactly how to apply it, we run into the same old material aid problem in another form. Nussbaum is very clear that providing and safeguarding all the capabilities costs money – there is no separation of social justice from economic justice. Therefore, she states, 'The only problem is how to raise the funds fairly, and how to allocate them fairly' (2019: 245). But that problem is a huge one. How is the money to be found? Nussbaum has said that states must levy taxes; but obviously poor states are less able to do this than wealthy ones. Yet redistributing money and resources from rich nations to poor ones is, Nussbaum says, unacceptably paternalistic and in any case inefficacious. Nussbaum does acknowledge that there is a problem here:

> Wherever we end up with regard to global duties of material aid – and Chapter 6 has argued that this is a complicated issue, given problems of paternalism and inefficacy – we must not approach these issues with the erroneous bifurcation of duties. If we follow the CA, we will not do so. (Nussbaum 2019: 245)

The trouble is that if we can't solve that complicated issue, we are forced into just such a bifurcation. For duties of justice can, at least to some extent, be fulfilled internationally, by United Nations rulings, sanctions, public opinion, petitions, consumer boycotts, online campaigns and so on. But if fulfilling duties of material aid is counterproductive, then on that front we're stymied.

Engagement with Contemporary Theorists

Nussbaum does mention the work of the contemporary ethical and political philosopher Peter Singer in her chapter titled 'The Tradition and Today's World', and that of 'other theorists of global justice' (2019: 223), although she does not name them. She cites Singer's recommendation of NGOs as the best way to deliver foreign aid and notes his efforts to identify and publicise the most efficient organisations. However, Nussbaum states that there are pitfalls in such an approach, enumerates them in the course of half a page, and moves on. But Singer has written very extensively about global justice and deserves more attention than this. His 2015 book, *The Most Good You Can Do: How Effective Altruism Is Changing Ideas About Living Morally*, is given in a footnote, but its actual proposals are not discussed. Since the publication of the book a whole Effective Altruism movement has sprung up (see https://www.effectivealtruism.org), which would have been worthy of some comment.

There is a rich and proliferating literature on the subject of global justice. Broadly, there are two sides in the debate: the liberal nationalists and the cosmopolitans. On the liberal nationalist side are those who think that justice is best thought of as applying *within* nation-states. Justice *between* states is a matter of observing international laws and not infringing the sovereignty of other states. We do not have direct duties of justice towards the indigent in other nations; their plight is the responsibility of their own government. We may, of course, provide humanitarian relief to other nations when they are struck by natural disasters or riven by war, but these are acts of beneficence rather than duties of strict justice. Representatives of this view would include John Rawls (1999), Thomas Nagel (2005) and David Miller (2012).

Nussbaum does not belong to this side. But she has something in common with them. Like them she puts high value on the nation-state: as she says, 'the nation is still the primary locus of human self-expression and human autonomy' (Nussbaum 2019: 140). However, she differs from them in one crucial particular, as she holds that we have direct duties to citizens of other countries.

The other side in the debate are the cosmopolitans. Nussbaum would presumably categorise herself as aligning with this side, since she believes duties of justice cross national borders. But most representatives of this group are cosmopolitan in a perhaps more full-blooded sense than that advocated by Nussbaum. They include Samuel Scheffler, who holds that special duties to one's nation can conflict with global justice (2002); Thomas Pogge, who argues that Western nations owe reparations to poorer countries as it is our fault they are poor, and that a massive reform of global institutions is demanded by justice (2008); and Gillian Brock (2009), who defends a cosmopolitan model of justice and recommends policies to move towards it. None of these cosmopolitans would wish to totally abolish the nation-state – at least not at the present time – but all accord it less moral importance than Nussbaum does and argue that its moral claims should be limited.

Moreover, Nussbaum's concession that, despite a clear duty of justice to assist the poor of other nations, we cannot in practice do much to deliver material aid means that, effectively, her position is not really so very far from that of the liberal nationalists. She is in a sense poised between liberal nationalists and cosmopolitans.

On the subject of asylum and migration she also seems to hover between two positions. Although she accepts in principle a duty towards asylum-seekers and migrants, she makes no concrete proposals about how to fulfil it. Nussbaum refers to the work of both Joseph Carens (2013), who puts the case for open borders (he likens the current arrangements to the medieval feudal system where peasants had no right to leave the land of their overlord – see Carens 2013: 226), and David Miller, who argues that nations have a right to restrict immigration to preserve national identity (2014: 370–1), and also to guard against over-population (2014: 371) – though Miller does say that states have a duty to accept refugees 'whose basic rights are being threatened or violated in their current place of residence' (2014: 372). Presumably, Nussbaum's position lies somewhere between Carens's and Miller's – perhaps slightly closer to Miller's, given the importance she attaches to national sovereignty – but she does not explicate this.

Investigating the ideas of these contemporary theorists could throw much light on the problems Nussbaum identifies. One feels that *The Cosmopolitan Tradition* is only the first half of an enquiry and needs a sequel. MacManus ended his review with the words: 'In the future, I hope for a more focused and deep take on cosmopolitan issues from her eloquent pen' (2021: 245). Given Nussbaum's prolificacy, energy and habit of returning to re-explore ideas, perhaps that sequel will be forthcoming.

Summary

The Cosmopolitan Tradition: A Noble but Flawed Ideal is an interesting, stimulating account of the development of an important and influential tradition, displaying Nussbaum's usual gifts of scholarship and narrative flair. It offers further evidence of the applicability of the capabilities approach, and it provides a theoretical underpinning for duties of global justice. However, it does not say enough about how those duties are to be fulfilled in the modern world. The concluding sections of the book pose problems rather than proposing solutions. The book is better seen as a contribution to an ongoing debate than a final statement of Nussbaum's position.

An Organic Whole

Having covered Nussbaum's thirty-five-year philosophical career, we are now in a position to see how her oeuvre constitutes an organic whole. As I said at the outset, she has made important contributions in many areas of philosophy. But those areas are not discrete. The connections between her ideas are manifold and strong.

For example, her work on Aristotle's ethics feeds into her capabilities approach, for that depends on an idea of human flourishing; her capabilities approach feeds into her work on animal rights, for that depends on supplying the capabilities appropriate to the nature of the species; the idea that each species has a nature which can flourish in a certain way connects back to Aristotle.

Or, again: Nussbaum's liberal philosophy underpins her theory of education as well as her theory of feminism as well as her defence of religious freedom. And her liberal philosophy finds its fullest expression in her capabilities approach which is applied to feminism, development, human rights, animal rights and global justice. Her contributions to different fields do not exist in isolation but are connected and mutually reinforcing.

Nussbaum herself notes that her work falls into two halves:

> My own work, like a lot of philosophical work in the past few decades, has discussed political institutions and laws, making general arguments about what justice is and what basic rights and entitlements all citizens have . . .
>
> The other half of my career has focused on the nature of the emotions and their role in our search for the good life. (2019: 12)

But these two halves are interconnected, too. For what basic rights and entitlements citizens ought to have depends on a claim about human emotional needs; and fulfilment of those emotional needs depends on just institutions.

The metaphor of an *organic* whole suggests a living organism, and that's an appropriate image for Nussbaum's work. For as well

185

as the internal coherence noted above, there is constant change and growth in Nussbaum's thought. For example, her conception of anger has changed. When she wrote *Sex and Social Justice* (1999) she conceived of anger as a positive emotion, necessary to effectuate change; 'justified anger' made it onto her list of capabilities, as an example of the range of emotions we should be capable of. By the time of *Anger and Forgiveness* (2016) she has revised her view and anger is now seen as normatively problematic – and is accordingly removed from the list.

Or consider the growing role that the capabilities approach itself has played in her work. At first it was applied only in the field of international development – as something to aim for *within* each developing nation. Subsequently she extended it to cover other species. By the time of *The Cosmopolitan Tradition* it is offered as a template for global justice – a goal for the whole international community, not just individual nation-states, to aim for.

Summing Up

Nussbaum has many virtues as a political theorist for our times. As has already been stressed, she is a gifted communicator, and the best way to disseminate ideas outside the academy is to make them accessible and enjoyable to read. Another of her strengths – increasingly rare in these divided times – is to make us aware of what unites rather than divides us. The universality of the capabilities approach stresses our common humanity (a phrase that has fallen out of fashion somewhat but should not have done). Nussbaum's embracingness is also evident in her openness to other disciplines. Philosophy by itself cannot come up with policy decisions, which is what she is ultimately interested in. Political actions in the real world are always context dependent, 'the fruit of a partnership between philosophy, history, political science, economics, law, and sociology' (Nussbaum 2019: 13).

Many philosophers are clever. There is nothing remarkable about that. But Martha Nussbaum is also wise – which is much rarer.

Recommended Reading

Nussbaum's oeuvre is so rich and extensive that a first-time reader might be daunted, uncertain where to begin. I'll conclude by recommending just four of her books, from successive stages of her career. They are:

- *The Fragility of Goodness*. First published in 1986, this is a fascinating and psychologically acute study of ancient Greek morality. Many of Nussbaum's key ideas can be found here: her conception of human flourishing, the high value placed on personal relationships, the conviction that philosophy's task is to illuminate the lives we lead. It is also a fine example of writing that is both scholarly and a pleasure to read.
- *Upheavals of Thought*. Published in 2001, this book is a complex, detailed, rich and readable study of the emotions. It rejects the familiar disjunction between reason and emotion and argues for a cognitive theory of emotions – that is to say, emotions involve propositional content which may be true or false. It's also an excellent example of the way Nussbaum philosophises through literature.
- *Frontiers of Justice*. Published in 2006, this is an excellent example of Nussbaum's liberal political philosophy applied to questions of global justice. It covers animal rights, the rights of disabled people and economic aid to developing nations. It also offers a sophisticated critique of contractarianism and utilitarianism, and presents the capabilities approach in its mature form.
- *Anger and Forgiveness*. Based on the John Locke lectures that Nussbaum gave in Oxford in 2014, *Anger and Forgiveness* (2016) is notable for its eye-opening reconsideration of morality and the emotions. Nussbaum gives us important new concepts to think with. Her radical views on anger and forgiveness are applied not only to personal morality but also to the public sphere and to law and policy.

Bibliography

Abbey, Ruth (2011), *The Return of Feminist Liberalism*, Durham: Acumen Publishing.

Alibhai-Brown, Yasmin (2015), 'As a Muslim Woman, I See the Veil as a Rejection of Progressive Values', *The Guardian*, 20 March.

Aviv, Rachel (2016), 'The Philosopher of Feeling', *The New Yorker*, 18 July.

Baber, Heather (2007), 'Adaptive Preference', *Social Theory and Practice*, 33:1, pp. 105–26. Available at http://home.sandiego.edu/~baber/research/ (accessed 26 May 2022).

Barry, Brian (2011), *Culture and Equality*, Cambridge: Polity.

Beard, Mary (2000), 'The Danger of Making Lists', *Times Literary Supplement*, 17 March, p. 6.

Becker, Lawrence C. (1998), *A New Stoicism*, Princeton NJ: Princeton University Press.

Bentham, Jeremy ([1789] 1961), *Principles of Morals and Legislation*, in *The Utilitarians*, London: Dolphin Books.

Blackford, Russell (2012), *Freedom of Religion and the Secular State*, Chichester: Wiley-Blackwell.

Blake, Michael (2003), 'Immigration', in R. Frey and C. Wellman (eds), *A Companion to Applied Ethics*, Malden, MA: Blackwell, pp. 224–37.

Blake, Michael (2013), 'Immigration, Jurisdiction, and Exclusion', *Philosophy and Public Affairs*, 41:2, pp. 103–30.

Bloom, Allan (1987), *The Closing of the American Mind: How Higher Education Has Failed Democracy and Impoverished the Souls of Today's Students*, New York: Simon & Schuster.

Brock, Gillian (2009), *Global Justice: A Cosmopolitan Account*, Oxford: Oxford University Press.

Butler, Judith (1990), *Gender Trouble*, New York: Routledge.

Butler, Judith (1999), *Gender Trouble: Feminism and the Subversion of Identity*, New York and London: Routledge.

Carens, Joseph (2013), *The Ethics of Immigration*, Oxford: Oxford University Press.

Delgado, Richard (ed.) (1995), *Critical Race Theory: The Cutting Edge*, Philadelphia: Temple University Press.

Diamond, Cora (2004), 'Eating Meat and Eating People', in Cass Sunstein and Martha Nussbaum (eds), *Animal Rights; Current Debates and New Directions*, Oxford: Oxford University Press, pp. 93–107.

DiAngelo, Robin (2018), *White Fragility*, Boston, MA: Beacon Press.

Eide, Stephen (2014), 'Martha Nussbaum: The Voice of Convention', *Academic Questions*, 27:2, pp. 185–98.

Elster, Jon (1983), *Sour Grapes: Studies in the Subversion of Rationality*, Cambridge: Cambridge University Press.

Epstein, Richard A. (2004), 'Animals as Objects, or Subjects, of Rights', in Cass Sunstein and Martha Nussbaum (eds), *Animal Rights; Current Debates and New Directions*, Oxford: Oxford University Press, pp. 143–61.

Forster, E. M. (1970), *Two Cheers for Democracy*, Harmondsworth: Penguin.

Francione, Gary L. (2004), 'Animals – Property or Persons?' in Cass Sunstein and Martha Nussbaum (eds), *Animal Rights; Current Debates and New Directions*, Oxford: Oxford University Press, pp. 108–42.

Frum, David (1998), 'Teaching the Young', Review of *Cultivating Humanity*', *The Public Interest*, 131 (Spring), Periodicals Archive Online.

Galeotti, Anna (2002) *Tolerance as Recognition*, Cambridge: Cambridge University Press.

Goldstein, Laurence (2007) '*Foreword: Martha Nussbaum and Her Critics*', in *The Ethics and Politics of Compassion and Capabilities*; lectures by Martha Nussbaum. Hochelaga Lectures 2005. Faculty of Law, University of Hong Kong.

Griswold, Charles L. (2007), *Forgiveness: A Philosophical Exploration*, Cambridge: Cambridge University Press.

Hadot, Pierre (1981), *Philosophy as a Way of Life*, Chichester: Wiley.

Harpham, Geoffrey Galt (2002), 'The Hunger of Martha Nussbaum', *Representations*, 77:1, pp. 58–81.

Holiday, Ryan (2016), *The Daily Stoic*, London: Profile Books.

Hosein, Adam (2013), 'Immigration and Freedom of Movement', *Ethics and Global Politics*, 6, pp. 25–37.

Hosein, Adam (2014), 'Immigration: the Case for Legalization', *Social Theory and Practice*, 40, pp. 609–30.

Hurka, Thomas (1993), *Perfectionism*, Oxford: Oxford University Press.

Hursthouse, Rosalind (1999), *On Virtue Ethics*, Oxford: Oxford University Press.

Ingram, George (2019), 'What Every American Should Know about US Foreign Aid'. Available at https://www.brookings.edu/policy2020/votervital/what-every-american-should-know-about-us-foreign-aid/ (accessed 26 May 2022).

Irvine, William B. (2008), *A Guide to the Good Life: The Ancient Art of Stoic Joy*, Oxford: Oxford University Press.

Jackson, Timothy P. (2018), 'Not Far from the Kingdom: Martha Nussbaum on Anger and Forgiveness', *Journal of Religious Ethics*, 46:4, pp. 749–70.

Kekes, John (2005), '*Hiding from Humanity: Shame, Disgust and the Law*', *Mind*, 114:454, pp. 439–44.

Khader, Serene J. (2011), *Adaptive Preferences and Women's Empowerment*, New York: Oxford University Press.

Klein, Daniel M. (2012), *Travels with Epicurus*, London: Oneworld.

Kymlicka, Will (1995), *Multicultural Citizenship*, Oxford: Clarendon Press.

Laborde, Cécile (2017), *Liberalism's Religion*, Cambridge, MA: Harvard University Press.

Legates, Marlene (2001), *In Their Time*, London: Routledge.

Locke, John ([1689] 2013), *Letter Concerning Toleration*, ed. Kerry Walters, Peterborough, ON: Broadview Press.

Locke, John ([1693] 1996), *Some Thoughts Concerning Education*, ed. Ruth W. Grant and Nathan Tarcov, Indianapolis, IN: Hackett.

Luk, Johnny (2021), 'The UK Is Still Better Than Most When It Comes to Overseas Aid', Aljazeera. Available at https://www.aljazeera.com/opinions/2021/7/29/the-uk-is-still-better-than-most-when-it-comes-to-overseas-aid (accessed 26 May, 2022).

MacManus, Matt (2021), 'A Review of Martha Nussbaum's *The Cosmopolitan Tradition: A Noble but Flawed Ideal*', *Human Rights Review*, 22, pp. 243–5, doi: 10.1007/s12142-021-00623-3.

Magee, Bryan (1988), *The Great Philosophers*, Oxford: Oxford University Press.

Magee, Bryan (2004), *Confessions of a Philosopher*, London: Phoenix.

Mill, John Stuart ([1869] 2008) *On the Subjection of Women*, London: Hesperus Press.

Miller, David (2012), *National Responsibility and Global Justice*, Oxford: Oxford University Press.

Miller, David (2014), 'Immigration: the Case for Limits', in Andrew Cohen and Christopher Wellman (eds), *Contemporary Debates in Applied Ethics*, Chichester: John Wiley and Sons, pp. 363–75.

Nagel, Thomas (1985), *Mortal Questions*, New York: Cambridge University Press, pp. 165–80.

Nagel, Thomas (2005), 'The Problem of Global Justice', *Philosophy and Public Affairs*, 33:2, pp. 113–47.

Nussbaum, Martha C. ([1986] 2013a), *The Fragility of Goodness*, Cambridge: Cambridge University Press.

Nussbaum, Martha C. ([1994] 2013b), *The Therapy of Desire*, Princeton, NJ: Princeton University Press.

Nussbaum, Martha C. (1997), *Cultivating Humanity*, Cambridge, MA: Harvard University Press.

Nussbaum, Martha C. (1999a), *Sex and Social Justice*, Oxford: Oxford University Press.

Nussbaum, Martha C. (1999b), 'The Professor of Parody: The Hip Defeatism of Judith Butler', *The New Republic*, 22 February.

Nussbaum, Martha C. (2000), *Women and Human Development*, Cambridge: Cambridge University Press.

Nussbaum, Martha C. (2001a), *Upheavals of Thought*, Cambridge: Cambridge University Press.

Nussbaum, Martha C. (2001b), 'Animal Rights: The Need for a Theoretical Basis (reviewing Steven M. Wise, *Rattling the Cage: Toward Legal Rights for Animals* (2000))', *Harvard Law Review*, 114:5, pp. 1506–49.

Nussbaum, Martha C. (2004a), *Hiding from Humanity*, Princeton, NJ: Princeton University Press.

Nussbaum, Martha C. (2004b), 'Beyond "Compassion and Humanity": Justice for Nonhuman Animals', in Cass Sunstein and Martha Nussbaum (eds), *Animal Rights; Current Debates and New Directions*, Oxford: Oxford University Press, pp. 291–320.

Nussbaum, Martha C. (2004c), 'Mill between Aristotle & Bentham', *Daedalus*, 133:2, pp. 60–8.

Nussbaum, Martha C. (2006), *Frontiers of Justice*, Cambridge, MA: Belknap Press.

Nussbaum, Martha C. (2008), *Liberty of Conscience: In Defence of America's Tradition of Religious Equality*, New York: Basic Books.

Nussbaum, Martha C. (2010), *Not for Profit*, Princeton, NJ: Princeton University Press.

Nussbaum, Martha C. (2012a), 'Undemocratic Vistas: ALLAN BLOOM (1987), The Closing of the American Mind: How Higher Education Has Failed Democracy and Impoverished the Souls of Today's Students', in *Philosophical Interventions: Reviews 1986–2011* (New York; published online May 2015). Oxford Scholarship Online: http://dx.doi.org.libezproxy.open.ac.uk/10.1093/acprof:osobl/9780199777853.003.0003 (accessed 14 March 2022).

Nussbaum, Martha C. (2012b), *The New Religious Intolerance*, Cambridge, MA: Belknap Press.

Nussbaum, Martha C. (2016), *Anger and Forgiveness*, Oxford: Oxford University Press.

Nussbaum, Martha C. (2018), *The Monarchy of Fear*, Oxford: Oxford University Press.

Nussbaum, Martha C. (2019), *The Cosmopolitan Tradition: A Noble but Flawed Ideal*, Cambridge, MA: Belknap Press.

Okin, Susan Moller (1999), 'Is Multiculturalism Bad for Women?', in J. Cohen, M. Howard and M. Nussbaum (eds), *Is Multiculturalism Bad for Women*, Princeton, NJ: Princeton University Press.

Peterson, Gregory R. (2021), 'Martha C. Nussbaum, Anger and Forgiveness: Resentment, Generosity, Justice', *Journal of Moral Philosophy*, 18:3, pp. 315–18.

Pigliucci, Massimo (2017), *How to Be a Stoic*, London: Ebury.

Plato ([c. 380 BCE] 2008), *The Republic*, trans. Robin Waterfield, Oxford: Oxford World's Classics.

Pogge, Thomas (2008), *World Poverty and Human Rights*, Cambridge: Polity.

Posner, Richard A. (2004), 'Animal Rights: Legal, Philosophical and Pragmatic Perspectives', in Cass Sunstein and Martha Nussbaum (eds), *Animal Rights; Current Debates and New Directions*, Oxford: Oxford University Press, pp. 51–77.

Quong, Jonathan (2011), *Liberalism Without Perfection*, Oxford: Oxford University Press.

Rachels, James (2001), 'Killing and Letting Die', in Lawrence Becker and Charlotte Becker (eds), *Encyclopedia of Ethics*, 2nd edition, New York: Routledge, vol. 2, pp. 947–50.

Rachels, James (2004), 'Drawing Lines', in Cass Sunstein and Martha Nussbaum (eds), *Animal Rights; Current Debates and New Directions*, Oxford:: Oxford University Press, pp. 162–74.

Rawls, John (1971), *A Theory of Justice*, Cambridge, MA: Belknap Press.

Rawls, John (1999), *The Law of Peoples*, Cambridge, MA: Harvard University Press.

Rawls, John ([1993] 2005), *Political Liberalism*, New York: Columbia University Press.

Raz, Joseph (2009), *The Morality of Freedom*, Oxford: Oxford University Press.

Robertson, Donald (2019), *Stoicism and the Art of Happiness*, London: Teach Yourself.

Robeyns, Ingrid and Morten Fibieger Byskov (2021), 'The Capability Approach', *The Stanford Encyclopedia of Philosophy* (Fall 2021 Edition), ed. Edward N. Zalta, available at https://plato.stanford.edu/archives/fall2021/entries/capability-approach/ (accessed 26 May 2022).

Robshaw, Brandon (2020), *Should a Liberal State Ban the Burqa?* London: Bloomsbury.

Rogers, Lesley J. and Gisela Kaplan (2004), 'All Animals Are *Not* Equal', in Cass Sunstein and Martha Nussbaum (eds), *Animal Rights; Current Debates and New Directions*, Oxford: Oxford University Press, pp. 175–202.

Said, Edward (1978), *Orientalism*, London: Pantheon.

Salzgeber, Jonas (2019), *The Little Book of Stoicism*, Jonas Salzgeber.

Scheffler, Israel (1973), *Teaching and Reason*, London: Routledge & Kegan Paul.

Scheffler, Samuel (2002), *Boundaries and Allegiances*, Oxford: Oxford University Press.

Schinkel, Anders (2008), 'Martha Nussbaum on Animal Rights', *Ethics and the Environment*, 13:1, pp. 41–69.

Sen, Amartya (1980), 'Equality of What?' in *Ethics and Economics II*, ed. Alan P. Hamlin, Cheltenham: Edward Elgar, pp. 257–80.

Sen, Amartya (1985), *Commodities and Capabilities*, Amsterdam: North-Holland.

Sen, Amartya (2005), 'Human Rights and Capabilities', *Journal of Human Development*, 6:2, pp. 151–66.

Shortt, Rupert (2012), *Christianophobia*, London: Random House.

Singer, Peter (2004), 'Ethics Beyond Species and Beyond Instincts: A Response to Richard Posner', in Cass Sunstein and Martha Nussbaum (eds), *Animal Rights; Current Debates and New Directions*, Oxford: Oxford University Press, pp. 78–92.

Singer, Peter (2015), *The Most Good You Can Do: How Effective Altruism Is Changing Ideas About Living Morally*, New Haven, CT: Yale University Press.

Sommers, Christina Hoff (1994), *Who Stole Feminism? How Women Have Betrayed Women*, New York: Simon & Schuster.

Sophocles (1996), *Antigone*, trans Brendan Kennelly, London: Bloodaxe Books.

Sunstein, Cass (2004), 'Can Animals Sue?', in Cass Sunstein and Martha Nussbaum (eds), *Animal Rights; Current Debates and New Directions*, Oxford: Oxford University Press, pp. 251–62.

Sunstein, Cass and Martha Nussbaum (2004), *Animal Rights; Current Debates and New Directions*, Oxford: Oxford University Press.

Taylor, Charles (1994), 'The Politics of Recognition', in Amy Gutmann (ed.), *Multiculturalism*, Princeton, NJ: Princeton University Press.

Vašák, Karel (1977), 'Human Rights: A Thirty-Year Struggle: The Sustained Efforts to give Force of law to the Universal Declaration of Human Rights', *UNESCO Courier*, 11, pp. 29–32.

Walzer, Michael (1983), *Spheres of Justice*, Princeton, NJ: Princeton University Press.

Wellman, Christopher H. (2015), 'Immigration', *Stanford Encyclopedia of Philosophy*, Stanford, CA: Metaphysics Research Lab, Center for the Study of Language and Information, Stanford University.

Williams, Bernard (1973), *Problems of the Self*, Cambridge: Cambridge University Press.

Williams, Bernard (1981), *Moral Luck*, Cambridge: Cambridge University Press.

Williams, Bernard (1994), 'Do Not Disturb', *The London Review of Books*, 16:20.

Wise, Steven M. (2004), 'Animal Rights, One Step at a Time', in Cass Sunstein and Martha Nussbaum (eds), *Animal Rights; Current Debates and New Directions*, Oxford: Oxford University Press, pp. 19–50.

Wolff, Jonathan and Avner De-Shalit (2007), *Disadvantage*, Oxford: Oxford University Press.

Index

EU representative:
Easy Access System Europe
Mustamäe tee 50, 10621 Tallinn, Estonia
Gpsr.requests@easproject.com

www.ingramcontent.com/pod-product-compliance
Lightning Source LLC
Chambersburg PA
CBHW071103280326
41928CB00051B/2776